The Rise of English Literary History

THE RISE

of English Literary History

B Y

René Wellek

CHAPEL HILL · 1941

The University of North Carolina Press

PREFACE

A "History of English Literary History"—awkward as such a title would sound—is a legitimate and even urgent task of English scholarship. We have histories of all the sciences, and there are several histories of political historiography, but no attempt has hitherto been made to trace the development of English literary history in any detail. Such a history, properly executed, would have more than antiquarian interest. It would not only satisfy the instinctive desire of men to commemorate the achievements of their predecessors, but would serve a practical purpose as well: it would help to show by what ways the present vantage-point, or *impasse*, of literary studies has been reached. It would elucidate present-day problems and increase a consciousness of the principles basic to our discipline. Ultimately it might serve as a starting-point for a general history of literary history in the main European countries. Further, an exposition of the peculiarities of the English development might throw some light on the whole question of the specific character of English scholarship and thus of the English mind in general.

The following pages are, however, only a very partial attempt to realize such a far-reaching program. I shall merely trace the origins and growth of English literary history from its beginnings during the Renaissance to Thomas Warton's *History of English Poetry* (1774–1781).

v

Warton's three large volumes were the first history of English literature "in form," and determined the whole future development of English literary history. They represent the culminating point of a long process which I have attempted to trace in some detail. A new volume devoted to a full study of literary history during the Romantic age down to Hallam's *Introduction to the Literature of Europe* (1837–1839) is in active preparation.

The following sketch is frankly based on the conviction that research is not enough and that the highest aim of the literary historian is the writing of literary history.* The book is thus not primarily a history of English scholarship and of the growth of English studies in general, though much attention has been devoted to the process by which the older literature was rediscovered and made accessible. Nor is the book a history of English criticism, though it has been necessary to notice changes of judgment on authors or periods of English literature. I am chiefly concerned with the programs and theoretical reflections of those engaged in literary history and, beyond these explicit avowals, with the underlying methods, ideals, and conceptions that governed the actual writing of the history of English literature.

So far as I know the only previous essay at tracing the history of English literary history is a little book by Gerard O'Leary (*English Literary History*, London, 1930), an unpretentious bibliographical handbook, elementary in its comments and evaluations. Nor do I know of any book in any other language which would present a parallel, with the exception of the Polish writer Sigmund Lempicki's *Ge-*

---

* For a full statement of the problems involved see my "Theory of Literary History," *Travaux du Cercle Linguistique de Prague*, VI (1936), 173-191 and a chapter "Literary History" in *Literary Scholarship: Its Aims and Methods* (ed. Norman Foerster), Chapel Hill, 1941.

schichte der deutschen Literaturwissenschaft (1920) concluding with a chapter on Herder, an instructive work of
somewhat different scope than this. I have learned more,
however, from the many monographs on individual authors
and from the books on allied subjects which are all cited in
the bibliography and the notes.

The need of a history of English scholarship was first im-
pressed on me during the years I taught English literature at
the Charles University of Prague, and took part in the
stimulating discussions on methods of literary study in the
Prague Linguistic Circle. The book was written during a
four-year stay in London (1935–1939) when I lectured on
Czech language and literature at the School of Slavonic
Studies in the University of London. It was substantially
ready for publication in May, 1939, and has been only revised and supplemented since then.

I must thank the British Museum for liberal access to its
treasures; and the libraries of University College, London,
of Yale University and the State University of Iowa, which
at different times were at my disposal. My thanks are also
due to Professor Ronald S. Crane of the University of Chicago, Professor Oliver Elton of Oxford, Professor John C.
McGalliard of the University of Iowa, Mr. James M. Osborn
of Yale University, Dr. Bruce Pattison of University College, London, and Professor Austin Warren and Dr. Curt A.
Zimansky of the University of Iowa, all of whom have read
the manuscript and made numerous valuable suggestions.
Finally I wish to express to Dean George Dinsmore Stod-
dard of the University of Iowa my gratitude for his gen-
erosity in aiding the publication of this book by a grant
from the funds of the Graduate College.

Iowa City, December, 1940

CONTENTS

The Origins

CHAPTER ONE

The Middle Ages and Renaissance

THE RISE OF LITERARY HISTORY was a slow process, incomprehensible unless we see it in close connection with the rise of modern criticism, biography, and historiography. It is part of (one of the greatest revolutions in the intellectual history of mankind) of the awakening of the historical sense and modern self-consciousness. Literary history in the more narrow sense developed, by an obvious process of specialization, from established forms like biography—which was not originally, of course, confined to literature—and from the criticism of individual works or the poetics of single genres, which were slowly expanded to include a historical survey of the past. Literary history as a distinct discipline arose only when biography and criticism coalesced and when, under the influence of political historiography, the narrative form began to be used. But this was a process which took almost two centuries. In early times we must look carefully to notice the seeds of ideas and forms which had a late flowering only in the eighteenth century.

There was no literary history in the Middle Ages, though some knowledge of the past of literature existed. The very conception of the aims of the poet, who was usually pictured as a humble craftsman in the service of his Maker, the widespread anonymity of literary creation, the prevalent "communism" both of subjects and forms, which shows that originality and individuality were not valued, the absence of any regard for the historicity of events: all these parallel symptoms of the medieval mentality explain the absence of any literary history proper. But, of course, rhetoric and poetics, largely derived from classical sources, were cultivated; and some biographical knowledge of the poets, with bibliography of their works, was preserved in lists of writers which through St. Jerome's *De Viris Illustribus* descend ultimately from Suetonius.[1] Sometimes these lists were elaborated into collections of short biographies. John of Boston, who was a monk at Bury St. Edmunds about 1440, compiled such a list [2] which included also "British" writers like Bede, Roger Bacon, John of Salisbury, and other theologians, scholastic philosophers, and church historians. Only slightly different as a type were collections of biographies of philosophers which descend ultimately from Diogenes Laertius. An Englishman, Gualterus Burlaeus (Walter Burley), who died about 1337, was the author of such a *Liber de Vita et Moribus Philosophorum*,[3] which includes also the Greek poets, Homer and Aeschylus.

Only with the dawn of the Renaissance conception of the poet as the maker, the rhetor and improver of a "rude" language could attention be drawn to the historical role of a great personality and to the contrast between the early times and the new art of "making" derived from Italy and France. Something like the faint outlines of a rudimentary history of English literature can be discerned in the first appreciations of the roles of Chaucer and Gower by their successors and disciples, for example, in Lydgate's, Occleve's, and Dunbar's well known verses in praise of their master, Chaucer.[4] They all agree not only in claiming for him superiority to all other English poets but also in assigning to him (and to Gower) the historical role of the introducer of rhetoric and eloquence to England. Not only do they know that Chaucer "illumined our rude speech"; he is also (as early as 1430) coupled with Dante and Petrarch as a founder, establisher, and maker of English poetry.[5] But there is nothing in the scattered medieval dicta on literature which would point to any clearer concept of the development of literature, and literature, on the whole, remained too deeply imbedded either in the craft of rhetoric or in the general learning of the age to receive much specific consideration.

No appreciable change came until the advent of Humanism and the Renaissance. Rhetoric and poetics assumed suddenly a central importance in the whole system of human values. The poet ceased to be the handmaid of nature. He became one who, "lifted up with the vigour of his own invention, doth grow in effect another nature." [6] Patriotism, though existing long before, now took pride in the scholarly and poetical achievements of its own nation in competition with the great men of classical antiquity. The Herald of England in a debate with France boasted of such famous "clerks and orators" as Chaucer, Gower, Lydgate, Linacre, Latimer, Coverdale.[7] The Reformation stressed and increased the feeling of difference from the continent and the medieval tradition radiating from Rome. The Christian philosophy of history, with the Last Judgment as the foreordained end, receded into the background, while new conceptions began to penetrate from abroad. The classical idea of a general decay of nature and man, though still alive throughout the seventeenth and eighteenth centuries, had little practical importance for the conceptions of literature. But the concept of progress began to emerge with all the generous hopes which animated a time of expansion and political victories. Bacon, who argued that the old times are in reality the youth of the world and that the present time is therefore wiser and more mature, was merely giving the clearest expression to a widespread notion.[8] The condemnation of the "rude and barbarous" Middle Ages was almost universal, and many authors, like Gabriel Harvey, hailed with pride the greatness of their own age, "the golden age to flourish now." [9]

The rudiments of literary history began to be established. The Reformation not only awakened a new form of patriotism, but also excited interest in early English history which was searched for proofs of English learning and wisdom. Even enthusiastic Protestants realized that the dissolution of the monasteries and the dispersal of their libraries necessitated a quick salvaging of anything that could be saved. These were the main motives that inspired the work of Leland and Bale. Thus Bale in his preface to Leland's *Laborious Journey* (1549) notes that "the proud Italians have always holden us for a barbarous nation . . . whereas if we had set our antiquities abroad," they must have "named Britain, a mother, a nurse, and a maintainer, not only of worthy men, but also of most excellent wits." [10] Of course these two great antiquaries were not primarily interested in literature, and still less in anything which could be called *belles lettres*. They rather continued and amplified the medieval tradition of the catalogue of writers which became the nucleus of the series of biographies and led logically to the form of Johnson's *Lives of the Poets* or Henry Morley's *English Writers*.

John Leland's catalogue of some six hundred names, written about 1545, was the earliest one, though it was not printed until 1709, by Anthony Hall. From Leland all the others derive either directly or indirectly. Leland has, at least, the germ of a historical conception not only in the use of an approximate chronological order, but also in his rather naïve attempts to discover the origin of literature in the Bards and Druids. His conception of English literature is the broadest possible, since it includes anything written in any language in the British Isles: the Welsh bards, the

Anglo-Saxon poets, the Latin church-writers and the English poets; but in practice, of course, theologians prevailed and Chaucer, Richard Rolle of Hampole, Gower and a few others are only islands in a sea of medieval church-writers and "learned" men.

The same is more or less true of John Bale's two catalogues, printed in the sixteenth century (1548 and 1557), and of his index, which was not published until 1902. The index, which represents the raw materials used in the later book, is alphabetical and therefore innocent of any historical viewpoint. Bale's earlier *Summarium* (1548), though partly based on Leland, shows a less scholarly mind than his predecessor's. Not only is the Reformation spirit with its virulent anti-Catholicism much more conspicuous (as one would expect from the author's experiences), but also a naïve genealogy, from Samothes Gigas, the brother of Homer, including the Egyptian Osiris, mars the early parts, and a childish endeavour to swell the number of names listed to six hundred with divisions into "centuries" characterizes Bale's mind as essentially medieval. This is true in spite of the fact that he includes for the first time (or at least in the same year as George Lily's *Virorum aliquot in Britannia Elogia*, 1548) a series of humanist biographies, not forgetting Leland and himself. The much larger *Catalogus* of 1557 is merely an expansion brought up to nine hundred writers, including some of the newest ones like Princess Elizabeth and containing much new extraneous matter such as a list of Church fathers, popes, emperors, etc. But in the second part, added in 1559, the extension to Irish and Scottish writers is significant though sketchy in performance, and one must always acknowledge the wealth of fairly accurate biographical and bibliographical information supplied by these catalogues.

But fuller and livelier biographies of literary men can be found in the sixteenth century elsewhere than in the dry catalogues of Leland and Bale. Of course, only rarely are these figures considered as men of literature; there is practically no literary criticism in the many individual lives of the period, some of which were reaching out to a psychological interpretation of personality. George Lily's *Virorum aliquot in Britannia Elogia* (1548) is in the true humanist tradition of eulogy. A series of lives of Colet, William Lily (the author's father), Linacre, Grocyn, Fisher, More, Latimer, etc., follows the familiar pattern, treating "family, first instruction, university, travel, last illness, and death." Similar lives of individual writers like Speght's well-known *Life of Chaucer* (1598) are modelled on the same Renaissance formula, but only in a few appear anything like literary considerations: Assheton's *Life of William Whitaker*, [11] for example, describes his writings as "res gestae" in martial metaphors. But life and literary criticism remain entirely unrelated, and the life and criticism themselves float *in vacuo*. A genre, however, had been established, which became one of the main traditions of literary-historical form in England, though most of the books discussed were written in Latin and treated writers outside the main tradition of English literature.

The same patriotic motive which inspired the work of Leland and Bale stimulated also the Anglo-Saxon studies of the Elizabethans. But it was combined with a desire to prove that there was a distinct vernacular Church in England before Rome had established its predominance. The leading spirit of the group, Archbishop Parker, collected Anglo-Saxon manuscripts which he later gave to Corpus Christi College at Cambridge. He must have suggested the first publication, *A Testimonie of Antiquitie* (1567), which reprinted

Aelfric's sermon for Easter Day, which was directed against the doctrine of transubstantiation, and quoted the Lord's Prayer, creed, and commandments in Anglo-Saxon. John Foxe in the second edition (1570) of his widely read *Acts and Monuments* used and quoted this little book and praised Aelfric. Foxe also wrote the Preface to the edition of the Anglo-Saxon Gospels, prepared by John Joscelyn, Parker's assistant, in 1577. There it is argued that the new Church is "no new reformation of things lately begun, but rather a reduction of the Church to the pristine state of old conformity." [12] A reprint of Asser's Latin *Life of Alfred* followed in 1574. William Lambarde had published the first collection of Anglo-Saxon laws in 1568. It has recently been discovered that several passages in this collection are interpolations and additions dating from the Elizabethan age, a striking proof that some Elizabethan, probably Laurence Nowell, knew Anglo-Saxon well enough to escape detection even under the searching eyes of nineteenth century scholarship.[13]

Besides the *Archaionomia*, Lambarde or Nowell translated also "Ohthere's Voyages" from Alfred's *Orosius* for Hakluyt's great collection of *Voyages* (1589). Camden in his *Remains* printed two versions of the Lord's Prayer in Anglo-Saxon with three other versions from the times of Henry II, Henry III, and Richard II, outlining the stages of development through which the English language had passed in the early Middle Ages. Most of these writers wanted to forge weapons in the polemical struggle with Roman Catholicism, but they incidentally aroused some genuine interest in Anglo-Saxon civilization and established a tradition of Old English studies which has never been completely interrupted.

There was no Middle English scholarship in the sixteenth century, even in the sense in which we can use the word in speaking of the Anglo-Saxon revival. But at least a tradition of printing Middle English poetry and prose was established when Caxton and his followers published Chaucer, Gower, Langland, Lydgate, and Malory. Among the editions of Chaucer, William Thynne's (1532) and Thomas Speght's (1598) collated manuscripts, and Speght's contained a glossary. William Thynne's son, Francis, irked by the aspersions cast on his father's edition by Speght, wrote a tract, known as the *Animadversions* (1598). This little book which unfortunately was not printed till 1810 can be regarded as the beginning of textual criticism on early English poetry. It corrects mistakes in Speght's biography and glossary, and suggests also definite emendations; it discusses all too briefly the Chaucer canon and refers to John of Salisbury as the source of the prologue to the *Wife of Bath's Tale*.[14] Thus, in the form of desultory criticisms on an edition, scholarly standards of editing were at least proclaimed and postulated.

We come much nearer to the living literature of the time in considering Elizabethan literary criticism. Criticism in England, as all over Europe, was, of course, mainly rhetorical and metrical. Thomas Wilson's *Arte of Rhetorique* (1553) is generally considered the earliest substantial work in English on criticism. It is strictly devoted to questions of oratory and diction and borrows largely from Cicero and Quintilian. It contains a few remarks on the history of rhetoric during the Middle Ages, referring to St. Augustine and to the elocution of the minstrels and Ausonius.[15]

The later rhetoric books of the Elizabethan age, especially Webbe's (1586) and Puttenham's (1587), two most comprehensive treatises, codify the historical knowledge current at the time. The sketches from classical literature (or rather lists of names) have been called rightly "but shreds of Horatian tradition or patchworks of Renaissance commentary." [16]

But the view of the history of English poetry contained or implied in them is necessarily more original and in itself not insignificant. The idea emerges of a uniform progress towards the glories of the present age: Surrey, Wyatt, and sometimes Lord Vaux had been early added to the roll of honour of English poets,[17] but the conception of uniform progress can be found in full bloom only in Webbe. He knows no memorable work written by "any poet in our English speech until twenty years past" and has nothing but contempt for the "brutish" poetry of rhyming which disgraced the Middle Ages.[18] In reality the harshness of this judgment is mitigated by his praise of Chaucer and by the curious exemption he makes for *Piers Plowman,* that it was not written in rhyme and was therefore presumably nearer to Elizabethan blank verse and the Latin hexameter. But Puttenham, while enumerating, rhetoric-wise, the best examples in every genre of poetry, gives something more than a mere roll-call. His stress on the importance of Wyatt and Surrey as the "first reformers of our English metre and style" [19] is nothing very remarkable and is well in line with the almost established conception of a uniform advance of English poetry, at that time largely understood as a refinement and regularization of diction and metre. More striking is Puttenham's attempt at a historical defence of rhyme, which includes an appeal to its existence in the poetry of American savages (derived from an Italian source) and implies the notion of a universal popular poetry from which Greek and Roman poetry is merely a deviation. Here can be discerned something like the dualism between primitive national poetry and the art of Greece and Rome which ultimately led to the distinction between Romantic and Classic. Puttenham seems to show some comprehension of the diversity of national traditions when he discusses Latin rhyming poetry in the Middle Ages. The "humours and appetites of men" appear "diverse and changeable . . . also in their learnings and arts," [20] from which conception something like a modern historical tolerance would seem to follow. Actually, however, the sketch of English poetry from Chaucer to Sidney is again conceived as a uniform advance, and the ethos behind Puttenham's consciousness of the difference of English poetry is purely patriotic and nationalistic. It is an argument that English poetry is older and more original, "coming by instinct of nature," [21] with no clear recognition of the far-reaching deductions which might have been made. But patriotism and nationalism were most important factors in the establishment of literary history, as they helped to create the concept of an independent national tradition and turned men's minds towards the search for an honorific past.

Samuel Daniel's *Defence of Rime* (published in 1607) shows an even stronger feeling for the historical process in literature. He mentions the Turks and Arabs, the Slavs and Hungarians as using rhymes; he appeals to the value of tradition or the "approbation of many ages"; [22] he even has a good word for the Goths, Vandals, and Langobards and mentions a civilized China which has never heard of Greece and Rome. He speaks of literary standards as "things that are continually in a wandering motion, carried with the violence of our uncertain likings, being but only the time that gives them their power," [23] and concludes rather wistfully: "This inordinate desire of innovation is but a character of that perpetual revolution which we see to be in all things that never remain the same: and we must herein be content to submit ourselves to the law of time, which in few years will make all that for which we now contend, Nothing." [24] Though these and similar passages show an extraordinary awareness of the passage of time, Daniel's main argument is not historical at all but rather an appeal to the eternal law of nature. "Custom and Nature: both defend rhyme." "Custom that is before Law: Nature that is above all art." Greece and Rome are no absolute authorities, because men are everywhere and all the time the same: a point of view which is exactly the opposite to any truly historical one. "We are the children of nature as well as they," he argues and so are the barbarians that have some special talents, e.g., in government, which prove them "not without judgment though without Greek and Latin." "There is but one learning, which *omnes gentes habent in cordibus suis*, one and the self-same spirit that worketh in all." [25] The differences of different times are, therefore, only slight and superficial; a basic sameness makes anything like a real progress or even change essentially unreal—Nothing. Daniel, in spite of his remarkable tolerance, is also a mind fundamentally unhistorical. The appeal to natural law remained an unhistorical principle even throughout the eighteenth century.

The other Elizabethan critics never go even as far as Puttenham or Daniel towards a general view of literary history. The natural-law argument is implied in all the many "defences" of poetry by proofs of its universality, which we find in Sidney and others. The constant parallels between English and classical authors (e.g., in Richard Carew's *Epistle* and in Meres' *Palladis Tamia*) do not show any comparative point of view, but rather a naïve patriotism which wants to match every single classical author with an English author who excelled in the same genre. Sir John Harington's interesting defence of Ariosto (in the preface to his translation of the *Orlando Furioso*, 1591) does not imply the recognition of a different artistic principle in Ariosto from that of Homer. If Ariosto deviates from the principles laid down by Aristotle "it is sufficient defence to say, Ariosto doth it." [26] But this obviously is not a defence of lawlessness or even of the originality of genius, but a proud claim that Ariosto is a classic who can establish precedents and new rules. Homer and Ariosto (like Ovid and Shakespeare in Meres) are visualized on the same plane, as living almost at the same time, with no consciousness of the gulf of ages and poetical traditions. Yet, in spite of the curiously original arguments in Puttenham and Daniel, literary conceptions in England were lagging behind those in Italy. This is only to be expected, as in most respects Elizabethan criticism is dependent on Italian Renaissance criticism. So far as the history of literature is concerned, no book was published in England which could be compared even with the historical parts of Crinitus, Scaliger, Gyraldus, or Patrizzi. In Webbe we find a short summary of Horace's *Epistle* with its stress on the increase and eventual decay of the arts,[27] but this seems to be the only conception of change to be found in Elizabethan criticism.

But there is one great exception: Bacon in his *Advancement of Learning* (and similarly, with important additions, in *De Augmentis*) [28] formulates the ideal of literary history. It has been doubted whether Bacon included poetry in his scheme, or whether he did not think merely of a history of learning. But, even if one grant that he looked at literature mainly as a record of intellectual advance, his suggestions seem scarcely less important. A history of literature as a history of the art of poetry was still something in the dim future, though conceptions of the advance of metrical refinement pointed the way. Bacon, for the first time in England, clearly conceived of literature as an expression of an age, and sketched even the methods by which such an evocation of the "spirit of an age" could be achieved: observation of the argument, style and method of presentation of individual books, and the "flourishings, decays, depressions, oblivions and removes" of schools, sects, and traditions. No doubt Bacon contemplated chiefly an intellectual history of mankind. He includes jurisprudence, mathematics, rhetoric, philosophy, etc., in his concept of learning, and he clearly recognized the deficiencies of purely political and diplomatic history. He sees that the history of learning was necessary to complete the picture. "Without it the history of the world seemeth to me to be as the statue of Polyphemus with his eye out; that part being wanting which doth most show the spirit and life of the person." But Bacon's scheme, which again demonstrates the greatness of his fertile mind "brooding on things to come," was unrealized. At least a century and a half elapsed before anything similar to his bold plan was attempted in England. Literary history in the seventeenth century lost sight, or rather never caught sight, of the high aims which were put before it by one of the greatest English minds, and had to grope its way slowly through new and increasing accumulations of materials.

CHAPTER TWO

The Seventeenth Century

THE SEVENTEENTH CENTURY, which has been called the "historical" century, cannot claim this name in England, as far as literary history is concerned. Methods of research in general historical scholarship improved beyond recognition. The names of Dugdale, Robert Brady, Henry Wharton, David Wilkins and many others still command the respect of modern scholars. But these advances concern almost wholly political and ecclesiastical history. No real attempt at literary history can be recorded, and there is nothing even comparable to Continental work in this field. Nevertheless the century was not altogether barren; especially towards its end there appeared conceptions and knowledge of facts which took literature out of the vacuum of rhetoric and poetics and prepared a genuinely historical approach.

In the main, the traditions established in the Renaissance continued with little change. But the little change which there was became important in the long run: both literary biography and criticism absorbed more and more matter strictly historical; their complete divorce, painfully evident in the sixteenth century, became less and less acute, and slowly there was prepared the union of the two forms which became one of the main traditional channels of English literary history. Biography in the early part of the seventeenth century simply continued the traditions established by Leland and Bale. John Pits' *Relationes Historicae de Re-*

bus Anglicis (written before 1613, published in 1619) is merely a version of Bale differentiated by the Catholic outlook of the exiled writer (he died as a Dean at Liverdun, Lorraine). The early parts with Britus Troianus and Cambria formosa, are equally fantastic, but at least the writers are carefully grouped according to calendar centuries. The virulence of the attack by Pits and his posthumous editor (W. Bishop) on Bale ("ut Idoli Bal ministrum facile dignoscas") [1] was, after all, only retaliation, for Bale was aptly called by Fuller "the angry wasp stinging all." It is, however, not quite true that Pits was "the idle drone stealing all." [2] In method he certainly does not constitute any advance, even if he contains original material on writers like Southwell and Campion, and laboriously compiles the names of Englishmen who went to Paris University or entered the Benedictine order. Thomas Dempster's list of Scottish writers (1620) is also little more than a "nomenclatura"; and so is Sir James Ware's book on the Irish writers (1639), which, though more valuable, is simply an expansion of the similar chapters in Bale, arranged according to calendar centuries. The biographies of Scottish writers including Langland, usually ascribed to David Buchanan, were published only in 1837 by the Bannatyne Club. [3] All these books were in Latin, and the decisive step of writing biographical collections in English was taken only by Thomas Fuller.

Before Fuller, however, the dramatist Thomas Heywood, in his *Hierarchy of the Blessed Angels* (1635) had promised "the Lives of all the Poets, foreign and modern, from the first before Homer, to the Novissimi and last, and what nation or language soever." [4] Probably little was lost when the plan fell through, as the remarks which preceded and followed these announcements show that Heywood had collected merely trivial anecdotes on the honours bestowed on poets and the calamities they had suffered.

The anglicization was important not only because of the easier accessibility to ordinary readers, but also for the necessary consequences of this change: the Latin churchwriters of the Middle Ages receded into the background, and actual English literature came to the fore. Fuller's early book, *Abel Redivivus* (1651), shows the source of this inspiration. It obviously flows from Foxe's highly popular *Book of Martyrs*, though it has a more literary twist. It includes lives of Wycliffe, Colet, Tindale, Latimer, Foxe, Lancelot, Andrewes, etc. *The Church History* (1655) contained biographies of Chaucer and Bacon. The best-known *Worthies of England* (1662) is much more literary in matter, though nothing like literary history could emerge from a collection based on a topographical plan purposely "interlaced with many delightful stories." While the book includes all kinds of "worthies," seamen and cardinals, writers of chirurgy and musicians, it shows some critical spirit in rejecting the "trash" of the first "centuries" of Bale and Pits [5] and a clear consciousness of the method adopted. The "ordering countywise" is based on the conviction that "*where* is as essential as *when* to a man's being," and the program (though hardly carried out in practice) of showing that "each county is innated with particular genius" [6] is important from our point of view, at least so far as it helped to take biography out of the thin air of Bale and give it a local habitation. A sense of connection with physical environment was a step towards historical interpretation.

The honour of having founded English biographical literary history must be reserved for Edward Phillips, Milton's much maligned nephew. In an early Latin work, *Tractatulus de Carmine Dramatico Poetarum Veterum* (1669), he had attempted something like a general sketch of literary history. He deals pretty fully with his ostensible topic, Greek and Latin tragedy, but then he rests satisfied with enumerating the mere names of Italian, Dutch, and German poets (referring only to those who have written in Latin). The English list is much fuller and states emphatically that English literature begins only at the time of Dante and Petrarch. Poets are listed under the various reigns since Edward III, sometimes with meagre comment and sometimes also with very hazy chronological notions. Churchyard appears as a contemporary of Occleve, and Marlowe is listed under the reign of Charles I! But a list of English poets right up to Milton and Dryden was at last established, longer and fuller than anywhere else.

This book served as the groundwork for the *Theatrum poetarum* (1675) in English. The preface is an interesting testimony to the break in poetical tradition created by the Civil Wars. "Let us look back as far as about 30 or 40 years, and we shall find a profound silence of the poets, except of some few dramatists." [7] It testifies also to the contemporary obsession with the "refinement" of the language and to the unbounded belief in progress. Phillips argues against the neglect of poets who had written in a language then obsolete, by forecasting a "double refinement" in two or three ages hence which will make contemporary poetry equally incomprehensible and antiquated. Phillips, of course, is against such time-serving, "What was *verum* and *bonum* once continues to be so always"; [8] and he has fine words of praise for Chaucer, Spenser, and Shakespeare. The biographies of writers which follow prove disappointing, however. They are arranged alphabetically, according to the Christian names of the authors, and are largely derived from Bale, Pits, and Fuller. Their value is in the notes on recent writers (of whom the youngest is Elkanah Settle) and in the oral tradition embodied in them. But their establishment of a choice of *English* writers—English in language—was an important precedent.

Phillips had remained satisfied with the dictionary arrangement, but this was at last discarded by William Winstanley in his *Lives of the most Famous English Poets* (1687). We may despise Winstanley, with Sir Egerton Brydges, as a "contemptible scribbler originally a barber, who stole all the characters of the English poets out of Phillips' book" or we may, with Haslewood, commend his "original information and entertaining anecdotes"; [9] a careful investigation of these claims is outside our purpose. But we must stress the importance of his having laid the foundations of a biographical history of English literature. Here are the main English writers from Robert of Gloucester (who, even in Warton, figures as the first English author) down to Dryden, Etherege and Wycherley. We may deplore the fanaticism of the comments on Milton, the "notorious traitor," whose "memory will always stink"; [10] but it is significant that we find quotations from Robert of Gloucester (extracted from Camden and Selden), from Lydgate, Occleve, Surrey, Wyatt, etc., the whole comprising an anthology which showed the way to many similar "ventures" of the eighteenth century.

From Winstanley there is a direct descent to Giles Jacob and Mrs. Cooper, and to Cibber's and Johnson's *Lives*. Just after Winstanley the biographical material concerning English poets was immensely enriched by the anecdotes and data collected by Aubrey and Anthony Wood. Aubrey's *Brief Lives*, accessible only since 1813, though used in MS by Wood, is arranged alphabetically and includes statesmen, soldiers, mathematicians, people of fashion, and personal friends. The zeal for collecting information and the knack of acquiring gossip, fair and foul, of this "shiftless person, roving and magotieheaded, and sometimes little better than crazed," [11] is that of a modern reporter. Anthony Wood's *Athenae Oxonienses: The History of the Writers of the University of Oxford, from the year of our Lord 1500* (1691–92) is a monument of minute seventeenth century learning, a mine which it took long to exhaust. But the book is limited by the fact that it records only the lives of Oxonians (or quasi-Oxonians) since 1500; and it extends, of course, far and wide beyond the region of fine literature. It is, in effect, an attempt at a biographical history of learning since the Renaissance, and the inclusion of many Cambridge men points to an ideal of completeness even beyond the superimposed limits. But the literary comments are extremely meagre and there is no historical perspective, except in the contempt for the darkness of the Middle Ages, in which "all studies of human learning, all the best arts and sciences, lay wasted and neglected." [12]

But before Winstanley's book became the established model, other methods of collective biography were tried, which introduced new variations. There is William Cave's *Scriptorum Ecclesiasticorum Historia Literaria* (1688)—as far as I know the first book by an Englishman to carry the name "Literary History" on its title-page. The Latin language and the limitation to theological writers are a reversion to the type of Bale. But as a new feature, the division into centuries, which are labelled with characteristic names like "Waldense" (the twelfth) or "Scholasticum" (the thirteenth) and introduced by a "Conspectus" of ecclesiastical history, shows a stronger sense of the writers' association with their respective times. Cave's book ends with the thirteenth century (which includes also Petrarch) but was con-

tinued up to 1517 on a similar plan by Dr. Henry Wharton.
Cave, though calling his book a literary history, is not literary in the modern sense; but Sir Thomas Pope Blount's
Censura Celebriorum Authorum (1690) is much more a history of *belles lettres*. The preface is rather remarkable, for
it expresses dissatisfaction with the merely biographical
method and for the first time recognizes the disadvantages of
the dictionary order. Blount arranges his authors chronologically because this alone makes it possible to observe
"fluxus et refluxus doctrinae." [13] The actual performance is,
however, disappointing; the book, which covers all the main
literatures since Hermes Trismegistos (considered a contemporary of Moses), is a mere scrapbook of quotations and
opinions. English literature is scarcely represented, as little
comment in Latin was available. But there are Chaucer, Barclay, Sidney, and the like, mostly buried under the mass of
humanists and philologists who predominate. The scheme,
a sort of history of world literature presented in short biographies, looks to a future age, but the mere collection of the
texts—without a single comment of the author—points back
to the "encyclopaedic" learning of the early seventeenth
century.

Blount's later book, *De Re Poetica* (1694), in English, is
again a scrap-heap of extracts, arranged first under the headings of the different genres and then under an alphabetical
list of authors, English and Continental. The list of English
poets is fairly full; and, as far as one can judge from the extracts, Blount accepted the current convention of English
poetical history, with Chaucer as the first reformer and
Waller as the ultimate refiner. That Blount was an ardent
believer in progress is obvious from his essay directed against
the theory of universal decay (in *Essays*, 1691), but his

books on literature are too impersonal, too much mere compilations, to have left a distinct trace behind them.

Blount ranges over the whole of literature; Gerard Langbaine in his *Momus Triumphans* (1688), and its expansion, *An Account of the English Dramatick Poets* (1691), narrows his field to the history of the drama. The book is an alphabetical list, a good deal of which is necessarily based on Fuller and Wood and the trade-lists of plays prepared by various publishers, but it has considerable value as bibliography and served as a basis for countless imitations.[14] However, it is no literary history, though Charles Gildon in his refurbishment, *The Lives and Characters of the English Dramatick Poets* (1698), is a little too severe in saying that "Langbaine seems to have known nothing of the matter, to have little or no taste of dramatic poetry." [15] Langbaine's original contribution is his full, or fairly full, list of sources, which he calls "thefts" or "plagiaries," and which it must have taken considerable time and pains to collect. Collective biography, then, had in Winstanley arrived at something like a scheme of specifically English literary history and in Blount at a scheme of something like universal literary history. But the actual performances were still mere catalogues of one kind or another and the materials quite isolated, so that many decades had to elapse before these schemes were filled out with the proper flesh and blood of true history.

This development was made possible by the independent growth of biography, antiquarianism, and criticism. Biography, even in the seventeenth century, largely remained "vacuum" biography, in Carlyle's term. Lives like Greville's *Sidney* (written about 1610) or even Sprat's *Cowley* (1668) are little more than sententious eulogies with scarcely any literary matter. In Fulke Greville there is, at least, an allusion to the distinction between classical and modern tragedy, and Sprat mentions the rise of Cowley's interest in poetry and speaks of the "likeness and the impression of the same mind" [16] in the most diverse of his writings. In John Gauden's *Life of Hooker* (1662) there is some literary discussion on style and matter. But all this is merely incidental, and the best biographies of the seventeenth century, Izaak Walton's four little classics, treat their heroes as saints and models of conduct and not as literary figures. The same is true also of Gilbert Burnet's *Life of Rochester* (1680), which makes of Rochester only a warning to sinners. More literary considerations can be found only in Dryden's *Life of Plutarch* (1683) where the works and their style have a place within the biographical scheme. Literary criticism and biography are there in simple juxtaposition. But new elements were being introduced into biography by devious ways: by the subtler introspection of diaries and autobiographies, by the general rise of psychology which, later in the eighteenth century, developed criteria of ultimate importance for literary history.

The antiquarian study of Anglo-Saxon remained even further outside the main tendency towards literary history. But, at least, the tradition was not interrupted even by the Civil Wars. William L'Isle, having struggled through High and Low Dutch, Middle English, and Middle Scots to acquire some knowledge of the language, published a treatise by Aelfric in 1623. Sir Henry Spelman established the first lectureship in Anglo-Saxon at Cambridge in 1623 and edited a sort of encyclopaedia of Anglo-Saxon law which contained the first Anglo-Saxon glossary. His son, John Spelman, wrote a life of King Alfred and edited the *Anglo-Saxon Psalter* (1640) very carefully, with good collations. Abraham Wheloc, the first holder of the lectureship, edited Bede with portions of the *Anglo-Saxon Chronicle* (1643), and re-edited Lambarde's edition of the *Laws* (1644) with further portions of the *Chronicle*. His successor, William Somner, is the author of the first *Anglo-Saxon-Latin-English Dictionary* (1659), and its preface contains the first account of earlier Anglo-Saxon scholarship. Interest in Anglo-Saxon was stimulated by the Hollander Franciscus Junius, who published *Caedmon* in 1655 at Amsterdam and the Gothic Bible in 1665 at Dortrecht. Thomas Marshall, who later became the teacher of Hickes, edited the Anglo-Saxon translation of the four gospels, in the same volume.

But interest in the language began definitely to revive only when a new lectureship had been established, this time at Queen's College, Oxford, in 1679. The leading spirit of the group was George Hickes, of Lincoln College, whose *Anglo-Saxon Grammar* (1689) was later incorporated almost unchanged in his great *Thesaurus* (1705). The first holder of the lectureship, William Nicolson, edited a *Historical Library*, surveying the older British historians; his successor, Edmund Gibson, published the *Anglo-Saxon Chronicle* (1692) in full for the first time, with a Latin translation; and Christopher Rawlinson edited Alfred's translation of *Boethius* (1698). Edward Thwaites's edition of the Anglo-Saxon *Heptateuch* (1698) contains *Judith*, which is, however, printed as prose and not recognized as a poem. This is typical of seventeenth century Anglo-Saxon scholarship; it is still completely unliterary: disguised in a Latin dress, it turns to law, history, and theology. The old polemical spirit of the Elizabethan antiquarians has disappeared. Little more was now done than editing, translating, and compiling grammars and dictionaries. But the seventeenth century prepared the ground and the material for the later development which reached its culmination in the nineteenth-century consciousness of the Anglo-Saxon foundations of English literature.

It is in literary criticism, however, that the gradual awakening of the historical sense can be felt most clearly. Literary criticism in England was almost stagnant for the first three quarters of the century, at least from the special point of view which we are considering. But it began to stir with sudden rapidity towards the end of the century, partly under the impact of Continental influences after the Restoration and partly through the advent of a few outstanding personalities like Rymer, Dryden, and Temple, who became the first English critics in any more technical sense of the term. These writers (together with a few minor figures) reflected the changed atmosphere that was reaching England from the Continent. The consideration of abstract poetics and rules gave way slowly to an analysis of the subjective impression of the reader or critic. This process of the "psychologization" of aesthetics has often been described, though usually with an unduly favourable stress on its value.[17] The new terms "gusto," "taste," "*je ne sais quoi*," and the like, important as they were as solvents of dogmatic neo-classicism, did not dispose of any problems, but rather fostered an anarchy of standards and a disregard for the actual work of art, though the extreme results of this attitude became a positive bane to genuine literary history only in the nineteenth century. The compromise solution of a "standard of taste," which comes from La Bruyère and Shaftesbury, temporarily retarded this tendency, which, of course, was only one of the many aspects of the great shifting of values from uniformity and generality towards individuality and diversity.

Far more important from the point of view of literary history was the whole movement of literary "Whiggery" which protested against the compliance with narrow rules and led to conceptions which can be described as "relativist." Dogmatism was being undermined by some sort of recognition that other ages had standards and viewpoints of their own. But "relativism" as such was not necessarily a preparation for the historical approach, though obviously it removed obstacles from the way. It frequently led rather to barren scepticism, to a mere assertion of despair, to the old and essentially vicious maxim of *De gustibus non est disputandum.* Besides, many pronouncements which in theory recognize the different standards of other nations and periods do not necessarily imply any real capacity for analyzing or understanding this difference. So neither the theory of taste nor relativism, which has frequently been misnamed the "historical point of view," were in themselves directly favourable to the rise of literary history.[18]

Genuine literary history became possible only when two main concepts began to be elaborated: *individuality* and *development.* These are complementary, since there is no understanding of historical individuality without a knowledge of its development, while, on the other hand, there is no true historical development outside a series of individualities. We must not, of course, understand individuality as referring only to the person of the poet. A comprehension of the uniqueness of a work of art increased with the new demands on "originality" or "invention." The old communism of subject-matter broke down, and "imitation" became slowly a term of reproach. A book like Langbaine's lists of "thefts" and "plagiaries" shows how sharply the so-called unoriginality of an older period was suddenly felt. The individuality of the poet was also stressed more and more: anonymity and community of authorship decline, at least in the higher ranges of literature; and the "genius" and "inspiration" of the writer comes more and more to be regarded as the essential factor in the creation of literature. "Creative" or "creation" are only other terms for the same concept. This sense of individuality and its value began to be extended also to types of art; the national peculiarities of one literary tradition began to be stressed in opposition to another; one type of drama was for the first time contrasted with another. The individuality of different epochs became recognized; the "spirit of the age" was such a new term much used in later analysis of the peculiar characteristics of each successive period in history.

Literature, besides, was slowly taken out of its vacuum and ceased to be a mere text for poetics. This was a necessary corollary of the growing sense of individuality, which cannot be comprehended or described except in its context or in contrast to some environment. Environment was first conceived during the seventeenth century in terms of physical climate. This was an unfortunate starting point, far away from the actualities of literary environment, but it led to considerations of the social milieu and the spiritual atmosphere. People began to discuss the influence of social stability, of peace or war, of liberty and decadence in literature; thus the concept of "national character" as a determining factor in literary creation was slowly taking shape.

Development, or at least a movement and change in time, was, however, the main concept which made literary history possible. Before the seventeenth century, with a few exceptions, Greece and Rome were considered as being on the same plane as contemporary England. Virgil and Ovid, Homer and Pindar, were discussed as almost contemporary writers. The germ of the concept of historical development is in the idea of progress which we have traced back to the Renaissance. But the idea of progress in itself was not sufficient to make literary history possible. It merely implied a uniform advance towards one ideal of perfection either in the present or in a more distant future; it rather tended to increase the contempt for the past and obliterated any distinction, except that of uniform improvement in the same kind, of the regularity of metre. Also the old idea of a "circular progress" implied an inevitable process of advance and decline, which it is difficult to reconcile with the actual diversity of the historical process. The modern concept of development could only arise when the idea of independent, individual, national literatures had become established and accepted.

At first, this process of growth was naturally conceived in close analogy with the ideas of contemporary biology. Literary evolution was "evolution" in the literal Latin sense of the term, a mere drawing-out of what was implicitly contained in the germ; it was a fixed and inevitable process of differentiation or of growth and decay. Such ideas did violence to the actual complex diversity of the literary process; but the problem was at least faced and formulated. This recognition of the diversity of different national traditions and their divergent courses of evolution was again only possible when past literature had been rediscovered and radically revalued. The slow opening-up of the treasures of Nordic poetry and the gradual unearthing of the older Romance literatures were broadening the literary horizon beyond the confines of the tradition descending from classical antiquity to the Renaissance. This formerly despised and therefore unexplored past began to be appreciated, at first with many reservations, and then so enthusiastically as to be exalted at the expense of the present.

This process was closely bound up with the spread of primitivism, a point of view which had never died out com-

pletely, because it was connected with such religious beliefs as the golden age and the decay of nature.[19] It should,
however, be stressed that the "historicity" of a given literary
phenomenon was felt for a long time merely as a limitation
and drawback and was usually used only as an apology for
the "faults" of older poetry and for its violations of the
"eternal," rational system of classical antiquity. A narrative
literary history became possible only when this dawn of the
historical sense had brightened to a full day. The process
which has been sketched here in abstract modern terms extends throughout the whole of the eighteenth century. All its
main elements were present even in the latter half of the
seventeenth century, though they were scattered in casual
pronouncements and their consequences were realized only
dimly by their authors or transmitters. In the eighteenth century, however, the different strands became disentangled,
the consciousness of the novelty of the new outlook and
criteria increased, and slowly the new conceptions began to
permeate and eventually to transform the traditional presentation of literary knowledge.

The subjective character that literary criticism was assum-
ing in the seventeenth century can best be illustrated by the
contrast between Rymer and Dryden. Rymer, in his *Tragedies of the Last Age* (1677), uses a hard-and-fast ideal of
drama as a measuring and chastising rod against the older
English drama. A rational plot which would resist all criticism on grounds of probability, decorum, and poetic justice becomes the standard. Any appreciation on grounds of
effect is expressly rejected. Critics who employ such methods seem to Rymer "a kind of stage-quacks and empericks
in Poetry who have got a receit to please." [20] His criticism
of Shakespeare and Beaumont and Fletcher, well known for
its carping literal-minded rationalism, is merely an applica-

tion of this principle. Dryden's two answers [21] argue against Rymer's dogmatism from the point of view of the reader's or spectator's psychology. It is empirically proved that "those plays which Rymer arraigns have moved both those passions (pity and terror) in a high degree." [22] The poet's business is to please the audience.

This point of view is an easy transition to arguments against the universal validity of the rules and in favour of a standard relative to time and place. Objections to the rules can be found in Oldham, Butler, Gildon, and many other writers of the time.[23] Dryden argues against Rymer that the "climate, the age, the disposition of the people, to whom a poet writes, may be so different that what pleased the Greeks would not satisfy an English audience." [24] John Dennis, in rejecting Rymer's model of tragedy, shows how inextricably this relativism was bound up with a clearer realization of literature's connection with its environment. "For setting up the Grecian method amongst us with success it is absolutely necessary to restore not only their religion and their polity, but to transport us to the same climate in which Sophocles and Euripides writ." [25] It is not necessary to accumulate further instances; they all point to the growth of an understanding of individuality, whether of a work of art, of a poet, or of a period, a type of style, or a national tradition.

The spread of "originality" and "genius" as terms of approval has been traced in detail,[26] and it is certainly no chance that Dennis was the foremost exponent of the "inspiration" theory. But for our immediate purpose the collective conceptions are far more important. "The spirit of the age" was such a concept which crystallized notions of historical individuality; it was used by Bacon, Bouhours, and Dryden.[27] Dryden speaks of it in the *Essay of Dramatic*

Poesy (1668), where he argues that the "genius of every age is different," [28] but apparently he does not yet understand the concept in the modern (Voltairian) sense of a pervading temper common to all cultural activities at a given time, but rather believes it to be the dominance of one particular kind of human endeavour in any one period. "Every age has a kind of universal genius, which inclined those that live in it to some particular studies." [29] In Greece it was the genius for the drama, in his own age the absorbing interest in natural science. But in speaking of Shakespeare and Fletcher as having written to the "genius of the age in which they lived," [30] Dryden assumes a sort of preestablished harmony between the successful author and his age, which hints at the important concept of the poet's "representativeness" for his time and nation.

The concept of a uniquely national style of writing is also frequently suggested at this time, again especially in Dryden. Neander's defence of the Elizabethans in the *Essay* points towards a double standard for the drama. The regularity and perfection of the French stage is contrasted with the "soul of poetry" in the English.[31] A parallel is drawn between the beauties of a statue, representing the French drama, and the beauty of a man, representing the English tradition. Here is the germ of such "romantic" concepts as the contrast between organic and inorganic form or between statuesque and picturesque art, which can be found in England for the first time in Coleridge. Obviously one should not press too far Dryden's suggestions of a greater "masculine vigour" and fancy in the English drama; their psychological source is often merely patriotic self-assertion, and in the whole body of Dryden's criticism they do not take up a really central position. Usually Dryden's discussion of French versus English drama is quite unhistorical, the arguments in favour of the English drama being merely patriotic, as in the passage where he refuses to be tried by the laws of another country "since it seems unjust that the French should prescribe till they have conquered." [32] Also to Rymer's criticism of the Elizabethans Dryden objected later (1693) that "it aims at the destruction of our poetical church and state." [33] According to the needs of the moment he turns against Elizabethan practices or attacks French conventions, and his own practice again is widely different either from that of Shakespeare and Jonson or from that of the French.[34]

But nationalism and speculations on national character (common in an age of character-writing) were an important factor in increasing the consciousness of national differences in the literary field. Rymer's introduction to Rapin's *Reflections on Aristotle's Treatise of Poesie* (1674) compares the different European languages in order to arrive at arguments for the superiority of the English language and English literature in general. Also the elaborate parallels among descriptions of night, quoted from Apollonius, Virgil, Tasso, Marino, Chapelain, and Le Moyne, which culminate in praise of a passage from Dryden's *Indian Emperor*, though partly derived from Scaliger, serve merely to bolster an argument inspired largely by patriotic assumptions.[35]

The increased consciousness of the dependence of literature on its environment was possibly of equal importance for the future of literary history. Unfortunately the critics of the seventeenth century started with the most remote and intangible influence on any literature, the climate. A smooth chain of causes and consequences was construed easily enough: a certain climate gives rise to a certain temper in a nation, and that produces certain types of institutions, which in their turn either favour or hamper the development of literature.

The influence of the climate on society is, of course, an old commonplace dating back to Plato, Aristotle, Vitruvius, Vegetius, Hippocrates, and Strabo. We find it again in Bacon and Montaigne, and it was most thoroughly elaborated by Bodin.[36] Throughout the seventeenth century the idea was echoed in England, for instance by Peacham, Barclay, Cowley, and Dryden; it is implied in Milton's invocation at the beginning of the ninth book of *Paradise Lost*, and it became one of the stock ideas of French critics like Bouhours, Fontenelle, and Fénelon.[37] The most elaborate statement of the theory in England is Sir William Temple's attempt in his essay *Of Poetry* (1690) to account for the (real or alleged) superiority of English comedy. This is explained by the diversity of English "humours," and the English propensity for humour is in its turn explained by the variable climate, "the native plenty of our soil, the unequalness of our climate, as well as the ease of our government, and the liberty of professing opinions and factions—plenty begets wantonness and pride; wantonness is apt to invent and pride scorns to imitate. Liberty begets stomach or heart, and stomach will not be constrained. Thus we have more originals, and more that appear that they are: we have more humour, because every man follows his own, and takes a pleasure, perhaps a pride, to show it." Not only the individualism of the Englishman but his alleged instability is ascribed to this same thing. "We are not only more unlike one another than any nation I know, but we are more unlike ourselves too at several times, and owe to our very air some ill qualities as well as many good." [38]

The particular formulas used by Temple, with their easy personifications and smooth chains of causes and effects, may seem naïve today, but a real question had been asked which has never since then disappeared from literary studies.

Temple's explanation must have appealed to his contemporaries very much, as it was, with slight modifications, repeated by Swift, Farquhar, Congreve, and Steele.[39] Congreve, for instance, embellishes it by adducing the big consumption of meat in England as a further cause of vigour and individualistic pride. The discussion quoted from Temple shows clearly that the explanation of national literature by climate was inextricably interwoven with an explanation from the state of society.

This social interpretation of literature was still far removed from a genuine comprehension of the actual social forces behind literature. But literature was, at least, felt to be in close interrelation with society. Sometimes even it was discovered that literature in its turn could be used as an elucidation of social history. The *Historia Histrionica* of James Wright (1699) declares that "old plays will always be read by the curious if it were only to discover the manners and behaviour of several ages: and how they altered. For plays are exactly like portraits drawn in the garb and fashion of the time when painted; . . . in the several fashions of behaviour and conversation, there is as much mutability as in that of clothes." [40]

Dryden in his *Discourse concerning the Original and Progress of Satire* (1693) is also clearly conscious of the relation of the satirist to his own time. He prefers Juvenal to Horace, because "Horace had the disadvantage of the times in which he lived: they were better for the man, but worse for the satirist." [41] But usually the influence of society on literature was stated more simply and crudely: peace and liberty are the prerequisites for any flowering of literature. Ovid and Virgil, of course, had praised the benefits of peace, and Bacon, Macchiavelli, and certainly many others repeated this obvious remark.[42] Cowley deplores "this warlike, various and tragical age which is the best to write of, but the worst to write in," [43] and Temple couples "long tranquillity of empire and government" with the advancement of knowledge and learning no less than with "exact Temperance in [the] races, great pureness of air and equality of climate." [44]

Liberty and letters had been closely associated by Longinus, and the idea was, with very different conceptions of the meaning of liberty, echoed by Milton and many others.[45] It played an important part in the debates on the superiority of English humour and English literature in general over the French. Wotton is especially emphatic on the supposed close association of democracy and literature.[46] Dennis and Shaftesbury were to make the most of this idea, which must, of course, always be understood in the context of the successful Whig revolution and its high expectations of an Augustan age, either in actual being or to come about in the near future.[47]

The idea of development is, however, at the very centre of the historical method. It could arise only when the static conception of the universe was breaking down. It would be outside the scope of this discussion to describe the process which replaced the closed world of antiquity by the diverse, imperfect, growing, and yet decaying world of modern conceptions.[48] The first idea of importance for the description of literature was that of a uniform progress. We have shown that it was in principle known already to the Renaissance.[49] Its obverse was the idea of universal decay, which, partly for religious reasons, never died out completely, even late in the eighteenth century.[50] Ben Jonson seems to have shared this view, and Henry Reynolds, who was interested in poetry primarily as a revelation of higher Platonic mysteries, speaks of the world as "decrepit, out of its age and doating estate." [51]

In practice, however, he knows, besides Chaucer, only fairly recent Elizabethan writers like Sidney, Spenser, Drayton and Daniel, whom he praises as secret philosophers to his taste.

Henry Peacham, who, in his *Compleat Gentleman* (1622), attempted a survey of English literature as a guide for young gentlemen, looks back also to the golden age of Elizabeth and accordingly extracts most of his information from Puttenham.[52] He has the conventional ideas about the "fogs of ignorance and barbarism" of the Middle Ages and musters the usual names of Chaucer, Gower, Lydgate (who is saddled with the authorship of *Piers Plowman!*), Hardyng, Skelton, Surrey, Wyatt, and the Elizabethans. In Michael Drayton's roll-call of English poets in his verse epistle to Reynolds (1627), Chaucer and Sidney assume the place of the great reformers of the English language, and similar lists of improvers can be found through Oldham and Denham right up to Addison's *Account of the Greatest English Poets* (1694). The complacent cocksureness of Addison's remarks on Chaucer, the "merry bard," and on Spenser, who "amused a barbarous age," have been quoted frequently enough.[53] Addison already voices the *fable convenue* of the time: that English poetry advanced steadily in refinement until it reached its perfection in Waller.

This is not the place to describe the rise of Waller's fame; he was, apparently, first singled out and elevated to a position parallel to that of Malherbe in France, in Soames' translation of Boileau's *L'Art poétique* (1683), for which Dryden chose the English equivalents.[54] But in the Preface to the 1690 edition of Waller's *Poems*, his claims were stated in the most extravagant way. Francis Atterbury, author of the Preface, says that Waller is the "parent of English verse and the first that showed our Tongue had Beauty and Numbers in it." [55] This view was accepted in substance by both Dryden and Rymer and became the foundation of their conception of the course of English literature.

In Rymer's *Short View of Tragedy* (1693) Chaucer is described as the first refiner of the language, though even after Chaucer it "retained something of the churl, something of the stiff and Gothish." Rymer explains: "In Queen Elizabeth's time it grew fine, but came not to an head and spirit, did not shine and sparkle till Mr. Waller set it a-running. But one may observe by his *Poem on the Navy, An. 1632*, that not the language only but his poetry then distinguished him from all his contemporaries, both in England and in other nations: and from all before him upwards to Horace and Virgil." [56]

Dryden was a firm believer in progress and argued from the advancement in natural science to a possible flowering of the arts. "If natural causes be more known now than in the time of Aristotle, because more studied, it follows that poesy and other arts, may with the same pains, arrive still nearer perfection." [57] Thus Dryden rejects the idea of a decay in nature [58] and in his Preface to the *Fables* (1700) describes the history of English poetry in these terms of an advance from Chaucer, who "first adorned and amplified our barren tongue," [59] through Spenser, Harington's *Orlando*, and Fairfax's Tasso to the perfection of Waller and Denham. This conception of the history of English poetry was even then not accepted universally. Attacks on Waller, by Dennis [60] and others show, however, the same fundamental assumption of a uniform advance towards polish of style and regularity of metre, even though they do not agree as to the merits of the particular individuals. Only Temple in his *Essay of Poetry* (1690) is a radical dissenter. He deplores the present "decline both of power and of honour" of poetry compared with its "former heights," and condemns the attempts at smoothness of language and style.[61]

But the idea of a uniform advance in technique and refinement was too tempting not to be accepted as the basis of an increasing number of sketches devoted to the history of individual genres. In Flecknoe's *Short Discourse of the English Stage* (1664) a scheme is hinted at which conceives of Shakespeare as the "inventor of the dramatick style, upon whom Jonson refined, while Beaumont and Fletcher first writ in the heroic way, upon whom Suckling and others endeavoured to refine again." [62] Rymer's *Short View of Tragedy* (1693) contains a sketch of the general history of the drama, which stresses the classical revival in France and Italy. Rymer is curiously silent on the Spanish stage, and his information on early English drama is meagre enough. But at least he quotes a report on a miracle play from Stow, mentions Heywood's interludes and Gascoigne, and is emphatic in his praise of *Gorboduc*. "It might have been a better direction to Shakespeare and Ben Jonson than any guide they have had the luck to follow." [63] His further criticism of Beaumont and Fletcher and of *Othello*, that "bloody farce," is obviously quite unhistorical in all its suppositions and conclusions. He makes no attempt to correlate his analyses with any time-sequence of the dramas discussed.

The same is true of Dryden's frequent discussion of the older English drama. The emphasis is shifting; Dryden lays it more upon the Elizabethans (though with many reservations and hesitations), but the praise he bestows on Jonson's *Silent Woman* [64] in preference to any other Elizabethan play shows that he did not himself transcend a narrow view of classical regularity in plot. Wright's *Historia Histrionica* (1699) also exemplifies the increased appreciation of the Elizabethans. Wright knows something about medieval mysteries, quoting from the Coventry plays and describing a Coventry pageant. He mentions Heywood's *Merry Play between the Pardoner and the Frere* (1533) and *Gammer Gurton's Needle*, which he wrongly assigns to the reign of Edward VI. He speaks of an advance "by little steps and degrees," [65] which shows that the idea of continuity, of *natura non facit saltum*, was invading literary history. Wright's *Country Conversations* (1694) contains an attack on Restoration Comedy which is not purely moralist and a defence of the unfashionable tragicomedy which shows that his preference for Shakespeare was not merely casual.

How much the idea of uniform progress meant as an approximation to truly historical considerations may be further demonstrated by the contrast between Davenant and Dryden. Davenant's *Discourse upon Gondibert* (1650) enumerates and criticizes great epic poems from a single point of view, their approximation to the ideal of "nature," as illustrated by their use of machinery. There is no sense of any difference in status between Homer and Virgil, Lucan, or Du Bartas. Exactly the same attitude is taken by Rymer in his survey of epic poetry prefixed to *Rapin's Reflections on Aristotle* (1674). Dryden's *Discourse concerning the Original and Progress of Satire* (1693) aims at something new in the history of genres; he tries to trace the "origin, the antiquity, the growth, the change and the complement of satire among the Romans." [66] Actually, he largely reproduces the views of Casaubon, Heinsius, and especially André Dacier, and hardly attempts more than to demonstrate that satire is of purely Latin origin, and that there are two branches of satire, making the usual comparisons among Horace, Persius and Juvenal. The modern history of satire is not even sketched except for the bare announcement that "thus I have given the history of satire, and derived it

as far as from Ennius to your Lordship (the Earl of Dorset):
that is from the first rudiments of barbarity to its last polish-
ing and perfection." [67] Even Dryden cannot escape the obsession of a uniform advance, and the fine program about
"growth and change" remains merely a distant ideal.

Universal and uniform progress, though by far the most
important idea in the actual consideration of literature at the
time, was not the only concept of change known to the
seventeenth century. Its insufficiency was sometimes clearly
realized, and hesitating attempts were made to use less rigid
conceptions. There was the old parallel of human institutions and contrivances with the growth and decay of an
animal or vegetable. Already Ascham in his *Scholemaster*
(1570) had paraphrased a passage in Velleius Paterculus,
saying quaintly that there is an analogy between civilization
and "fruits, plums, and cherries, but more sensibly" with
"flowers as roses and such like. . . . For what naturally can
go no higher, must naturally yield and stoop again." [68] Sir
William Davenant later transferred this idea to language in
Discourse upon Gondibert (1651). "Language," he wrote,
"which is the only creature of man's creation, hath like a
plant seasons of flourishing and decay, like plants is removed
from one soil to another, and by being so transplanted, does
often gather vigour and increase." [69]

Such analogies led easily to the ancient theory of circular
progress. We find it in Plato, Aristotle, and Seneca, and it
was revived by Bodin and most fully by Le Roy. Bacon,
Feltham, and Barclay discuss it, and Hakewill devoted almost a whole book to it. It occurs in Bouhours and Fontenelle.[70] We find it implied in many casual pronouncements,
for example in Dryden, when he compares the history of
English poetry with the history of a human individual and
at the same time draws a rigid parallel to it in the supposedly

analogous development of Latin poetry. "Chaucer," he says in the preface to the *Fables*, "lived in the infancy of our poetry. . . . We must be children before we grow men. There was an Ennius, and in process of time a Lucilius and a Lucretius before Virgil and Horace: even after Chaucer there was a Spenser, a Harington, a Fairfax, before Waller and Denham were in being." [71] The biological parallel drives Dryden relentlessly to look down on Chaucer as on a child and to excuse Spenser as an immature youngster. The implication that English and Latin poetry ran exactly the same course is not developed; no deductions are yet made from this very far-reaching theory of closed circles repeating each other with inexorable necessity.

The imitations of Boileau's *L'Art poétique* worked in the same direction. Soames' translation had, with Dryden's advice, substituted English names in the sketch of the history of French poetry (1683). "Imitation" of this style was a perfectly harmless game of ingenuity, but it implied a conviction that the course of English and French literatures is parallel. In this translation Fairfax takes the place of Villon; Spenser that of Marot; Davenant that of Ronsard; and Waller that of Malherbe. Ozell's revision of Soames for the collected edition of Boileau in English (1712) substituted Chaucer for Fairfax, as Chaucer obviously came closer to Villon in his relative chronological position than Fairfax. But the fitness of these parallels and even the value of Boileau's original scheme are not under discussion; the important facts are that the history of English poetry could be conceived in such terms, and that these imitations strengthened both the conception of a uniform advance towards the goal of metrical correctness and the close parallelism with an analogous development in France.

But here is nevertheless the germ of the evolutionary concepts, derived from biology, which were to play such an important part in literary history of the future. Dryden, like many before him, thinks of the Greek drama from Thespis to Aristophanes as having had "time enough to be born, to grow up and to flourish in maturity," [72] but the pronouncement is merely incidental and he makes no attempt to apply the biological analogy either to the development of English literature or to the growth of literature in general.

Only Sir William Temple makes these ideas the very basis of his literary conceptions. Temple, epicurean in outlook and temperament, could not bring himself to believe in the vaunted progress of modern times. He saw human nature as essentially the same in all ages and countries and looked with ironical satisfaction at the coming and going of civilizations. He read much on China, Peru, the Turkish Empire, and the old Germanic North and drew from the rise and decay of empires and civilizations the lesson that "our modern learned" are wrong "who will have the world to be ever improving" and believe that "nothing is forgotten that ever was known among mankind. . . ." [73] These empires, like natural bodies, grow for a certain time, and to a certain size, which they are not to exceed." [74] Temple immediately applied these ideas to the vicissitudes of literature. "Science and the arts have run their circles and had their periods in the several parts of the world." [75] They migrated from the East to the West through Greece and Rome to Italy and France. There is no reason why there should have been any advance. The flowering of the arts "falls in one country or one age, and rises again in others, but never beyond a certain pitch." [76]

Here, then, the almost Spenglerian theory of closed cycles of culture is embraced with real conviction and set into a harmonious context of moral philosophy and historical insight. The idea in itself was, of course, classical. The life of a nation had been frequently compared with the life of an individual, and the necessary stages of youth, maturity, and old age had been early detected in national as in individual life, for example by Florus and by St. Augustine. Moreover, the similar classical teaching of a necessary cycle of political institutions, which can be found in Plato, Aristotle, and Polybius, had been revived by Macchiavelli and Bodin.[77] But its application to literature by Temple was new, at least in England. Temple, unfortunately, did not develop it completely in his well-known attempt to sketch the history of poetry in order to observe "the antiquity, the uses, the changes, the decays, that have attended this great empire of wit." [78] Like Dryden, he cannot escape in practice the idea of one single progress or decay of literature. When he speaks of the history of mankind in a metaphor [79] of a man who declines between his thirtieth and fiftieth year and recovers afterwards without regaining the full vigour of youth, Temple is back to the conception of a present "old age" or "decay" of nature and has abandoned his theory of individual cycles.

Temple's sketch of the history of literature, important as it was made by the breadth of his literary horizon, does not use the idea of independent civilizations which run or have run their cycles, but merely adopts an "undulatory" view of the changes. Temple describes the rise of ancient prose through Longus, Petronius, Heliodorus and Lucian, and accounts for the decay of Rome with arguments based on the prevalence of war and the "fierceness of the Gothic humour" together with the "unequal mixture of the modern languages." [80] He conceives of medieval Latin poetry as influenced by "Gothic imitation" and then displays information unusual for his time on the old Germanic poetry which he calls "Runic." All he knows seems to come from a reading of the Danish antiquarian, Ole Worm, though elsewhere he shows direct acquaintance with Snorri's prose *Edda* in Resenius' Latin version (1665).[81] But in quoting and praising the song of Ragnar Lodbrog, which he recommends to those who love in poetry "to consider the several stamps of that coin, according to several ages and climates," [82] he cannot dispense with the apologetic tone of superiority usual in his age. He praises the truly poetical vein of poetry, "taking it with the allowance of the different climates, fashions, opinions, and languages of such distant countries." [83] He also traces the Spanish romances and all romantic machinery like fairies and elves to the same Nordic source and looks for the remnants of Runic poetry, even in Irish. He sees clearly that the Renaissance was not merely a return to classical antiquity, since rhyme in itself, in Petrarch, Ronsard, Spenser, Ariosto, and Tasso, constitutes a large innovation which links these poets definitely with the medieval past. The last stages of literary history he sees as unmitigated decay: he describes the predilection for small genres like the song, the sonnet, and the ode as something peculiarly modern, and he deplores both the vogue of the burlesque (Scarron) and the attempts at mere smoothness of language and style.

In Temple, then, we find the germs of many of the most influential future conceptions underlying literary history, and we see the broadening of the literary horizon which could not but accompany the breakdown of the old purely humanistic traditions. Temple is a child of his age in remaining half-heartedly tied to the older tradition. He even, ironically enough, became the champion of classical antiquity in the much discussed and overrated controversy between the Ancients and Moderns. His ignorant contempt for scientific discoveries and his impatience with the complacent prophets of unlimited progress had driven him into a position which was really uncongenial to his modern mind. His part in the controversy and his unfortunate blunder about the Phalaris letters have hitherto largely obscured the position of Temple, who is among the chief heralds of the historical method.[84]

In Dryden's various and variable criticism we find, it is true, many of the same themes scattered through his prefaces in casual pronouncements, which show that he also was susceptible to these new influences and helped to prepare a new mental atmosphere. The most conservative mind among these critics was Rymer, who clung in general to the rigid, unhistorical standards of neo-classicism. But even he felt the new wave of interest in the past; we see this in his sketch of the history of drama and in the well-known pages of a *Short View of Tragedy* (1693), that stress the importance of Provençal poetry, from which not only Italian poetry (Petrarch) but "in truth all our modern poetry comes...." [85] Rymer's knowledge is largely based on the notes to Redi's dithyramb *Bacco in Toscana* (1685), and Jehan de Nostredame's *Vies des plus Célèbres et Anciens Poètes Provençeaux* (1575) which he knew in the Italian translation of Giovanni Giudici.[86] He happened here upon a topic destined to become one of the central themes of literary history in the eighteenth century: the origin of "romantic," or rather medieval, poetry. In the seventeenth century all these suggestions remained uncorrelated, unsystematic, with no proper realization of their consequences and implications. But the seeds scattered were soon to shoot most luxuriantly.

The Eighteenth Century

CHAPTER THREE

Ideas on Literary History

THE EIGHTEENTH CENTURY completed the process whose beginnings we have traced. The tendencies described gathered momentum only very slowly, and the year 1774 had arrived before Thomas Warton's first volume was published. Warton's *History of English Poetry* was the first history of English literature "in form," as he said,[1] the first narrative history to cover any long period and most literary types systematically and fully. But Warton was not the great innovator he is sometimes declared to be.[2] He was rather the man of the moment, who had the ability to organize the materials accumulated by a century and to interpret them in the light of literary ideas elaborated by a century of intensive thinking. His great achievement became possible only when both scholarship and theories reached a certain consolidation not likely to be disturbed for some time, when, on the one hand, bibliographies, biographies, editions and commentaries had prepared the material, and on the other hand, a body of opinion, of concepts concerning the study of literature and its development, had been clearly formulated. The two lines of interest were not, of course, completely independent before they met in the mind of Warton. The motives which turned people to a study of old manuscripts, black letter-books, and pre-Restoration literature in general, were part of the process of literary revaluation that had been going on for a century; and, conversely, the conceptions of literary history were made possible only by the materials supplied by antiquaries and editors. Scholarship and criticism, which in the seventeenth century could be described as almost independent of each other, had begun to coalesce long before Warton. General conceptions of literary history had filtered through purely antiquarian work, and new materials had broadened the horizons of speculative thinkers. There is no simple chain of cause and effect, but instead a complex process, inside which we can observe mutual interdependences acting in all directions. Any presentation in a logical sequence like the following must necessarily simplify the complexity of reality. The only practicable method of studying the complex process is to disentangle the threads of the pattern. We shall, therefore, examine the relevant literary ideas, then the achievements of scholarship, and finally the successive attempts at true history. It would, however, be misleading to suggest that a simple process of "thesis, antithesis, and synthesis" had actually occurred.

The rise of literary history was dependent on a general growth of the "historical sense" which can be described as a recognition of individuality in its historical setting and an appreciation of the historical process into which individualities fit. It is sufficient to allude to some of the factors that turned attention to literary individuality at the end of the seventeenth and the beginning of the eighteenth century. Under the influence of Cartesianism, philosophical interest had begun to shift from the cosmological problem to the problem of consciousness and its growth. The problem of knowledge was to become the central concern of English philosophy from Locke onwards. As the approach of Locke and his followers was psychological rather than strictly epistemological, psychology became a new and fundamental science. Religious individualism led to increased emphasis on personal experience. In political life, the growing respect for the rights of the individual, points, at least theoretically, to liberalism. In ethics, concepts like the "moral sense" or Butler's "conscience" show the same trend towards subjectivist standards.

If we turn to aesthetic and literary concepts, we see the same movement away from the abstract and towards the individual, subjective and concrete—to the unique which has been once and will never be again. The poet becomes an "original," "creative" genius, a "second maker; a just Prometheus under Jove" in Shaftesbury's widely quoted terms.[3] Addison, in a well-known essay in the *Spectator*, had contrasted "natural genius" with *"bel esprit"*;[4] Welsted insisted that "no performance can be valuable which is not an Original";[5] and after 1755 there were books by William Sharpe, William Duff, and Alexander Gerard expressly devoted to the exaltation of original genius.[6]

The growth of interest in the poet as an individual is shown by the increased interest in biography, not only as a history of external facts, but as a picture of the poet's mental peculiarities and their rise in the individual history of his mind. Attention, which in earlier times was concentrated on the impersonal product of the poet's art, turned for the first time to the process of creation. Since this process was conceived as something individual, something intimately bound up with the personality of the author, "originality" became the slogan against imitation, against observance of the rules and exact conformance with established types. Edward Young's *Conjectures on Original Composition* (1759) is the *locus classicus*. It asserts that all men are born "originals," that "no two faces, no two minds, are just alike."[7] The process of creation, not being easily observable or measurable, was thus conceived as something fundamentally irrational, a result of the subconscious forces of the human mind, a product of feeling and volition, even of enthusiasm, passion, and inspiration. Such a process of creation was considered ideal; it was projected into the past as the process by which original genuine poetry was produced, in contrast to the mechanical, cerebral way of composing recent poetry.

Not only was the process of creation conceived as something irrational, but, logically enough, also its result, the work of art. More and more voices described it as incomprehensible, as something parallel to a piece of nature, even to a "vegetable," to something "grown, not made." [8] This irrationalism naturally invaded explanations of the enjoyment of poetry. Aesthetics in itself represents such turning to the individual state of mind of the reader or listener. The spread of terms like "gusto" and "taste" shows how the concept of abstract beauty was discarded in favour of an individual standard. At first these terms did little more than point to this problem of individuality and leave it unsolved and unexpressed. They shifted, however, the interest from intellect to sentiment, to the subrational powers of the human mind, or, as Dubos, the foremost exponent of eighteenth-century sentimentalism, called it, to a "sixth sense." This concept of taste as that of "original genius" or the "vegetable" work of art fostered that anarchy, that mere irresponsible dilettantism and caprice, which was, after all, one of the characteristics of much eighteenth-century interest in older literature. But the concept of "taste" was, in spite of these ultimate consequences, at first most valuable in deflecting attention from speculations on beauty, ideal genres, and the like, to a more careful analysis of the individual or national response to a work of art. It was thus one aspect of the whole movement towards the individual and particular.

Its dangerous anarchism, being soon perceived, was com-
batted by the concept of a "standard of taste." In England
this seems first to occur in Shaftesbury, who was essentially
a Neoplatonist. "Taste" and "Judgment" were identified by
him and Welsted; [9] they intellectualized the concept of taste
and thus prepared the way for Kant's *Critique of Judgment*.
Hume based the standard of taste on the uniform consent
and experience of the nations,[10] and Burke, Hogarth, Kames,
Reynolds, and especially Gerard tried hard to support this
standard by rational arguments from general qualities of human nature and attempted thus to retard a development un-
profitable for a systematic study of literature.

The very same turn from formalism to emotionalism can
be traced in the aesthetics of music. One could even suspect
that music was the art which helped most to subvert the old
theory of imitation. As soon as people began seriously to
think about music, they saw that the theory of imitation
would not hold, even though they tried to stretch it to include an imitation of the passions. Thus James Harris, in his
remarkable *Three Treatises* (1744), recognized that "music
derives its efficacy from another source than imitation" and
that it raises the affections "by a sort of natural sympathy." [11]
Charles Avison's *Essay on Musical Expression* (1752) acknowledged that imitation without expression is nothing,
and that the imitation of nature is not essential to music.[12]
Adam Smith similarly argued that "music is certainly less an
imitative art than any other which merits that appellation"
and concluded that "the principal effect of music arises from
powers altogether different from those of imitation." [13] Sir
William Jones in an *Essay on the Arts commonly called Imitative* (1772) accepted these arguments completely and extended them to poetry. Neither poetry nor music can be
thus called imitative, as they are rather "expressive of the

passions and operate on our minds by sympathy." [14] Beattie merely drew the logical conclusion when, apologetically enough, he wanted to remove music from the imitative arts, without meaning "any disrespect" for music or Aristotle.[15]

In the theory of painting the old ideas of imitation or of Neoplatonic ideal beauty died much harder for obvious reasons. Reynolds and Daniel Webb, who took many ideas on the *Beauties of Painting* from that rather ineffective German "classicist" Raphael Mengs, remained completely under the spell of Neoplatonic ideas.[16] These must always imply an unhistorical approach; it is, therefore, not chance that the first book in England which can be described as a history of painting should have been such a poor compilation as the lectures of James Barry,[17] while music found two extensive and, on the whole, penetrating historians in Sir John Hawkins and Dr. Burney, only a short time after Warton wrote. But we cannot discuss the history of aesthetics in England as such; for the purposes of our survey it is sufficient to realize the importance of the problem of individuality and of the closely related emotionalism. Without it, the whole new conception of true and primitive poetry is incomprehensible.

The individual in isolation is ineffable. "Taste," "Genius," "Inspiration," "Creation," "Expression," are fundamentally irrational concepts, pointers towards a problem which remained unsolved. They heightened the value of individuality and focussed attention on its mystery. But individuality could be studied, at first, only in relation to its environment. Nothing is more frequent in the eighteenth century than insistence on studying the environment of the poet, on entering sympathetically into his mind and conditions. Thus John Husbands asked in 1731, while pleading for Hebrew poetry, "what strange work should we make of the most modern of the Greek and Latin authors, if we endeavoured to read them without regarding the genius or customs of the people to whom they were written." [18] Theobald, in introducing his edition of Shakespeare (1734), realized that "the critic must be well versed in the history and manners of his author's age, if he aims at doing him a service." [19] Dr. Johnson, in his *Observations on Macbeth* (1745), also joins in the chorus: "In order to make a true estimate of the abilities and merit of a writer, it is always necessary to examine the genius of his age, and the opinions of his contemporaries." [20]

Lowth, in his *Lectures on Hebrew Poetry* (1753), most eloquently and finely advocated more than a mere knowledge of the language, the manners, disciplines, rites, and ceremonies of the people studied. He proposed to investigate their inmost sentiments, the manner and connexion of their thoughts. "In one word, we must see all things with their eyes, estimate all things by their opinions." We must imagine ourselves "exactly situated as the persons for whom the poetry was written, or even as the writers themselves." [21] Joseph Warton in his *Essay on Pope* (1756) stated that "we can never completely relish, or adequately understand any author, especially any ancient, except we constantly keep in our eye his climate, his country and his age." [22] Hume asked the critic to "place himself in the same situation as the audience." [23] Edward Gibbon, in his early French essay *On the Study of Literature* (1761), asked us to "place ourselves in the point of view with the Greeks and Romans." [24] Dr. Johnson, in the preface to his edition of Shakespeare, wanted us to compare the performances of every man "with the state of the age in which he lived." [25] A book like Robert Wood's on Homer (1769) proposed to "approach as near as possible to the time and place, when and where he wrote." [26]

The idea was repeated almost everywhere, but it is impossible to consider its mere expression as the accomplishment of the historical method.[27] Similar pronouncements can be found in the early Italian defenders of Ariosto and even in such non-romantic writers as Jean Chapelain.[28] After all, it amounts to little more than a recommendation to pay proper attention to "decorum," "costume" or, as Pope says, to study the poet's

> fable, subject, scope in every page;
> Religion, country, genius of the age.[29]

The natural consequence of this attention to environment was the increasing regard for the relativity of critical standards. It permeated all the many debates on Shakespeare's observance of the unities or Spenser's principles of composition and led to greater and greater tolerance for different types of art. It had thus a most important effect on the increasing interest in early and foreign literature. It found possibly its sharpest expression in Goldsmith's demand that "English taste, like English liberty, should be restrained only by laws of its own promoting." Criticism must "understand the nature of the climate and country, before it gives rules to direct taste. In other words, every country should have a national system of criticism." [30]

In early times this attention to "manners" remained largely an aspiration. It assumed flesh and blood only when environment was analyzed in detail. Though great advances were made during the eighteenth century, much still remained very vague and general, remote from the concrete conditions of the analyzed work. The most common approach was through the theory of climate, popularized by Temple. Generally speaking, only a few rather crude and dogmatic

solutions were current. The mild climate of the South was
contrasted with the rigours of the North, while extreme
heat was considered detrimental to the growth of literature.
Or sometimes East and West were contrasted, in which
case the East was identified with the South and considered
favourable to the "warmth of imagination." Thus Pope
complimented Lady Mary Montagu on having been "en-
lightened by the same sun that inspired the father of poetry,"
Homer, and on the fact that she "glowed under the same
climate that animated him," when she stayed at Constan-
tinople.[31] Addison assigned "extravagant imagery" to the
"warmer climates." [32] Husbands in 1731 spoke of the "Genius
of the east" which "soars upon stronger wings, and takes a
loftier flight than the Muse of Greece and Rome." [33] Blackwell, in his book on Homer (1735), praised the climate of
Asia Minor as one of the favourable causes accounting for
the supreme genius of Homer.[34] John Brown connected the
rise of the pastoral with the fertility of the Sicilian vales; [35]
and Wood, in his *Homer* (1769), was, like Blackwell, emphatic on the advantages of the Greek climate in comparison
with the Egyptian which makes people sluggish and in-
capable of producing great literature.[36]

Goldsmith was one of the most fervent believers in the
decisive influence of climate and reproduced all the more
extravagant arguments of Buffon, in essays only recently
identified as his. "It is climate alone which tinctures the
negro's skin: that makes the Italian effeminate, and the
Briton brave." [37] It was, of course, felt that a more precise
explanation of this influence of climate was wanting. Therefore Addison, or whoever wrote *A Discourse on Ancient
and Modern Learning* (1739), tried to account a little more
concretely for its influence by suggesting that it "causes an
alteration of the animal spirits and of the organs of hear-

ing." [38] Goldsmith explained the English temper which he described not as spleen, but as "the gloom of solid felicity," by a climate that produced more meat than drink, for meat-consumption increased severity of outlook.[39] Sir William Jones praised the climate of Yemen in recommending Arabian poetry and spoke of the immoderate heat of the East as disposing the Eastern people to a life of indolence, which gives them full leisure to cultivate their talents. He made the alternative suggestion that the sun has a direct, physical influence on the imagination.[40]

But such arguments must have sounded unconvincing to a northern people justly proud of their great imaginative poetry. Sir Kenelm Digby, who died in 1665, had argued that "Spenser's works are evidence that a northern climate may give life to as well-tempered a brain, and to as rich a mind as where the sun shines fairest." [41] Similarly, Addison agreed that genius can be found also in the "colder regions of the world." [42] An early poem of Gray on the *Alliance of Education and Government* (1748)—significantly enough to be preceded by a dedicatory ode to Montesquieu—had accepted the theory of climate,[43] but in a letter to John Brown, Gray argued, remembering Ossian, that "imagination dwelt many hundred years ago in all her pomp on the cold and barren mountains of Scotland," and thus cannot be a result of heat.[44] Thomas Seward (1750), in explaining the superiority of English poetry, was frankly puzzled by the argument that "England's frozen foggy genius" should rather paralyze the "nobler and fiercer flame of poetry." [45]

More thoroughgoing sceptics rejected the whole principle. Hume categorically rejected Temple's notion that climate could have caused the instability and uncertainty of the English character, and merely allowed that southerners have a stronger amorous propensity and northerners a greater love of liquor.[46] Also Sterne made elaborate fun of Temple's theory in *Tristram Shandy*, ascribing humours rather to the blood and experience than to wind and air.[47] Dr. Johnson chided Milton for fearing the climate of his country might be "too cold for flights of imagination" [48] and scornfully rejected the view that "a luckless mortal may be born in a degree of latitude too high or too low for wisdom or for wit." [49] Kames argued against the influence of climate. Against Buffon and Goldsmith he urged that it "cannot account for the copper colour of Americans" and similar racial distinctions.[50] The helplessness of even a shrewd historian like Robertson, in dealing with these problems, is well illustrated by his *History of America* (1777). He made a great deal of climate and the grandeur of the natural objects that America presents to the sight, but in his description of the Indian tribes confused hopelessly zones and landscapes. But the prestige of "scientific causation," the fame of Montesquieu (who took some of his ideas on the influence of the air from a pamphlet by Arbuthnot),[51] and the example of Dubos made even empirically-minded Englishmen and Scotsmen delude themselves with such literally "airy" speculations.

The climate theory came nearer to actual literature only when it was expanded and reinterpreted so as to include general geographical conditions and landscape. Lowth's fine *Lectures on Hebrew Poetry* (1753) explained the particular cast of Hebrew poetry by the influences of the surrounding objects of nature. This gave pleasant and, on the whole, legitimate opportunities for tracing the sources of Bible imagery. Robert Wood actually travelled in the land of Homer and saw the country around Troy. He studied it with great care, in order to verify the correctness of every detail in Homer and to demonstrate that he was "the most constant and faithful copier after nature." [52] The enthusiasm for Nordic poetry and Ossian suggested that there was a direct relation between the gloom and wildness of the northern landscape and the sublime melancholy of these poems. The scenes and pictures actually before the poet's mind were, after all, directly mirrored in his poetry.

But we come nearer to the actual determinants of literary evolution if we consider the influence of social conditions. In an earlier age these were conceived largely in terms of political conditions, as an age proud of its recent achievement of constitutional liberty could not help visualizing all such problems in terms of a simple contrast between liberty and despotism. Shaftesbury was the main exponent of this age-old view. The Greeks, "with their liberty not only lost their force of eloquence, but even their style and language. . . . The high spirit of poetry can ill subsist where the spirit of liberty is wanting." That is why the "vastest empires governed by force and despotism" are barren in literature.[53] Thus the intimate association of liberty and letters favoured high hopes for the near future. A new Augustan age was confidently expected. Welsted sings in 1724 "I see arise a new Augustan Age"; [54] and Blackwell, a great admirer of Shaftesbury, states that the present age in England is "a happy instance of the connexion between Liberty and Learning." [55] Blackwell's book on Homer argues that Homer lived at a time most favourable to poetry; he saw "cities spirited with liberty." But "Greece was ill-settled. Violence prevailed in many places," and he lived "amidst the confusion of wandering tribes." He saw "towns taken and plundered, the men put to the sword, the women made slaves." [56] No contradiction or incongruity between these statements was apparently felt by Blackwell; liberty as a condition for the flowering of the arts was understood by

Shaftesbury in a constitutional sense, while in Blackwell it begins to assume the meaning of freedom from social restraint, of the turmoil and anarchy of primitive manners. The conventional view was emphatically stated by John Upton in his *Observations on Shakespeare* (1746). He stressed the "reciprocal dependence and mutual connexion between civil liberty and polite literature," and ascribed the flowering of Elizabethan literature entirely to the dawn of liberty (apparently religious). If Britain should ever become a tyranny, then "we must bid farewell to our Miltons and Shakespeares and take up contentedly again with Popish mysteries and moralities." [57]

Goldsmith is one of the many later writers who accepts the close association of liberty and letters, and who accounts for the failure of the Carolingian Renaissance by the lack of "permanence of the state and freedom." [58] Also Kames agreed that "taste could not long flourish in a despotic government" and that despotism is alone sufficient "to account for the decline of Greek sculpture and painting." [59] But again the sceptical intellect of Hume subjected the principle to a closer scrutiny. He saw that against the association of liberty and letters might be argued the undoubted splendours of the Ages of Louis XIV and the Medici, and he propounded a compromise solution: learning flourishes better in republics, the arts in monarchies. Hume threw doubt on the whole value of causal explanation; with an apparent allusion to Blackwell, he thought that a man "who should enquire, why such a particular poet as Homer, for instance, existed, at such a place, in such a time, would throw himself headlong into chimaera," and he concluded that there was something "accidental in the first rise and progress of the arts in any nation." [60]

Lord Chesterfield rejected the whole principle completely;

he could not see why the "despotism of a government should cramp the genius of a mathematician, an astronomer, a poet or an orator." He curiously enough thought that tyranny deprived writers only of such topics as bawdry, blasphemy, and sedition—to do this was a good thing in any case—and he argued more convincingly that the Revival of Letters was not owing to a free government but to an absolute Pope like Leo X, or a despotic Prince like Francis I.[61] Dr. Johnson, too, in commenting on Gray's "Progress of Poesy," which spoke of the Muses as "scorning the pomp of tyrant power," observed that "in the time of Dante and Petrarch, from whom Gray derives our first school of poetry, Italy was overrun by tyrant power and coward vice: nor was our state much better when we first borrowed the Italian arts." [62] Thus, the crude solution that the best influence on literature is a free constitutional government was abandoned fairly early. Possibly the theory was discredited by the disappointment of hopes for a new Augustan Age.

Another common approach to the influence of society on literature was the association of literary production with religion. The main exponent of this view was John Dennis, who argued that "Grecian Poetry flourished with their religion and failed with their religion." [63] This idea was fostered by the growing regard for the Bible as poetry and was the foundation of John Husbands' plea for religious poetry.[64] It underlay Lowth's praise of Hebrew poetry, and cropped up occasionally in a different context. Thus Thomas Seward (1750) accounted for the greatness of Elizabethan poetry by its religious inspiration, by the "spirit of God," the "Sun of Righteousness," and more concretely by the fact that the "noblest poems that were ever wrote in the world, those of Job, David, Isaiah and all the Prophets, were daily read" in churches and homes.[65]

But both these theories were soon completely over-shadowed by the point of view which we have learned to call primitivism. As this has been fully discussed by several recent writers, it is not necessary to stress how widespread it was, long before Rousseau.[66] Its connexion with the Lockian psychology which, by the assumption of a *tabula rasa*, weakened the idea of original sin, and with Shaftes-bury's ethical sentimentalism, is obvious. Applied to litera-ture, it led to the all-important contrast between primitive poetry, universal and sentimental, and modern literature, ra-tionalist and refined. The conditions for the production of true poetry were seen in the simple life rather than in mod-ern luxury; in life inspired by religion rather than in the godless life of modern society; in rude, and even barbarous, manners rather than in refined polite conventions; in a so-ciety which encouraged the open expressions of feelings and enthusiasm, rather than in modern hypocrisy and cold ra-tionality; in an atmosphere that supported the belief in su-pernatural beings, and even in downright superstition rather than in a time when the daylight of reason had dissipated elves, fairies, and witches; in picturesque, colourful manners rather than the drabness, monotony, and commercialism of the modern age.

There is nothing peculiar in a nostalgia for simple manners or even in a desire for a return to "nature" in poetry. The pastoral movement, which pervades the whole sixteenth and seventeenth centuries, is such a symptom of an age-old long-ing. Even Donne thought that he wrote more naturally than the Petrarchans, and Dryden felt himself a poet of nature compared with the metaphysical writers. But the particular, very uniform conception of nature and natural poetry which prevailed in the eighteenth century was something new. The main thesis, "simple manners foster true poetry," was in itself merely a retort to the believers in progress in the arts. The interesting problems arise only when we examine the concrete meaning of "simple" and of "true." These meanings are very different in different writers, but the very fact that the most varied manners were considered simple and the most varied poetry "primitive," made this crude dichotomy possible.

If, in the meantime, we turn our attention only to one part of this question, to the manners or the social influences which were then considered most conducive to great poetry, we notice a clear movement towards an increasing stress on more and more primitive and even savage stages of society—a progress which was, however, not quite universal. An early writer like Blackwell, whose book on Homer seems to have been one of the main sources of primitivist ideas in the century, was still fairly sober on this point. Though he praised Homer's "representation of natural and simple manners" and thought that "wealth and luxury disguise nature" he did not place Homer—who to him was the greatest poet —in a savage society. Homer lived rather in a state of transition, when manners were passing "from the stage of rudeness to the polite stage." Blackwell was typically hesitant (and we suspect simply confused) about the social status of his hero. Once he calls him a "strolling indigent bard," elsewhere he described his position as highly respected and important, and rejected comparison with the Irish or Highland "Rüners" as a slur on Homer.[67] In Lowth, the Hebrews, who produced "the only specimens of primeval and genuine poetry," [68] were also depicted rather as a simple, grave, temperate nation of husbandmen and shepherds with nothing savage about them. A compromise between the old belief in progress and primitivism was first elaborated in Hurd's dialogue on the *Golden Age of Queen Elizabeth* (1759).

He tries to show that the most favourable time for the purposes of poetry "lies somewhere between the rude essays and uncorrected fancy, on the one hand, and the refinements of reason and science, on the other. And such appears to have been the condition of our language in the age of Elizabeth." [69]

But apparently the enormous success of Ossian made these compromises unnecessary and encouraged the opinion that aboriginal manners are most favourable to poetry. Hugh Blair's *Dissertation on the Poems of Ossian* (1763) was the fullest exposition of the view that the "times which we call barbarous" were most "favourable to the poetical spirit," and that "imagination was most glowing and animated in the first ages of society." [70] Similarly William Duff (1767) agreed that the "early and uncultivated periods of society are peculiarly favourable to the display of original poetical genius." He explained: "The earliest and least cultivated period of society is most favourable, as every object is new, imagination free, as there is no criticism and tradition, and as the manners are simple and uniform and thus, in poetical description, must appeal universally." There is leisure and tranquillity. "The poet," he dreamt, "wanders with a serene, contented heart, through walks and groves consecrated to the Muses." [71] Robert Wood, in 1769, trying to account for the greatness of Homer, abandoned the more careful view of Blackwell and described the rude state of Homeric society in terms of the Arab civilization which he had seen in the countries he visited on his travels.

In all these later writers the complete confusion about the states of society supposed to be primitive is the most remarkable feature for the modern observer. The early stages of Greek civilization, the society depicted in the Old Testament, the Arabs, and the dim dark ages in which Ossian was imagined to have lived, were all on a level. Richard Hurd then added to this list even the feudal civilization of the Middle Ages. The earlier dialogue on the Age of Elizabeth had not yet drawn these extreme conclusions. But in the *Letters on Chivalry and Romance* (1762) he had apparently taken courage from Jean Chapelain's defence of the romances, which he must have read sometime after writing the dialogues.[72] Hurd there expounded not only the "agreement between the heroic (Homeric) and Gothic manners," but insisted on the "preeminence of the Gothic manners and fictions as adapted to the ends of poetry, above the classic." The Gothic manners and fictions "are the more poetical for being Gothic."

The main arguments in favour of this contention were that the gallantry of feudal times was more poetical than the "simple and uncontrolled ferocity" of the Grecian, and that the enchanters and witches, the "machinery" of the medieval past, were more "sublime, more terrible and alarming than those of the classic fablers." [73] Pity and terror, even "alarm," induced by whatever methods, were in this theory of effects considered as superior to any contemplation of beauty. Thus a simple, rude, or at least picturesque and superstitious society was fully established as the social structure most favourable to the flowering of poetry. The influence of society on literature was thus acknowledged, but an actual analysis of this influence was almost impossible as long as the catchwords "simple manners," "heroic manners," "Gothic manners," all considered as almost interchangeable, obscured a view of the actual social conditions in which literature is produced. Only very rarely do we find other more concrete views suggested. Thus Dennis early (1702) contrasted the reign of poetry and pleasure under Charles II with the reign of politics and business under Queen Anne and reflected on its consequences to literature.[74] Gildon suggested, in passing, the genuinely sociological view that "in England plays began at the very bottom of the people, and mounted by degrees to the state we now see them in." [75] Shakespearean criticism sometimes referred to the influence of the "illiterate, low-minded mechanics" who were supposed to have composed the audience of Shakespeare,[76] and Warton's *Observations on Spenser* (1754) made much of Spenser's acquaintance with pageants, masques, and even tapestry.[77] The author of the *Poetical Balance*, sometimes supposed to be Goldsmith, contrasted Sidney, the poet of the court, with Spenser, the poet of the country.[78] But all these and similar suggestions remained only incidental hints. Much work had to be done, much closer analyses of actual social conditions made, before a sociological method could throw any light on the real process of literature.

It was thus difficult in the eighteenth century to illuminate literature by social history. The converse use of literature for the illustration of social history was simpler and easier. Obviously, literature was not always studied by people with literary interests but a good deal by historians and antiquarians. Much miscellaneous information about costumes and customs, historical events, and topography could be gleaned from *belles lettres*. The commentaries on Shakespeare, Jonson, and Spenser are full of digressions into fields which today would fall under a "History of Everyday Things in England." It would be tedious to quote the many examples of writers on literature who used such information rather as illustration of social history. Especially later, the scholars interested in romance continually excused their preoccupation with such a trivial topic by the hopes they entertained of throwing light on ancient manners. Even Campbell in the *Polite Correspondence* (1741), one of the earliest accounts of old English poetry, recommended translation from Anglo-Saxon as serving to "illustrate many dark passages in our ancient history." [79] But, before Warton, no systematic attempt was made to use Chaucer, Shakespeare, or Spenser for a picture of the age. On the whole, literature was searched for odd, quaint, or unusual references to disused customs rather than for the materials of social history.

The concepts of change, progress, and finally development invaded literature as we have shown before. The original contribution of the early eighteenth century was the idea of a general history of literature. Such a history was made possible by the conviction that poetry is universal and that primitive poetry is uniform. Thus the origins and even the early stages in the development of poetry were everywhere the same. The Bible, Homer, Ossian, the Welsh bards, the Lapland and Indian songs, the Scottish ballads, the Provençal "ditties" and even chivalrous romances appeared on one common level as testimonies for the universality of poetry. Steele's praise of the Lapland love songs and Addison's of *Chevy Chase* were most influential. [80] But one must beware of Addison's terminology; he labours hard to show that *Chevy Chase* is written on a classical pattern and has a universal appeal just because of its simplicity which he contrasts with the "Gothic manner" of writing, appealing only to a peculiar taste and full of false wit and extravagant fancies. In Addison there is no primitivism in the later sense, for he wanted to bridge the gulf between the old ballad and Virgil. What he called the "Gothic manner of writing" is, as the reference to Cowley shows, rather something that we today would call Baroque.

The primitivist combination of Laplanders, Eddic odes as quoted by Temple, Taliessin's Welsh odes, and the poetry of the Bible appears only in John Husbands' remarkable Preface (1731). The *Polite Correspondence* (1741) mentions Orpheus and Homer, the odes of Taliessin, Scottish bards, and the Indians. Anglo-Saxon poetry fits into the scheme, as do Pindarics, the Lapland odes, or the poems of Ramsay's *Evergreen*. It is all the same, as long as all these poems have a metaphorical style, obscure composition, and abrupt transitions. Blair in his *Dissertation on the Poems of Ossian* (1763) was clearest and most systematic about the uniformity and universality of primitive poetry. He stressed "the degree of resemblance among all the most ancient poetical productions, from whatever country they have proceeded," and considered their common style, which he called the "oriental vein of poetry," as "characteristical of an age rather than a country." [81] He quoted *Ragnar Lodbrog* in full and described the Lapland songs. Ossian he felt to be in complete agreement with the main traits of universal poetry, though Blair preferred his "tenderness and delicacy of sentiment," his "humanity, magnanimity and virtuous feelings of every kind" [82] to Homer's rougher manners. In a letter addressed to John Brown, Gray, in 1763, agreed with this point of view: "The truth," he believed, "is that, without respect of climates, imagination reigns in all nascent societies of men, when the necessities of life force everyone to think and act much for himself." [83]

David Hume, with his more rationalist intellect, was one of the few who saw essential distinctions among the so-called primitives. His paper, *Of the Authenticity of Ossian's Poems*, unfortunately not published until 1875, argued from this "extreme delicacy" against the genuineness of Ossian. He rightly demonstrated that the style and genius of these poems was quite different from the "savage rudeness" of the Lapland and Runic odes.[84] China, Peru and India, the Iroquois, Ossian and the Edda, Homer and Theocritus, the ancient Hebrews, and the Irish bards were all mixed up in the original union of poetry described by John Brown.[85] Gray, in the later notes to the *Progress of Poesy* (1768), quotes also the Erse, Norwegian, and Welsh fragments, alongside of Lapland and American songs, as proof of the "extensive influence of poetic genius over the remotest and most un-civilized nations." [86] And Thomas Hawkins refers to Runic odes, to Scheffer's Lapland songs, and the Iroquois poetry described by Lafiteau as evidence for the independent origin of poetry in many nations.[87]

But the first man who contemplated primitive poetry as a whole was Thomas Percy. He planned a collection of *Specimens of the Ancient Poetry of Different Nations*,[88] and his whole life-work was an attempt to carry out this plan based on a conception of the substantial identity of all primitive poetry. Percy himself considered most of his publications as contributions to such a symposium of all the nations: his two publications of (indirect) translations from Chinese, his *Five Pieces of Runic Poetry* (1763), his paraphrase of the *Song of Songs* (1764) as a "sample of Hebrew Poetry," the whole of the *Reliques* (1765) which include also specimens of Spanish romances, and the *Ancient Songs, chiefly on Moorish Subjects* [89] which were ready for the press in 1775. He wrote to Evan Evans that he considered his *Poetry of the Ancient Welsh Bards* (1764) part of the scheme, and told him that he had "*in petto* Arabic Poetry, Greenland Poetry, Lapland Poetry, Northamerican, Peruvian, etc." [90] His plans for a new three-volume collection of *Ancient English and Scottish Poems*, for an edition of metrical romances, and for one of Surrey, meant only a slight shifting of interest towards the modern age, since in Percy's eyes even the chivalric romances and Surrey, like many very late poems in the

Reliques, had the essential quality of spontaneity, of "pleasing simplicity and artless graces." [91]

This conception of a universal, essentially uniform, primitive poetry almost demanded a new answer to the question of the origins of poetry. It had to be explained from universal mental needs. It was impossible to rest content with such old views, held even by Bentley, as that tragedy was simply invented by Thespis and comedy by Margites. A grossly rationalist view, like that of Lewis Crusius' *Lives of the Roman Poets* (1726), became an exception. According to Crusius, "wise men observing how far that which touches our passions, and moves our affections, prevails above the voice of naked truth and reason, and consulting the good and happiness of mankind, were desirous to make our imperfections contribute to our improvement: they therefore artfully blended truth with fiction, gilding the bitter pill of instruction to make it go down better. Thus the oldest poems are pieces of morality, historical accounts of the actions of great and famous men, or the praises of God." [92] Samuel Cobb spoke of poetry in Paradise and of Moses as the first of poets.[93] Even Shaftesbury, who in many points was one of the inspirers of the historical movement, thought that Homer "introduced" the natural and simple style, in opposition to the earliest poets, who wrote in an extremely metaphorical manner. From Homer derived both tragedy and comedy, which "first lay in a kind of chaos intermixed with other kinds." [94] But more naturalistic theories of the origin of poetry were common very early. Joseph Trapp, for instance, who cannot be described as sympathizing with the primitivist point of view, agreed with Vossius that poetry took its rise from Love, but owed its increase and progress to Religion. Harvest thanksgiving poems were the oldest poems, and shepherds found out the use of poetry in Greece; thus the lyric was the oldest kind of poetry and shepherds were the first poets.[95] But the established theory of the origin of poetry assigned it to a simple "overflow of emotion" in primitive man which somehow "of itself," as Blair says, assumed a poetical turn.[96] Lowth thus considered the ode as the most ancient species of poetry and almost coeval with human nature itself. The ode was the "offspring of the most vivid, and the most agreeable passions of the mind, of love, joy and admiration." [97]

A series of articles in the *British Magazine* (1762), which have been ascribed both to Goldsmith and Smollett, contains a most characteristic discussion of the origin of poetry.[98] The author distinguished between poetry which sprang from ease (apparently the pastorals) and another "species which owed its rise to inspiration and enthusiasm. . . . The admiration and awe" of primitive man before the beauties of nature "would break forth in exclamations expressive of the passion produced." For instance, seeing the sun, he would speak "O glorious luminary," etc., all in the approved sentimental rhetorical style. A number of individuals would join in these orisons which would be accompanied by corresponding gesticulations of the body. The sounds and gestures would "naturally" fall into measured cadence. "Thus the song and the dance would be produced, and a system of worship being formed, the Muse would be consecrated to the purposes of religion." The poetry of the bards and Chinese poetry were cited to show "poetry as a universal vehicle." The poet's share in the creation of mythology was stressed, and satire was derived quite simply from the festivals of the gods. These produced good cheer, which led to mirth and buffoonery: "hence satire." [99] The account of the origin of poetry in the preface to *A Poetical Dictionary*

(1761), very doubtfully ascribed to Goldsmith, is similar. Early "man felt an inward acknowledgment of the immensity and omnipotence of that supreme being, to whom he owed his nature and perfections: and that acknowledgment broke forth in numbers of harmony." Thus "the throne of poetry was founded upon religion." [100]

Hugh Blair (1763) and William Duff (1767) were the extravagant exponents of the purely emotional origin of poetry, "the effusion of a glowing fancy and an impassioned heart which will be perfectly natural and original." [101] This theory was elaborated in more detail in Sir William Jones's *Essay on the Arts commonly called Imitative* (1772). Like Goldsmith, he derives poetry purely from emotional needs. It was "originally no more than a strong, and animated expression of the human passions, of joy and grief, love and hate, admiration and anger." For no particular reason, except a belief in man's innate religiosity, he decided that "the most ancient sort of poetry consisted in praising the deity." He imagined, like Goldsmith, a primitive man, in face of the wonders of nature, "bursting into an extasy of joy, and pouring his praises to the creator of those wonders, and the author of his happiness." The next source of poetry was "probably love." Hence arose "the most agreeable odes and love-songs." Then came grief, which found expression, first in dirges and later in elegies. "As soon as vice began to prevail in the world," there was, of course, detestation for it, and this evoked moral poetry. "Where there is vice, there must be hate," and hate led to satire. Thus drama was derived from religion, lyrical poetry from love, and the epic from the detestation of vice and admiration for virtue, since "it illustrates some moral truth by the examples of heroes and kings." Sir William Jones then defined "original and native poetry" (the main examples of which he found in the Bible) as "the language of the violent passions, expressed in exact measure, with strong accents and significant words." [102]

This theory of the origin of poetry, which one may call the "spontaneous generation" theory, was part of the whole conception of a "natural" evolution of poetry in terms of a biological organism. We have shown how old are these originally metaphorical analogies. They recur in several variations; Hugh Blair, for example, drew a parallel between the youth of man and the early stages of poetry.[103] Mrs. Cooper, or whoever wrote the comments in the *Muses' Library* (1737), compared the tracing of the progress of English poetry with the scientist's study of a series of fossils, "leading step by step from nature in her crudest state to the most refined." [104]

The necessity of the evolutionary process was stressed repeatedly; Shaftesbury spoke of the succession of genres in Greece as happening "not by chance, but rather through necessity, and from the reason and nature of things." [105] Most common, however, was the analogy with the flowering of a fruit or vegetable or the aging of a man, an idea that easily led to the conception of a closed cycle of evolution, repeating itself over and over again. We have shown that the idea came from antiquity and found its main exponent in Temple.[106] Hume adopted this view, paraphrasing Velleius Paterculus fairly closely. "When the arts and sciences come to perfection in any state," he says in the *Essay on the Rise and Progress of the Arts and Sciences*, "from that moment they naturally, or rather necessarily decline, and seldom or never revive in that nation, where they formerly flourished." He recognized implicitly the "cycle" theory when he concluded that "arts and sciences, like some plants require a fresh soil" in order to flower and to decay again.[107]

This conception permeated the curious book by Goldsmith on the *Present State of Polite Learning* (1759), which assumed a circular theory similar to Temple's. He accepted a close, necessary parallel between ancient and modern literature enabling us to perceive that period of antiquity which the present age most resembles. Hence we shall learn "whether we are making advances towards excellence or retiring again to primeval obscurity: we shall by their example, be taught to acquiesce in those defects which it is impossible to prevent." This strange fatalism led to a pessimistic view of the present state of polite learning in England. The prevalence of criticism (Goldsmith complains that there were as many as two literary reviews in London!) marks the "natural decay of politeness," a decay which "may be deplored but cannot be prevented." [108] In the *Citizen of the World* (1760) Goldsmith echoed Hume: "This decay," he thought, "is surely from nature, and not the result of voluntary degeneracy. . . . Fatigued nature again begins to repose for some succeeding effort." [109]

This almost biological fatalism was not, of course, accepted generally. Other explanations for decadence were easily available, such as the paralyzing influence of a very great master or the exhaustion which drives artists to search for novelty at any price. This point of view was expressed fully by Kames in his *Sketches of the History of Man*. There he attacked Velleius Paterculus and Winckelmann for adopting a "reason not a little ridiculous." Winckelmann is a significant name in our context as he was the first to write a history of Greek art which was not merely a list of artists, but he was apparently the first and last to utter this opinion for a long time to come, and the problem receded again into the background.

Kames argued against the necessity of decay which he ascribed to "a performance so much superior to all of the kind as to extinguish emulation," and judged that "supposing a language to have acquired its utmost perfection, I see nothing that should necessarily occasion any change," except some external agency, like a political revolution.[110] Kames thus, for the first time, clearly formulated the ever-recurring opposition to the idea of a necessary internal evolution. In these and similar ideas was the germ of a purely deductive, general, speculative history of poetry, which could be constructed from a knowledge of human nature, without regard to particular times or places.

Many eighteenth-century minds pursued this seductive vision; it came obviously immediately from Montesquieu and Condillac and ultimately from Vico. Adam Smith early contemplated such a general "history of human improvement" to account for the origin of the different sciences and arts and show "by what chain has the mind been led from their first rudiments to their last and most refined improvements." [111] His *History of Astronomy* was planned as such a conjectural history or "histoire raisonnée," and he sketched a history of language in this style. Unfortunately, nothing has remained of his lectures on English literature, given as early as 1748–49 in Edinburgh, though it is hardly likely that they contained more than an outline of rhetoric.[112] Only from other later papers can we learn that Adam Smith conceived poetry, music and dancing as three sister arts "which originally went perhaps together." [113]

All these ideas met in John Brown's remarkable attempt at a general history of poetry, called *Dissertation on the Rise, Union and Power, the Progressions, Separations and Corruptions of Poetry and Music* (1763).[114] Brown is a primitivist with a clear consciousness of the uniform nature of savage life, and he recommends a study of the "principles of savage nature" as the starting-point for a history of poetry. He collects his examples from all over the world, from Greece, Ossianic Scotland, Bardic Ireland, Scaldic Iceland, Peru, India, China and America without much distinction, though he admits that allowance must be made for differences of soil and climate. But, first of all, he pretends to arrive at a general history of poetry purely by speculation on its universal, necessary derivation. The passions of primitive people find a natural expression in a mere "chaos of gestures, voice and speech." Then the "natural love of measured melody, which time and experience produce, throws the voice into song, the gesture into dance, the speech into verse or numbers."

Thus arose, among all nations, a union of song, dance and poetry, an original song-feast, something like the Wagnerian "Gesamkunstwerk." It was produced by the most eminent people among the tribe, by the chieftains, who were thus at first legislators, musicians, and poets all rolled into one. At this stage, the earliest histories, laws, and proverbs would be written in verse. Verse was thus before prose, not for any mnemotechnic reasons, but because the "natural passion for melody and dance necessarily throws the accompanying song into a correspondent rhythm." The religious rites of the early people would also naturally be accompanied by dance and song.

But this ideal state of affairs could not last: with the advance of civilization the three arts would separate and, in Brown's view, degenerate from their original union, in which the "several kinds would lie confused, in a sort of undistinguished mass, mingled in the same composition." The union of poet, musician and legislator would dissolve. Thus the individual arts, dance, music, and poetry would arise, beginning with dance, which is the first art to become distinct. Poetry would, at first, be a confusion of all genres, "a rapturous mixture of hymns, history, fable and mythology, thrown out by the enthusiastic bard in legislative songs." Then the individual kinds would arise. First would come lyrical poetry, odes or hymns, because poetry is "in the simple state, but a kind of rapturous exclamations, of joy, grief, triumph or exaltation."

The epic poem would arise next, for the earliest histories would be written in verse. Then, from the union of these two (an unexplained, retrograde step), a certain rude outline of tragedy would arise, also, of course "naturally." A bard would celebrate the deeds of a hero, and the "surrounding choir would answer him at intervals, by shouts of sympathy or concurrent approbation." This "barbarous scene" would "improve" into a more perfect form, he says—rather inconsistently in view of his general theory of deterioration all along the line. "Instead of relating they would probably represent, by action and song united, those great and terrible achievements which their heroes had performed." Not only can tragedy thus be shown to be a necessary result of evolution, but every detail of tragedy can be deduced similarly. "If the choir should be established by general use, and should animate the solemnity by dance as well as song, the melody, dance, and song would, of course, regulate each other and the Ode or Song would fall into stanzas." The continuous presence of a choir must lead to the unities of place and time. Thus having accounted for the rise of all main kinds of poetry, the further development can be described only as a process of further fission: a process of specialization and, in Brown's eyes, of degeneration closely connected with a general corruption of manners.

Brown asserted and believed that he had "deduced" this whole ingenious scheme on purely general, or as we would say today, abstract "sociological" principles. His numbered propositions follow each other seemingly with the same rigour as the propositions in Spinoza's *Ethics*, deduced "more geometrico." Brown then tries to demonstrate that empirical evidence from all countries tallies exactly with the outline deduced. Greece is the first example, most fully elaborated, and as the scheme was obviously composed with an eye on Greece, it is not very difficult for Brown to show that every detail corroborates his theory. There is the original union of all the three arts, the high status of early bards like Orpheus or Homer, the rise of Orphic hymns, of the Hesiodic and Homeric epic, and finally of tragedy, all nicely agreeing, point by point, with the general scheme.

A new feature is an acknowledgment to the genius of Aeschylus, whose inventive power added a second person to the drama; and this recognition of individual initiative somewhat contradicts the collectivist theory the author professes. The description of the rise of comedy is also new. Comedy arose from narrative poems of the invective or comic kind, which in their turn arose from casual strokes of raillery in the original choirs at song-festivals. The narrative would easily slide into dramatic representation. The dissolute comedy of Aristophanes corresponds to the rule of a dissolute populace. All "these causes clearly account for the establishment of the old comedy, at that very period it took place." The new comedy with its unpolitical, generalized satire is due to the suppression of the excesses committed by the old.

Brown then looks for corroboration of his scheme among the northern nations, though he has to admit gaps in the chain owing to the paucity of evidence. The only example, doubtful at that, of the union of legislator and bard is Snorri Sturluson. All other Nordic poetry arose during the second stage of separation between legislator and bard. Thus Ossian is quoted as "a noble confirmation to many principles advanced in this analysis." Especially he serves as an example of the original union of kinds, because *Fingal* is chiefly epic yet mixed with hymns. The same principles are then shown to be illustrated by the history of the Irish bards, by Chinese conditions, by quotations from Garcilaso de la Vega on Peru and by an account of the coast of Coromandel. The natural union of melody and song and the progressive stages of their separation are then illustrated from Hebrew poetry, and conditions in Rome are cited as examples of an advanced stage of disintegration.

The Middle Ages, so far as they were not accounted for by the references to Ossian, the Edda, and the Irish bards, are passed over as barbarous; nor can the Renaissance present a cheerful picture to Brown. On the Revival of Learning, the three greater kinds of poetry were, in many instances, necessarily divorced from music, for the Greek and Roman poets, being the only approved models, could be read and imitated by scholars only. Thus tragedy and the ode were divorced from their assistant arts and became the "languid amusement of the closet," and "tragedies that cannot be acted and odes that cannot be sung" were the final result of the separation, which in music is paralleled by the rise of counterpoint and thus of instrumental music.

The whole history of poetry appears thus as a regular process of disintegration and a gradual dissociation of an original ideal union. But Brown was not merely a passive observer and historian of poetry; he was also a reformer who wanted to accomplish a reunion of poetry and music in the very teeth of his theory. Though he had just tried to establish the inevitability of the whole process, he would himself like to reverse the course of events. He, therefore, traces the several attempts to reunite poetry and music: the song, the opera, the motet, and the oratorio, all and sundry of which he criticizes as imperfect unions. Songs, and especially Scotch airs, are praised, but criticized as "divorced from important topics." The opera is condemned as an unnatural revival of Roman tragedy. "It is an exhibition altogether out of nature, and repugnant to the universal genius of modern customs and manners." Opera emerged only at a time "when the general state of manners in Europe could not naturally produce it." In the motets and oratorios poetry is completely subordinated to music. So Brown proposes a reunion of poetry and music through odes in the style of Dryden, with musical accompaniment. He elaborates the scheme of an academy to be established for this purpose and furnishes himself a specimen of such an ode, which is, however, a rather dreary example of Pindarics on a Biblical theme.

All these practical suggestions seem a disappointing anticlimax to a remarkable theory which in many ways anticipates the arguments of Nietzsche and Wagner. It fitted, however, very closely into a contemporary movement which tried to combine poetry and music under many forms. Benda's melodrama, Gluck's operas, Algarotti's writings, and in England such attempts as Mason's choral tragedies, point in the same direction.[115] Brown's own ideas of a reunion are particularly academic and lifeless, and his pattern of evolution is too simple, too hard and fast, for the modern mind. But it is important not only for his consistently ethnographic approach to poetry, but mainly because his rigid scheme of evolution was the first attempt at a history of poetry without names of individual poets. It foreshadowed the concept of collective creation which led to the romantic ideas of "communal" authorship, and it sketched, or at least implied, the idea of an internal, self-propelled movement of poetry, which was much later most clearly formulated in Hegelian dialectics.

Though we could not accept the easy rationalist formulas suggested by Brown, the problem itself has been unduly neglected in recent decades. Only a book like the Chadwicks' *Growth of Literature* shows that it is still as topical as ever and that it is well worth attempting with a present-day knowledge of primitive oral poetry. In Brown the rigid scheme of evolution, precisely because it aspires to be absolutely general and applicable to any time or society, is detrimental to an actual comprehension of the much more complex historical process.

The opinions expressed by Brown in another book, on Shaftesbury's *Characteristics* (1751), support this diagnosis fully. There he says that there is but "one unvaried language or style in painting. Its foundation is in the senses and reason of mankind: and it is therefore the same in every age and nation." Though there are fashions in literary style, which are "relative, local and capricious," the only good style is that of "unadorned simplicity," free of every local, peculiar, and grotesque ornament, as we find it in the Bible. It is significant of the curiously common eighteenth-century lack of discrimination that Brown enumerates as great simple writers not only Homer, Virgil, etc., but also Demosthenes and Cicero, Dante and Boileau, Shakespeare and Milton. In particular, Milton had, according to Brown, "formed himself entirely on the simple model of the best Greek writers and the sacred Scriptures." [116] Though all these details show Brown's unhistorical mentality, and though his principle of evolution is thus only a uniform process of disintegration, the fact that such a general history was attempted at all shows how the idea of development had entered general consciousness.

Brown was by no means without influence. John Gregory's curious medley called *Comparative View of the State and Faculties of Man* (1765) reproduced Brown quite closely,[117] and Daniel Webb's *Observations on the Correspondence between Poetry and Music* (1769) combined Brown's evolution of poetry with a theory of the origin of language, based purely on imitation of sound. "Passion produced song; . . . passion and song gave birth to measure"; in the early stages of society the "characters of the poet and musician would be united in the same person"—these are statements which we could find also in Brown. Webb had a confused theory about the rise of verse from the impressions of sentiment and of the necessary succession of metres; iamb and trochee were the original metres, from which dactyl and anapaest were derived. The next step of evolution was a mixture of iambic and trochaic verses. As an example of the earliest stage a Peruvian rhymeless sonnet is quoted, while the mixture of metre is proved from *Chevy Chase*.

Webb was frankly puzzled by ancient lyrical poetry and by the problem of quantitative measures with musical accompaniment. He was even sceptical about the traditional glories of ancient music, but accepted an original union and common rhythm of poetry and music "where measure flows from the laws of musical pronunciation." [118] Evan Evans [119] and Percy [120] also referred to Brown, and some of his concepts can be found in Wood's book on Homer. Wood stressed the oral transmission of the Homeric poems [121] and the idea that the priest was originally a law-giver, a poet, and a musician all in one.[122]

A slightly different evolutionary conception was expounded by Adam Ferguson in his *Essay on the History of Civil Society* (1767). Ferguson's interests were largely "sociological," and his comments on literature are rather meagre.

But he worked the development of poetry into his scheme. On the whole, he accepted the primitivist point of view. Man is a "poet by nature," and poetry arose out of universal psychological needs, out of delight in sound and the desire to memorize the record of events more easily. He accepted Blair's and Brown's thesis that the "early history of all nations was uniform in this particular: priests, statesmen and philosophers in the first ages of Greece delivered their instructions in poetry, and mixed with the dealers in music and heroic fable." Then a sorting-out took place, an emancipation of poetry from mere instruction in politics, history, and other subjects.

Ferguson had unfortunately little to say on the concrete process of this progressive division of labour, beyond a general affirmation that literature develops in close contact with society and that, therefore, retirement is not favourable to the production of great literature. Literature revived "among the turbulent states of Italy" in times of acute conflict and dissensions. Ferguson showed an understanding of the change of social forms by growing social differentiation, and he suggested that the process of literature could be linked up with this social development. [123] He has, therefore, been called the first "sociologist," and Auguste Comte frequently referred to him as a predecessor.[124] But the concept of development in Ferguson was just as anti-individualist as in Brown, and thus equally blocked the way to a more concrete understanding of literary evolution. Later, however, these speculations assumed a very great importance in literary history and paved the way for Hippolyte Taine and Brunetière, and for the most consistent "evolutionist" in England, John Addington Symonds, whose *Shakspere's Predecessors* (1884) well illustrates both the successes and dangers of this approach.

Throughout the preceding sketch we have only incidentally referred to contemporary theories of language, its nature, its origin and evolution, though these were obviously of the highest importance for the rise of similar theories on literature. Eighteenth century ideas on language merit a specially close consideration, not only as an almost exact parallel to the ideas held about literary individuality and development, but also as the model which influenced the establishment and acceptance of the theories of literary history sketched above. Language and literature are inseparable, and the art of poetry, in particular, could not be dissociated from the language and diction in which it was written. In linguistics, as in aesthetics, we see the same turn from rationalism to psychologism. Descartes, Delgarno, Leibniz and, in England, John Wilkins [125] worked for a "universal" language: a language of fixed signs, which would fulfill intellectualist demands for clarity, a single meaning for every sign, etc. This is an ideal that has led since to many attempts at constructing an artificial language and has helped the achievements of modern "symbolic logic."

Locke seems to have been the first to "psychologize" language, to understand it as an operation of the mind, both as to origin and function. But he still was a rationalist, since he considered language merely as a means to the end of knowledge. Berkeley was a most extreme nominalist, thinking of language not as an instrument of thought but more as a hindrance to the advancement of science. "We need only draw the curtain of words, to behold the fairest tree of knowledge." [126] This negative attitude to language did not, however, impede the concrete study of language. On the contrary, by denying the one-to-one relation of linguistic symbol and object, and by maligning the cognitive power of language, attention was turned away from language as a copy of existent qualities of things and directed to language as a mirror of individual and national conceptions of things. It is exactly the same process as that by which the apparently anarchic concept of "taste" became fruitful for the study of literature.

Already Bacon had characterized the advantages and disadvantages of individual languages.[127] Analyses of Greek, Latin, and Hebrew, and sometimes even comparison of them with English, date back to the Renaissance, though their value was impaired by superstitious veneration for the classical languages and by the prevalence of vague ideas about the structure and history of the English language. But patriotic pride did much to offset the weight of tradition, just as it did in literary criticism, and there were innumerable comparisons between English and French to the disadvantage of the latter.[128] Something like a description of national style thus became possible.

With the growing sense of individuality a comprehension of the shades of individual style increased considerably. Already Puttenham in a remarkable passage had spoken about style as "the image of man, *mentis character*. . . . For man is but his mind, and as his mind is tempered and qualified, so are his speeches and language at large, and his inward conceits be the metal of his mind, and his manner of utterance the very warp and woof of his conceits." [129] Similarly Ben Jonson had spoken about "*oratio, imago animi.*" [130] However, in spite of this theoretical conception, we rarely meet with any clear description of style, though the tradition of ancient rhetoric supplied at least some of the instruments and criteria. But more common were almost purely instinctive characterizations of the effects of style and manner. Thus, for instance, the author of a series of papers in the *Literary Magazine* (1758) called the "History of our own

Language" showed considerable ingenuity in characterizing the style of the most important prose writers of the seventeenth and eighteenth centuries from the point of view of an ideal of perspicacity and grace.[131]

There must be everywhere in criticism thousands of such pronouncements, and a study of translations would be profitable if carried out with this growth of stylistic sense in mind. The contrast between Pope's Homer and, for instance, Cary's Dante, the result of about a century's evolution, is striking and should be considered apart from the different abilities of the two men.

Locke's theory of language, which admitted the collaboration of minds in "mixed modes," had shown that "universal" grammar was an illusion. He had stressed the impossibility of exact translations and demonstrated that "very few words correspond exactly in different languages." [132] He had thus opened the gate to pure subjectivism, as the concept of taste did in aesthetics. But, just as the "standard of taste" was a reaction against this extreme subjectivism, a similar reaction came also in linguistics. It has the same source: Neoplatonism and Shaftesbury. James Harris, Shaftesbury's fervent admirer, led the way. His *Hermes* (1751) was, according to the subtitle, another attempt at universal grammar. There was a rationalist element in him, which was, however, far outweighed by Neoplatonic ideas. Language was to him a system of symbols, expressing general ideas, which are conceived as subsisting in a Platonic world. Hence he was led to a discussion of individual languages, as "nations like single men, have their peculiar ideas." These peculiar ideas become "the genius of their language, since the symbol must, of course, correspond to its archetype." [133] Harris thus could characterize the individual languages, concluding with a eulogy of Greek as "conformable to the transcendent and universal genius" of its people.

For Harris, every language has its national genius, its own peculiar form-giving principle, an idea which led to the German "Sprachgeist" and is only one step removed from the conception of a peculiar genius in every national literature. Harris found the genius of the language in its form, in the intelligible, "internal" form—a Neoplatonic concept which had been reintroduced by Shaftesbury and the Cambridge Platonists. This internal form was not conceived as something outside the mind of man, but as a function of its workings. In a *Treatise concerning Art* (1744) Harris had described art not as a finished product but as an "energy." In *Hermes* he spoke of language not as an invention, but as a creation, an unfinished process. Art and language were to Harris not merely ornaments of the mind. He addressed art: "Thou art more truly mind itself—'tis mind thou art, most perfect mind." [134] Here in Harris were the germs of conceptions that much later came back to England in German elaboration: the "spirit of language," "internal form," art as the activity and expression of the national soul.

These ideas remained in Harris, however, largely static, divorced from a conception of the origin and development of language. Even to Harris language was mainly an instrument of knowledge. This view changed only when the genetic approach defeated intellectualism and established an emotional conception of language. The latter was, of course, not an entirely new idea. Already Epicurus had derived language from "pathos," from feeling, dislike and like, and Lucretius stressed the desire for sensual expression.[135] The notion was elaborated by Vico, who, directly or indirectly, must have influenced the whole century with his emotionalist theory of language and its origin. A scientific theory of the

origin of language was only possible when the account in
Genesis had been discarded. As late a writer as Monboddo
had to make elaborate subterfuges to hide the irreconcil-
ability of his theory with the Bible. But many earlier writers
simply proceeded on the assumption of a natural origin of
language; Mandeville gave a naturalistic account of the slow
rise of language from gestures and sounds like weeping;[136]
Blackwell tried to account for it from "rude accidental
sounds" uttered under the pressure of some passion. The
primitive parts of language consisted of rough, undeclined,
impersonal monosyllables expressive commonly of the highest
passions. Chinese and the supposedly monosyllabic northern
tongues are quoted as examples of such rude aboriginal languages.

This emotional theory of the origin of language explained
the supposed characteristic of all primitive languages (and
thus all primitive poetry), its figurativeness. "From this de-
duction it is plain," said Blackwell, "that any language
formed as described above, must be full of metaphor. We
must imagine the speech of savages to be broken, unequal
and boisterous." The Turks, Arabs and Indians are described
as taciturn people, who, when they open their mouths and
"give loose to a fiery imagination, are poetical and full of
metaphors." The Preambles to the *Arabian Nights*, knowledge of which was then just spreading through Galland's
translation, are quoted as an example. Blackwell, though elsewhere drawing the conclusion that a "polished language is
not fit for a great poet," still thought of metaphor largely
as a "real defect" of speech, as a necessary makeshift at a
stage when vocabulary was still limited.[137]

This rationalist view was most vigorously expounded in
William Warburton's *Divine Legation of Moses* (1741).
There he indignantly rejected the idea of a rise of language

from confused and indistinct noises and appealed to the scriptural account of its origin in divine instruction. But in practice he traced a history of language through sign (gesture) to parable, simile, metaphor and epithet in a logical succession. Metaphor was not due, "as it is commonly supposed," to the "warmth of a florid and improved fancy," but solely to a "want," to a "rusticity of conception." American savages, ancient Gauls, and the love of proverbs among peasants are mentioned. The whole process was paralleled in the history of writing. Against those who interpreted the Egyptian hieroglyphics as signs of mysterious wisdom, Warburton argues that they are mere picture-writing, and thus more primitive, more metaphorical, and an essentially defective means of communication.[138]

In Harris's *Hermes* (1751), another very rationalistic theory of the origin of the Oriental, metaphorical style was suggested. The words of Orientals were consonant with their servile ideas. They knew only "tyrants" and "slaves" and talked of kings as gods. Thus hyperbole was introduced, exaggeration which sometimes ascended into the great and magnificent and even sublime, as in the Scriptures, but also "frequently degenerated into tumid and bumbast (sic)." [139] Lowth's whole book on Hebrew poetry (1753) was based on Harris's ideas of the "peculiar genius and character of each language," which determines "to a great measure the style and colour of the poetic diction." [140] The different metaphors, similes, etc. of Hebrew poetry were analyzed on the assumption that primitive poetry must and should be metaphorical.

This idea recurred in many eighteenth-century books and was invariably used to characterize early poetry. Blair, in the *Dissertation on Ossian* (1763), combined the rationalist with the emotionalist explanation of the origins of language.

"Figurative language," he said, "owes its rise chiefly to two causes: to the want of proper names for objects and to the influence of imagination and passion over the form of expression." [141] In William Duff, who is one of the most extreme primitivists of the time, "bold and glowing metaphors" [142] were associated with early poetry and found, without much distinction, in Homer and Ossian, in the Bible and Oriental poetry, and in the Nordic scalds and Shakespeare. Kames tried to show that figurative language was part and parcel of the early development of mankind. "During the infancy of taste, imagination is suffered to roam, as in sleep, without control. Wonder is the passion of savages and rustics." Thus "giants, and magicians, fairy-land and enchantment" were invented first. As a second stage, closer to modern refinement, after gigantic fiction had been banished, there remained the taste for "gigantic similes, metaphors and allegories." Folk-lore and folk-mythology is worked into a general scheme of history as a preparatory stage to metaphorical style by an easy equivocation of the word "gigantic."

The *Song of Solomon* is quoted as an example of the metaphorical stage, and the theory that figurative language is due to the force of imagination in a warm climate is rejected. "In every climate, hot and cold, the figurative style is carried to extravagance, during a certain period of writing. Even in the bitter cold country of Iceland we are at no loss for examples," Kames argues, and he quotes a number of *kenningar* from the *Edda*.[143] We must not forget that even the highly ornate and to our mind extremely artificial style of Gray's odes was a conscious attempt to recapture that "oriental," elevated, sublime, metaphorical style which was supposed to be nearest to the language of the heart and thus to the poetry of original unspoilt natural man. The obscurity, deliberate allusiveness, and abruptness of these odes were all considered well in harmony with ancient ballads, Welsh odes, Scaldic poetry, and Pindarics.

A more careful, almost physiological statement of the origin of figurative speech can be found in Daniel Webb's *Observations on the Correspondence between Poetry and Music* (1769). Webb, too, rejected the idea that language had its source in contract. Language in its earliest stages is most "expressive," since it is mostly the "offspring of sensation." It arises from the imitation of natural sounds, a theory which was elaborated by Webb in great detail and still finds some adherents among philologists. This theory alone seemed to Webb satisfactory to "deduce the invention of language, in its first spring, from a simple and almost mechanical exertion of our faculties." The most simple words are thus the most original. Only when imitation failed, "compact" must have taken place. Webb then tried to explain why imagery is the language of passion and suggests that imagination can be quite literally heated with the animal spirits.[144]

The eighteenth-century stress on visual metaphor was one of the consequences of the Cartesian psychology with its high valuation of sight. "Imagination" in Addison and many others means little more than the visualizing faculty as "our sight is the most perfect and most delightful of all senses." [145] The principle of *ut pictura poesis* and the whole efflorescence of purely descriptive poetry are symptoms of the same attitude. The enthusiasm for metaphor is also explainable from the stress contemporary psychology put on the power of association. Genius was sometimes, especially by Muratori, defined as a combinatory power, as the faculty of discovering similarities even between dissimilar things. Thus wit, metaphor, and genius are constantly associated in the eighteenth century; the common bond of the three terms is in inventiveness, which is frequently itself described as a power of combination. The invention of a centaur was highly valued as a proof of genius; Shakespeare's Caliban or Pope's Rosicrucian elves in the *Rape of the Lock* were generally admired as supreme examples of genius. The speech of primitive people was thus naturally considered the nourishing soil of genius.

This simple and widespread conception of a derivation of language and of the metaphorical style from emotion was not accepted by many more speculative thinkers. Many were no more content with the crude dualism between metaphorical and modern rationalist language than they were with the dualism between primitive and polished poetry. The idea of an evolution of language was actually more easily conceivable than that of an evolution of literature. The parallel between language and a vegetable had been drawn by Davenant and Temple. It was repeated by Welsted. "It is with languages, as it is with animals, vegetables, and all other things: they have their rise, progress, their maturity, and their decay." [146] Dr. Johnson, too, admits implicitly the internal development of language when he rejects any attempt to explain the loss of forms and terminations in the transition from Old English to Middle English by external causes, such as the intermixture of languages.[147] Joseph Priestley in his *Course of Lectures on the Theory of Language* (1762) accepted the idea of a "regular growth and corruption of languages" [148] and drew the parallel between language and the development of an animal or plant. Though he admits the force of external historical influences, such as migrations, on the history of language, he rejects the idea that language could be artificially directed or corrected.

This spread of an "organic" conception of language, the

victory of those who would explain it rather *physei* than *thesei,* could also be illustrated by the almost general abandonment of the idea of an English academy, or other methods of "ascertaining and fixing our language forever," for which Swift had hoped.[149] The supposed critical dictator of the eighteenth century, Dr. Johnson, professed in the Preface to his *Dictionary* (1755) that he had to give up "his early hopes of stabilizing the language." [150] He accepted change as gradual and inevitable, though he reasonably enough recommended, and himself assisted, efforts to retard an evolution which elicited widespread fears that "such as Chaucer is, shall Dryden be." [151]

But professional thinkers tried to trace the actual detailed general evolution of language in exactly the same manner as Brown had tried to trace the general history of poetry. Adam Smith constructed such a conjectural history of language in his *Considerations concerning the first Formation of Languages* (1767).[152] He saw the history of language as a process of increasing abstraction, as a movement from the concrete to the abstract. He traced a sequence of denominations from proper nouns to common names, hence to adjectives and so on through all parts of speech. Prepositions signifying abstract relations appear as the last stage. Logically, Adam Smith should have considered this disintegration of language into component parts (such as the isolation of prepositions, compared with the older suffixes) as a sign of progress. But, under the influence of traditional respect for the classical languages, Smith decided that they were still superior to a language like English, though he saw that the "simplification of machines" meant progress.[153] The reasons given for this decision are the alleged prolixity and disagreeable sound of synthetic languages like English. He was similarly inconsistent in his opinion on the causes of this development. His whole theory was based on the conception of a necessary, logical development from the concrete to the abstract, but in practice he decided that the mixture of languages was the cause for the loss of complexity. Only Jeremy Bentham was later consistent enough in his Utilitarianism to welcome the evolution towards the synthetic type unreservedly.

Another elaborate attempt to describe this general necessary history of language was Monboddo's *Origin and Progress of Language* (1773), where language was set into the framework of a conjectural history of society. Monboddo adopted the ideas of Harris, though he combined them with an evolutionism unknown to the static Platonism of his predecessor. Monboddo, like Harris, was anti-Lockian in his outlook, a Platonic idealist who saw in language the product of mental creation. The development of language was described by him as an evolution from a sort of pre-speech, inarticulate cries and gestures, to an artificial language, which he saw developed to highest perfection in a language like Greek. The beginnings of language were described as wholly emotional expression, which slowly changed towards greater abstraction and complexity (and not towards simplification as in Adam Smith). Monboddo was no straightforward primitivist, but could rather be described as a "perfectibilist." He stressed the gradual progress in arts and manners and the diversity of mankind. "Man so far from continuing the same creature, has varied more than any other being that we know in Nature." [154] Monboddo used much ethnographical knowledge for his arguments and quoted extensively from missionaries' reports on Indian languages. But the freakishness of his insistence that the orangutan is a primitive man, the one thing everybody seems to know about Monboddo's book today, should not obscure the merits and significance of his synthesis of Platonism and evolutionism.

These paragraphs on the theory of language have led us seemingly far afield. But their value as a parallel to the history of poetry is obvious; we see in linguistics the same shift towards emotionalism and a theory of expression which we could describe in aesthetics. We see the rise of the genetic approach in considerations of the origins of both language and of poetry; the description of early figurative, emotional language combined with the conception of early poetry has helped to define the dualism of primitive poetry versus polished poetry which permeated all literary considerations in the later eighteenth century. We see finally, how the concept of internal, necessary evolution emerged from biological analogies in descriptions of the history of language; how language ceased to be looked upon as a simple contrivance of human ingenuity, but came to be seen as part and parcel of the human mind, of its development and growth, and thus of the evolution of humanity itself. The very same idea emerged in literary history; books ceased to be bibliographical items and became members of a series, of which it thus became possible to write, for the first time, a history that was not only a catalogue of books or a collection of lives, but the development of an *art*, an activity of a nation and of mankind. But history could not have been written if the materials had not been accumulated by the curiosity and diligence of editors and antiquarians, and if the literary horizon had not broadened so widely that all these ideas had examples and materials to work upon. Now we have examined the warp, let us look at the woof.

CHAPTER FOUR

The Study of Early Literature

IN THE EIGHTEENTH CENTURY, revived interest in early English centred first in the English Renaissance. The reasons for the preference are obvious. The language was still comprehensible without special effort. There was no break in the tradition of printing of many Renaissance authors, and their reputation and influence had never suffered total eclipse. The vicissitudes of Shakespeare's fame have been traced so frequently that we can well spare the repetition of evidence to show that Shakespeare was never little known or appreciated, that his plays were acted without interruption on the English stage and reprinted with scarcely any pause. But there is no denying that the reasons for appreciating Shakespeare changed considerably, that admiration for him increased in fervour, that his plays were acted with a stricter regard to his text, and that editions of his works assumed a new character. The growing "idolatry" of Shakespeare slowly spread to his contemporaries and predecessors, and Shakespearean studies became a rallying point of any study of older English literature. Together with Milton, Shakespeare was the first English author who was thought to deserve the honour of textual criticism.

The reputation of this new technique had considerably increased in England, mainly through the success of Bentley, and Bentley's methods were in the minds of the first textual critics of Shakespeare, long before Bentley applied them himself, so unluckily, to a correction of the text of Milton. The actual corruption of Shakespeare's text and its very real linguistic difficulties encouraged "corrective" or "conjectural" criticism, in Shakespeare as in the classics.[1] The new method was used for the first time, with some manner of consistency, by Pope and Theobald.[2] It amounted to a collation of all accessible editions (quartos and folios) without much system or much discrimination as to their value, and to the construction of an eclectic text, for which aesthetic considerations, or preconceptions about correct metre and grammar, were decisive. It has been pointed out that the method imitated classical scholarship, which quite legitimately used all manuscripts preserved because they might represent very different traditions. "It simply never occurred to men like Pope, Theobald, and Capell that the Shakespeare quartos were not in the same position with respect to the author's original text as the classical manuscripts were." [3]

Though Dr. Johnson had recognized the authority of the first Folio as early as in the prospectus for his edition in 1756, only Edmond Malone established a canon of authoritative quartos and the superiority of the first Folio over the others by careful collations. Textual criticism, apart from its own considerable value, had the merit of studying the text of Shakespeare closely and thus of turning attention away from the old generalities on Shakespeare as "nature," on his attitude toward rules and unities, to a closer examination of the individual plays. As Morgann said, reflecting the drift towards particular knowledge: "General criticism is as uninstructive as it is easy: Shakespeare deserves to be considered in detail." [4] Real interpretation remained obviously impossible without the use of contemporary documents. Theobald especially led the way with quotations from Elizabethan drama, chronicles and voyages. Dr. Johnson's *Proposals for Printing the Dramatick Works of William Shakespear* (1756) expounded a very full program of interpretation from contemporary literature of Shakespeare's allusions, language, and relation to sources, and he fulfilled partially, at least, this plan in his edition. Johnson hopes that by "comparing the works of Shakespeare with those of writers who lived at the same time, immediately preceded, or immediately followed him, [he] shall be able to ascertain his ambiguities, disentangle his intricacies, and recover the meaning of words now lost in the darkness of antiquity." [5] Thus Shakespeare criticism could, for the first time, solve the problem of his learning, which was indissolubly bound up with questions of his originality, with the debate about his ignorance of the unities, his observance of poetical justice, and so on.

Those who read Shakespeare, like Warburton, with their heads full of classical tags, misinterpreted and misunderstood him constantly. Richard Farmer, in his deft *Essay on the Learning of Shakespeare* (1767), clearly demonstrated Shakespeare's almost complete dependence on modern translations and defended the method of "all such reading that was never read" as the reading necessary for a comment on Shakespeare. "Nothing but an intimate acquaintance with the writers of the time, who are frequently of no other value, can point out his allusions, and ascertain his phraseology." [6] Shakespeare's sources had been partly known to Langbaine as examples of "plagiary," and Rymer had censured Shakespeare severely for his use of Cinthio's story for *Othello*. Dryden, Rowe, Gildon, Pope and, more systematically, Theobald refer to Shakespeare's sources. Mrs. Charlotte Lennox published, with the blessing of a preface by Dr. Johnson, her *Shakespear Illustrated* (1753), which brought together for the first time a considerable number of Shakespeare's sources and laid them open to the inspection of all. Discussion of Shakespeare was thus diverted from the old vague stress on invention, which amounted to a praise of his fairies and witches, to the question of his subtler originality in handling a traditional plot. Johnson recognized that "Shakespeare's excellence is not the fiction of the tale, but the representation of life." [7] In his edition he makes full use of the material assembled by Mrs. Lennox, though he sometimes disapproves of her opinion. But he adds nothing of his own, and he barely hints at the actual artistic problems raised by the comparisons now made possible.

Thus plenty was done for the elucidation of Shakespeare's text and the collection of his sources. But up to 1794, we have no serious analysis of his style [8] and nothing about his social relations, except some generalities on "unhappy Shakespeare who lived in an age unworthy of him." [9] But the criticism of individual plays both increased and changed its direction with the new attention to a study of Shakespeare's characters. This began early in the century with Hughes discussing *Othello* (1713), or Theobald *Lear* (1715),[10] and can be welcomed as a further symptom of more concrete interest in Shakespeare. But eventually they produced consequences dangerous to any insight into Shakespeare's mind and art. The characters were soon judged, mostly under the influence of stage-performances, as independent of the play, as real, historical persons. Morgann's much overrated essay on Falstaff (1777), with its absurd speculations on Falstaff's early life, led the way to the romantic analyses of Schlegel, Coleridge, Hazlitt, and others, which frequently lost all contact with the actual text of Shakespeare. Up to 1778 there was practically no discussion of the development

of Shakespeare's art and almost none of his relations to contemporaries.

But the interest in Shakespeare widened to include his
contemporaries, successors, and predecessors. The first two
had never completely ceased to be acted, adapted, and reprinted. There are plenty of eighteenth-century editions of
Ben Jonson, both of collected and of individual plays, and
Peter Whalley was the first to produce an edition of Jonson
(1756) with some materials prepared by Theobald and notes
on his sources and classical parallels, where he could apply
his learning to better purpose than in his misdirected arguments on Shakespeare's supposed classical achievements.[11]
He rejects the "improving" technique of editing, remarking
sensibly that "the mere improvement of a writer's words can
never authorize the alteration of his words." [12] In the same
year W. R. Chetwood published his paltry *Memoirs of the
Life and Writings of Ben Jonson*, which were planned to
precede a new edition of the plays, but included only a reprint of the spurious *Widow* and of *Eastward Hoe*. Thomas
Coxeter's collected edition of Massinger was published post-
humously in 1761, preceded by *Critical Reflections on the
Old English Dramatists*, written by George Colman the
elder, which plead to Garrick for an extension of his reper-
tory of roles to dramatists outside of Shakespeare. Colman
argues in favour of the minor dramatists with the same arguments used for Shakespeare: "Experience has proved the
effect of such fictions on our minds," even if the plots are
"uncouth" and the characters very different from present-
day humanity.[13]

Beaumont and Fletcher received most attention in the
period in question; Pope seems to have thought of editing
their works and actually compiled an index to his copy of

the 1679 Folio.[14] An edition by another, otherwise unknown Colman [15] in 1711 had been very defective, but that of 1750 seems one of the best eighteenth-century efforts. It is again based on work by Theobald, who had already planned it in 1742, and had actually done work amounting to about a fifth of the ten volumes. It was finished by Thomas Seward and John Sympson, in Theobald's spirit, which is apparent in a preface extolling the great importance of textual criticism. "Verbal Criticism very justly holds the palm from every other species of criticism," [16] Seward says, almost in the style of Bentley, who thought that "conjecture can cure all—conjecture, whose performances are for the most part more certain than anything, that we can exhibit from the authority of old manuscripts." [17] Seward stresses, not altogether unjustly, "the merit of criticism in establishing the taste of the age, in raising respect in the contemptuous, and attention in the careless readers of our old poets." [18] But he does not see the other side of the question: editors could not have become busy on their collations, if the respect and attention for the early authors had not already increased.

Besides Beaumont and Fletcher, Jonson and Massinger, few editions of any of Shakespeare's contemporaries or successors were published. About two hundred pre-Restoration plays were quoted in Hayward's *British Muse* (1738), apparently from extracts supplied by Oldys; and, from the time of Theobald onward, Elizabethan plays were widely used by commentators on Shakespeare and Milton. Robert Dodsley's *Select Collection of Old Plays* (1744) contained five plays by Massinger, Webster's *White Devil*, Ford's *'Tis Pity She's a Whore*, Marston's *Malcontent*, Dekker's *Honest Whore*, Heywood's *Woman Killed with Kindness*, Marlowe's *Edward II*, and some Shirley, Killigrew, etc. W. R. Chetwood's curious medley *A Select Collection of Old Plays*

(1750) reprinted *Fair Em*, Brewer's *Love-Sick King*, Middleton's *Blurt Master Constable*, together with Davenant's *Salmacida Spolia* and four interludes. Edward Jacob reprinted *Arden of Feversham* ascribing it to Shakespeare (1770), and Edward Capell included a careful reprint of *Edward III* in his *Prolusions* (1760) which, on the whole, represent the best in eighteenth-century technique of editing. But there was very little criticism on all these authors throughout the century. Giles Jacob registers merely names and titles; Cibber's *Lives* in general reprint only information from Wood, Winstanley, etc., while a remark like W. R. Chetwood's in 1749 praising Thomas Heywood strikes us with a certain freshness only because it shows some independent judgment arrived at by actual reading.[19]

The pre-Shakespearean drama was an even more obscure region. *Gorboduc* had been reprinted by Spence as early as 1736, and Pope had praised it, after Rymer, for its "much purer style than Shakespeare's was in several of his first plays." [20] It reappears in Dodsley together with *Gammer Gurton*, Lilly's *Campaspe*, and Kyd's *Spanish Tragedy*. The introduction to Dodsley mentions Richard Edwards and quotes Sidney on the drama with approval. John Bowle prints *The Troublesome Reigne of King John*, in his *Miscellaneous Pieces of Ancient English Poetry* (1764) and D. E. Baker repeats the information of Dodsley with slight additions. Only Thomas Hawkins in the *Origin of the English Drama* (1773) attempted some sort of sketch of pre-Shakespearean drama. Kyd and Peele are praised, and he reprints not only *Gammer Gurton*, *Gorboduc*, and *the Spanish Tragedy*, but also Gascoigne's *Supposes*, Preston's *King Cambises*, Peele's *David and Bethsabe* and Kyd's *Soliman and Perseda*. The material for a history of English drama was then, with some gaps, already assembled.

Interest in Renaissance literature outside the drama centred necessarily in Spenser. Revival of interest in him, as shown in imitations and appreciations, has been described frequently.[21] For our purposes it is sufficient to note that Spenser received also early editorial attention in the new style. John Hughes's edition (1715) is an "improving edition" which preceded Pope's Shakespeare, Urry's Chaucer, and Bentley's Milton. Its importance lies in the preface, which stressed the chivalric influence on Spenser and drew a parallel between Gothic architecture and the composition of the *Fairie Queene*. His defence of Spenser, derived from the Italian apologies for Ariosto, and demanding that Spenser should be tried by his own rules, was, in England, one of the very earliest statements of the contrast between classical unity and "romantic diversity."

Spenser thus became the starting-point for any literary discussion of chivalry and of "romantic" composition, in an age which, at first, knew scarcely any genuine medieval romance. Spenser was, like Shakespeare, the happy-hunting-ground of commentators, as his special language, even more archaic to an age that had not yet experienced the revival of Elizabethan diction, his many allusions, proper names and fairly obvious adaptations and borrowings were so many incitements to literary research. John Jortin's *Remarks on Spenser's Poems* (1734) is such a collection of notes with classical parallels; and John Upton, in a *Letter concerning a New Edition of Spenser's Fairie Queene* (1751), anticipated, at least broadly, the program of Warton's *Observations on the Fairie Queene* (1754). Upton has the same plan as Warton of tracing Spenser's debt to Ovid, Chaucer, Ariosto and Tasso. His edition, which came out only after Warton's book, in 1758, contains a defence of Spenser's composition as conforming to classical rules, some attempts at the interpretation of his political allegory, already noticed by Hughes, and many parallels not noticed by Warton. The same year brought another edition by Ralph Church, with a careful life, apparently written by William Oldys, and briefer notes.

But the critical discussion of Spenser scarcely changed even with Hurd's *Letters on Chivalry and Romance* (1762). Hurd's whole interest is still concentrated on the question of composition. He repeats Hughes in essence when he says that the *Fairie Queene* should be "read and criticized under this idea of a Gothic, not a classical poem." [22] He draws again the parallel with Gothic architecture, "which has its own rules," [23] and he finds a unity of another sort than the classical, a unity of design and not of action, in the whole epic poem. But the novelty is rather in the boldness of the formulation than in the actual thought. How curious the confusions as to periods and their styles were in the eighteenth century is illustrated by Hurd's other parallel with Spenser's plan. He compares it to a formal garden, which he describes as laid out on the "Gothic method of design," [24] with avenues converging on a centre. This he contrasts with the more natural, artless and simple landscape-gardening of William Kent, which we have been taught to regard as "preromantic." The composition of the *Fairie Queene* has, in reality, nothing whatever to do with Gothic architecture and only very little with the design of a Renaissance garden. Hurd himself realizes that Spenser's *Fairie Queene* differs also from the composition of a medieval romance. He probably knew little of the romances at first hand, though he mentions *Amadis, Sir Lancelot of the Lake*, and Chaucer's *Squire's Tale*. When he speaks of Milton's being attracted "not by the composition of the books of chivalry, but the manners described in them," [25] he defines his own attitude and that of all the early romance scholars, like Percy or Warton. They looked in it for pictures of bygone times, and since they still felt very strongly the demands of regular composition on a classical pattern, they either tried to find it in the "romantic" poems admired by them, as Addison did in *Chevy Chase*, or Percy in *Libius Disconius;* or, as a last resort, they tentatively began to advocate a special principle of composition, parallel to that of Gothic architecture, which would enable them to discover a new regularity.

Spenser thus became the centre of much literary discussion. With him was bound up the whole problem of romance, the debate on non-classical composition, discussions on the admissibility of allegory and the "fairy way of writing." But other problems in Spenser, especially outside the *Fairie Queene*, were scarcely noted,[26] since, on the whole, literary problems in the eighteenth century were largely limited to a number of set topics that elicited astonishingly uniform answers. These answers were rarely "neo-classical" or "romantic" in any later sense; they were rather empirical, haphazard, and sometimes curiously compromising, hesitant and even self-contradictory. But, by their very bewilderment, they were important for the increasing grasp on the realities of early poetry.

Spenser, as the centre of Renaissance poetry, was only the main figure on a crowded stage. The memory of a hero like Sidney could never have completely faded. An *Arcadia*, modernized by Mrs. Stanley, appeared in 1724–1725, *The Defence of Poesy* in 1752, and Mrs. Cooper's *Muses' Library* reprinted two poems which she ascribed to Sidney in her first anthology of Elizabethan poetry of any size and fullness.[27] She knows and quotes from William Warner, George Gascoigne, Thomas Nash, George Turberville, Fulke Greville, Sir Walter Raleigh, Sir John Harington, Sir John

Davies, Edward Fairfax and Samuel Daniel, giving short biographies and appreciations. Snippets from many other writers, including Campion, appeared in Thomas Hayward's *British Muse* (1738),[28] an old-fashioned type of anthology with headings like "Courtship," and "Virginity" and with a marked preponderance of erotic passages. William Oldys wrote for it a *Critical Review of all the Collections of this Kind ever published* which begins with *England's Parnassus* (1600). Later Percy's *Reliques* (1765) is in part an anthology of Elizabethan poetry. It includes much matter from the Elizabethan miscellanies, first explored by Oldys, many poems from the dramatists, and pieces by Warner, Drayton, and Gascoigne.

Fuller reprints of Elizabethan poets were not really uncommon in the eighteenth century. Sir John Davies's poem *Nosce Teipsum* had been published frequently in the seventeenth century and throughout the eighteenth. It attracted the attention of theologians by its arguments in favour of immortality. One of the early editors claims to have been converted by Davies "from a brutish habit of twenty eight years intemperance to a sober life" and Dr. Thomas Sheridan appended his own essay on immortality to the poem, as late as 1733.[29] We can speak of literary interest in Davies only with Capell's excellent edition in the *Prolusions* (1760). The collected works of William Drummond of Hawthornden were edited by Sage and Ruddiman with Ben Jonson's *Conversations* in 1711. There was an edition of Daniel's *Poetical Works* with a Memoir (1718) which recommends the reprinting of old English poets, "even if they have not that turn of versification which is the pride of our modern attempters." [30]

Drayton was also reprinted: John Oldmixon thought it necessary to versify the *Heroical Epistles* as *Amores Britan-*

nici (1703) because the language seemed to him now "obsolete, his verses rude and unharmonious, his thoughts often poor and vulgar, affected and unnatural." [31] The *Heroical Epistles* were reprinted by Dodsley in 1737, and *Nimphidia* was published in Dryden's *Miscellany* and as *The History of Queen Mab*, independently in 1751. A large folio with Drayton's *Works* appeared in 1748, with a highly laudatory "Essay," probably by Charles Coffey.[32] There we find, for the first time, the suggestion, later taken up by Horace Walpole, that the *Mirror for Magistrates* is the source of the English historical play. Another *Life of Drayton* was written by William Oldys for the *Biographia Britannica* (1750). It pointed out omissions in the 1748 Folio which were then added in the 1753 reprint of the *Works* in four octavo volumes. Campbell in the *Polite Correspondence* (1741) praised Drayton as a "patriot and poet," but Pope disparaged him as a "very mediocre poet" and Goldsmith's "Citizen of the World" had never heard of him before he saw his tomb in Westminster Abbey.[33] Tusser's *Points of Husbandry*, Churchyard's *Worthiness of Wales*, the *Works* of William Browne, Fairfax's translation of Tasso, Hall's and Marston's satires and Phineas Fletcher's *Piscatory Eclogues* may conclude this remarkable list, which may not even be complete.[34] A number of these reprints were "improving" editions, in which the editors quite unscrupulously changed the metre, the syntax and even the vocabulary of the originals in order to bring the texts closer to eighteenth-century requirements of smoothness, correctness and decorum. This practice, paralleled in Pope's Shakespeare and Urry's Chaucer, can be traced back to Edward Phillips' edition of Drummond (1656) which even then modernized the grammar and diction quite thoroughly.[35]

John Donne, who chronologically belongs to the Elizabethans and possibly the other pre-Civil war metaphysicals, might be considered as falling within this survey of the revival of early English literature. But as the metaphysicals' reputation in the eighteenth century has been discussed recently in detail [35a] it may be sufficient to point out that Donne and his immediate followers suffered from the reaction against them initiated in the age of Dryden, and that no critical situation had yet arisen before Warton which would have changed the unfavourable verdict on their style and versification. It was even more trenchantly summed up and enlarged in Johnson's "Life of Cowley." The metaphysicals, of course, had not yet acquired the patina of antiquity which made the revival of much early literature possible. But there were survivals of the deferential attitude to Donne even in the eighteenth century, especially in the biographical dictionaries like those of Giles Jacob and Cibber, and the *Biographia Britannica.* Donne was known best as a satirist, but the refurbishment of his satires by Pope and Parnell in 1731 was applauded by everybody, including Thomas Warton, because "his asperities were such as wanted and would bear the chisel." [35b] Donne the lyrical poet was either unknown or despised for his unnatural wit, a situation which did not change even after the reprint of his poems in 1779. An imitation, without acknowledgement, of "Go and catch a falling star" in 1741 and occasional laudatory references from such unlikely quarters as Warburton and Richard Hurd, represent only small reservations in the general condemnation of his bad taste and extravagance. As we are not writing a history of taste, it is more central to our purpose to turn to the more distant past.

This interest in Renaissance poetry extended naturally to pre-Elizabethan poetry, though it was for obvious reasons fainter. There was a very poor reprint of Tottel's *Miscellany* by George Sewell in 1717, and this defect was not remedied till 1815. Percy planned an edition in 1763 and worked on it intermittently for many years. It was to include the other works of Surrey and Wyatt and showed a much more scholarly editorial practice than his *Reliques*. The whole edition was ready in 1808, when it was destroyed by fire with the exception of a few copies which allow us to form an opinion of its unusual value.[36]

Barclay, Skelton, Surrey and Wyatt are extensively represented in the *Muses' Library*. Percy's *Reliques* too quote from Tottel, Skelton, and Hawes's *Pastime of Pleasure*. There was a special reprint of Skelton, to whom Pope alludes as "beastly," [37] in well-known verses. *The Tunnyng of Elynour Runnyng* was printed in 1719 and in the *Harleian Miscellany* (1744). Sackville's *Induction* appeared, in full, in the *Muses' Library* (1737) and in Capell's *Prolusions* (1760).

During the eighteenth century early prose literature was not widely studied or criticized, though some writers never needed revival. James Upton, John Upton's father, published Ascham's *Scholemaster* in 1711, and James Bennet edited in 1761, Ascham's *English Works* with a Life by Dr. Johnson, which quoted Puttenham on Surrey. More's *Utopia* was, of course, frequently reprinted, and there are *Memoirs* of his life by Ferdinando Warner.[38] Samuel Knight wrote a *Life of Colet* (1724). John Lewis was the author of a full *Life of John Fisher*, which remained, however, in manuscript until 1855. Richard Hooker's works were frequently reprinted, and there was a first large collection of Bacon's Latin works in 1730. David Mallet's *Life of Bacon* (1740) was of some value, though the incidental sketches of scholastic philosophy and Bacon's thought were very meager. Sir Walter Raleigh was most fortunate among the Elizabethans, with two editions by Oldys (1736) and

Thomas Birch (1751) and two Lives, of which the older, by Oldys, was a high achievement in point of accuracy and fullness. It was no mean compliment to it that Gibbon, who had planned a *Life of Raleigh*, came to the conclusion that he could give only little more than an abridgment of Oldys.[39]

Imaginative prose of the sixteenth century was, however, almost completely neglected. Outside Sidney, there was only a badly modernized *Euphues* dating from as early as 1718. The author of the preface to Dodsley had seen and read *Euphues* and condemned its "unnatural affected jargon and stiff bombast," [40] an opinion repeated by D. E. Baker and Peter Whalley. But otherwise, outside of chroniclers and antiquaries, there is scarcely any trace of a knowledge of Elizabethan prose, though abstracts of rare works, including Elyot's *Gouvernor*, More's *English Works* and even Webbe's *Discourse on English Poetry*, can be found in Oldys' short-lived *British Librarian* (1737). Nevertheless, if we also take into account the fact that old books were then still easily and cheaply procurable, the materials for a history of Elizabethan literature were assembled. A list of the authors quoted by Johnson in the *Dictionary* would show that he dipped into almost all who have been enumerated here.[41]

Of Middle-English literature Chaucer is the only author who never passed completely from the minds of Englishmen. Dryden's and Pope's paraphrases helped to revive interest in him. In 1721 appeared Urry's edition which wanted to restore Chaucer "to his feet again," regularizing the metre by an arbitrary and wrong-headed system that followed from the current misinterpretation of his pronunciation. There were other modernizations, a new, fragmentary edition by Thomas Morell (1737), and both Dr. Johnson and Thomas Warton planned editions of Chaucer. Dr. John-

son's Chaucer was to be similar to his Shakespeare, for it was
to contain "remarks on his language, and the changes it had
undergone from the earliest times to his age, and from his to
the present, with notes explanatory of customs etc. and references to Boccace, and other authors from whom he has
borrowed, with an account of the liberties he has taken in
telling the stories." [42] Warton laid his plan aside in favour of
the *History*. [43]

Thus the field was free for Tyrwhitt, who, together with
Warton, was the first since Dryden to give any serious
criticism of Chaucer. The many references in every book
touching older English literature, all repeating the tag about
the father of English poetry and the bibliographical information collected by Thomas Hearne, scarcely compensate
for the almost complete lack of any criticism at the time.[44]
Only Dr. Johnson in the Preface to the *Dictionary* discusses
with some fullness the old question of Chaucer's Gallicisms,
deciding, as we would decide today, that Chaucer's innova-
tions have been overrated and that he shares them with his
contemporaries. The studies of sources most prominent in
Shakespeare and Spenser scholarship, began also to affect
Chaucer. Thus Richard Farmer discovered the *Teseide* as
the source of *Knight's Tale*, a fact which was known before to
Thynne in 1598.[44a] Apparently only Tyrwhitt described
Filostrato as the source of *Troilus*. It was, of course, known
that the *Romaunt of the Rose* is a translation from the
French.[45] Gower survived, though rarely more than his
name and his association with Chaucer. Pope remarked to
Spence that "there is little that is worth reading in Gower:
he wants the spirit of poetry and the descriptiveness that are
in Chaucer." [46] Mrs. Cooper considers him a "man of learning who does not appear to have much genius" and calls his
whole work "little better than a cool translation from other

authors." [47] She reprints a passage from the *Confessio Amantis*. Only Johnson seems to value his historical position highly, considering Chaucer Gower's disciple and thus Gower the true father of English poetry.[48] But an actual study of Gower began only with Warton.

Piers Plowman attracted somewhat more attention. Hickes quotes it as an example of alliterative poetry and the author in the *Muses' Mercury* (1709) quotes a passage describing the metre as blank verse. "Robert de Longland" lived, he thinks, some seventy years before Chaucer. The *Muses' Library* (1737) praises Langland highly as "the first of the English poets." "No writer, except Chaucer and Spenser, for many ages, had more of real inspiration." [49] Langland is also correctly put into the reign of Edward III or Richard II; the book is described and extracts are given, though complaints are made about the metre and the "hardly intelligible dialect." [50] In Cibber's *Lives* (1753) we find high praise for Langland, though his style is called "equally unmusical and obsolete with Chaucer's." [51] Finally, Percy, in a little essay *On the Metre of Pierce Plowman's Visions* recognizes, at least in principle, that alliteration is not merely an ornament but the foundation of Langland's metre, and puts it into the tradition descending from Nordic poetry. He has also high praise for his "strong allegoric painting, great humour, spirit and fancy." [52]

Fourteenth-century literature, outside Chaucer, Gower and Langland, remained *terra incognita* before Warton. There were, however, two reprints of Mandeville,[53] and the Wyclifite New Testament was edited by John Lewis (1731). Metrical romances remained completely unknown, though most of them were listed in the Cottonian, Oxford, and Harleian Catalogues. Again, Percy is the first to make use of these lists and to transcribe six romances for his own use.[54] The *Essay on the Ancient Metrical Romances* (1765) gives a list of thirty-nine romances and a description of *Libius Disconius*. Percy later planned an edition, but it was again and again held up and finally forestalled by Ritson's *Ancient Engleish Metrical Romanceës* (1802) which contains ten romances out of a total of thirteen known to Percy.[55]

The Chaucerians of the fifteenth century never disappeared from sight so completely. The editions of Chaucer contained a liberal sprinkling of fifteenth-century poetry, like the *Flower and the Leaf*, also modernized by Dryden, and Lydgate's *Siege of Thebes*.[56] Tanner has a full discussion of the Lydgate canon largely based on Bale. *The Muses' Mercury* (1709) praises him as more regular, more polished and more intelligible than his master Chaucer, and he is mentioned by Gildon, Giles Jacob, Pope, Cibber, and John Husbands. But Mrs. Cooper complains that she gave "a considerable price for his works, and waded through a large folio," but found only a "modest disciple" of Chaucer.[57] Johnson quotes from the *Falls of Princes* to show "that our language was then not written by caprice, but was in a settled state." [58] The study of Lydgate can be said to have begun only with Gray, whose paper was not, however, published till 1815. It is based purely on the *Falls of Princes* and is largely descriptive, though it pays attention to the question of sources and metre. It is a model handbook exposition, though scarcely very critical in the preference for Lydgate over Gower and Occleve. The last was apparently unknown to Johnson and Mrs. Cooper.[59] Otherwise only Hardyng's *Chronicle* seems to have survived, since it was praised by Winstanley. But Mrs. Cooper dismisses it as unimportant, and Cibber's *Lives* calls it "totally destitute of poetry." [60]

English fifteenth-century prose was represented at least by an edition of Sir John Fortescue's *On the Governance of the Kingdom of England* (1714), a book which was also analyzed by Oldys and quoted by Dr. Johnson. The Preface to the 1714 edition by John Fortescue-Aland, a descendant of the author, pleaded for the study of the Anglo-Saxon language and laws with great patriotic fervour.[61] John Lewis wrote a full *Life of Reynold Pecock* (1744) with stress on ecclesiastical matters, and a *Life of Caxton* (1737), which was, however, soon superseded by the *Life of Caxton* written by Oldys for the *Biographia Britannica* (1748). Caxton, of course, attracted the interest of everybody who wrote on early printing, like Ames or Conyers Middleton. Only Ames, in his *Typographical Antiquities* (1749), describes Malory's *Morte d'Arthur*,[62] but one cannot speak of interest in its contents.

Fifteenth-century Scottish literature also began to be appreciated again. This revival was, at first, confined to Scotland, where it had its own specific sources in Scottish nationalism and Jacobitism. Sir Robert Sibbald planned a *Historia Literaria Gentis Scotorum* as early as 1702, but the few fragments which are preserved, seem to show that he would have done little more than expanded David Buchanan and Dempster.[63] Also George Mackenzie's *Lives and Characters of the Most Eminent Writers of the Scots Nation* (1708–1722) is scarcely an advance on the older biographical methods; it is full of irrelevant padding and the material is almost always second-hand. Especially the part of William Nicolson's *Historical Library* devoted to Scottish authors was laid under heavy contribution.[64]

Older Scottish literature continued to be reprinted, in some measure, throughout the seventeenth century as patriotic reading for the masses. Sir David Lyndsay's works,

Barbour's *Bruce*, and Blind Harry's *Wallace* were reprinted until late into the eighteenth century in poorly modernized editions. *Christ's Kirk on the Green* appeared as early as 1691 in an edition by Edmund Gibson of *Polemo-middinia*, a "macaronic" poem ascribed to William Drummond of Hawthornden, as a sort of philological joke with plentiful etymological notes. It reappeared in James Watson's and Allan Ramsay's collections and was reprinted elsewhere in the eighteenth century.

Other older Scottish poetry including Montgomerie's *Cherry and the Slae* appeared in James Watson's *Choice Collection of Comic and Serious Scots Poems* (1706–1711). But the first full-length publication of some scholarly pretensions was Thomas Ruddiman's edition of Gavin Douglas's *Aeneid* (1710) with a "Life" by Bishop Sage and a very full glossary which for a long time to come remained the only Middle Scots dictionary. Allan Ramsay was, however, the first to tap the resources of the Bannatyne manuscript in his *Evergreen* (1724). Dunbar's *Golden Terge*, fables by Henryson, and much other matter were printed for the first time, though very great liberties were taken with the text. Ramsay even added stanzas to Dunbar's *Lament for the Makars* foretelling his own advent and wrote himself a *Vision* which he boldly ascribed to Alexander Scott. Blind Harry's *Wallace* was very badly modernized by William Hamilton of Gilbertfield in 1722; Francis Fawkes did better with the Prologues to Douglas's *Aeneid*.[65] This interest in Middle Scots literature spread then to England. Scraps from Lyndsay appear, for the first time, in Hayward's *British Muse* (1738). Campbell in *Polite Correspondence* (1741) praises Douglas as "by far the ablest translator who ever attempted the works of this prince of Latin poets" and "knows nothing equal to it, unless it be Chapman's Homer." [66]

Also, Gray had read the *Aeneid* and "was much pleased," particularly with the "poetical prefaces to each book," and he had the *Palice of Honor* copied out for his use.[67] Thomas Warton, in a collection called *The Union or Select Scots and English Poems* (1753), reprinted Dunbar's *Thistle and the Rose* and Lyndsay's *Prologue to the Dreme*. But Sir David Dalrymple (later Lord Hailes) was the first scholarly editor of a fuller selection from the Bannatyne manuscript. His *Ancient Scottish Poems* (1770) made Warton's sketch possible and earned him the encouragement to write a *History of Scotch Poetry*.[68]

Material on medieval drama was slowly accumulating. Nobody seems to have noticed at the time the mystery play on Noah's Ark, printed in Henry Bourne's *History of Newcastle-Upon-Tyne* (1736), probably because it was buried in a local history book. Gildon, Jacob, etc., do not even make use of the information contained in Wright's *Historia Histrionica* (1699), a work which must have become pretty scarce, for Oldys reprints it in the *British Librarian* only thirty-eight years after its publication, and it reappears in the eleventh volume of Dodsley. The Preface to Dodsley's *Old Plays* (1744) is still very severe on the mysteries as representing "in a senseless manner" some miraculous history from the Bible. In the moralities the author finds "some shadow of meaning, something of design, a fable and moral." But the whole subject is still dismissed because "a more particular knowledge of these things was so little worth preserving that the loss of it is scarcely to be regretted." [69] The body of Dodsley's texts contains Rastell's *Four Elements*, Heywood's *Four P's* and the *New Custom*. The *Harlein Miscellany* printed an *Interlude on St. John the Baptist* by Bale, while D. E. Baker simply, even literally, reproduced Dodsley's Preface.

Percy's *Essay on the Origin of the English Stage* (1765) makes the first considerable advance. He describes *The Slaughter of the Innocents* from the Digby mysteries, Wever's *Lusty Juventus*, and *Everyman*. He points especially to the supposed observance of the unities in *Everyman* just as he had looked for classical composition in *Libius Disconius*. In describing *Hick Scorner* he stresses its progress towards presenting real characters. All these plays were then, for the first time, printed in Thomas Hawkins's *Origin of the English Drama* (1773), which contains also a description of the Chester plays, based on the Harleian Catalogue, and a few more appreciative remarks on mysteries and moralities.

The further we go into the past the dimmer knowledge becomes, not only in proportion to the actual difficulties of reconstruction and the scarcity of documents, but also because of the flagging interest of a century that still struggled hard with the script and language. Hickes called the language of the time semi-Saxon or corrupt Saxon and quoted from the *Poema Morale*, from *Cokaygne*, and from an early *Life of St. Margaret*. An English translation of Geoffrey of Monmouth was published by Aaron Thompson in 1718, and Thomas Hearne followed with his editions of Robert of Gloucester (1724) and the second part of Robert Mannyng of Brunne (1725). Attention was concentrated purely on the rhymed chronicles, which were treated rightly as mere historical documents and scarcely poetry. Thus Percy complains to Shenstone that the rhymes of Robert of Gloucester are "to the last degree mean and contemptible," and refers to "frightful" specimens in Selden's notes to Drayton.[70] But Robert of Gloucester remained the only early Middle English text quoted widely in the *Muses' Mercury* and elsewhere.

The *Muses' Library* (1737) shows knowledge also of a

Charter of Edward II, in which, for reasons too mysterious to probe, it finds some similarity to a "relique of the ancient British Druids," [71] also of some lines on Bath and verses on the death of Henry I, which are obviously of very much later date.[72] Dr. Johnson quotes *Cokaygne* and the *Life of St. Margaret* from Hickes; otherwise he quotes only the ubiquitous Robert of Gloucester.[73] Nothing else was known at the time: Wanley's catalogue lists *Ormulum*, without recognizing its verse form, and the *Owl and the Nightingale* as a "Poema Normanno-Saxonicum." Early Middle English was thus completely left to historians and antiquaries.

This was, after all, the tradition of Anglo-Saxon studies, which also, as Warton complains, were divorced from "taste and genius." [74] A few halting steps were taken to give literary interpretation to Anglo-Saxon remains, but they were not advanced enough to prevent Warton ignoring or almost ignoring Anglo-Saxon literature and beginning his history only after the Conquest. Warton confesses that this "jejune and intricate subject" would almost have doubled his labour and states that Saxon poetry has "no connexion with the nature and the purpose of his present undertaking." [75] Thus the fateful gulf between Anglo-Saxon and Middle-English was never bridged in the eighteenth century. The late seventeenth-century studies of Anglo-Saxon culminated early in the eighteenth century in George Hickes's monumental *Linguarum Veterum Septentrionalium Thesaurus Grammatico-Criticus et Archeologicus* (1705) which contains an Anglo-Saxon, a Gothic, an Old High German and an Icelandic Grammar, and was supplemented by Humphrey Wanley's Catalogue of Anglo-Saxon, early Middle-English and Icelandic manuscripts in English libraries which even today has not been superseded by any work of similar scope.

The book (or rather books) are completely philological

and antiquarian in purpose and method, and Hickes's dissertation on the utility of studies in Old Northern Literature (1703) stresses their help in explaining law and institutions like the jury, in topography, etymology, etc. There is no mention of genuinely literary interests. But in the text of the *Thesaurus* literary considerations are not altogether absent: the chapter on Anglo-Saxon poetry quotes Alfred's Boethius, *Judith*, *Athelstan's Victory*, and the *Fight at Finnsburg*, the manuscript of which has since been lost. Hickes also makes an attempt to explain the system of Anglo-Saxon verse. He suspected it of being based on an elaborate system of quantity, whose principles had been forgotten, while alliteration, though fully recognized as important, is justified merely by quotations of purely ornamental alliteration in Homer, Virgil, Spenser, Donne, Dryden, etc. Wanleys' catalogue contained the first mention of the *Exeter Book* and *Beowulf* described as a "tractatus nobilissimus poetice scriptus" and as "egregium exemplum poesis Anglo-Saxonicae." [76] But more than a century was to elapse before the manuscript was published by a Dane.

Hickes was connected as a teacher and by marriage with the two Elstobs. The brother, William Elstob, who died early, edited Wulfstan, while his sister Elizabeth published *Rudiments of Grammar for the English-Saxon Tongue* (1715), the first Anglo-Saxon grammar in English. She had edited also an *English-Saxon Homily on the Birth-day of St. Gregory* (1708) and had planned a large-scale edition of the Saxon Homilies, for which she appealed for subscriptions and the printing of which was actually begun.[77] Hickes praises her "attempt to prove the uncorrupted state of the primitive English church" for use in controversies with the Papists, a motive which harks back to Matthew Parker and his group, but there was a patriotic and also mildly feminist touch in her hopes to "invite the Ladies to be acquainted with the language of their predecessors and the original of their mother-tongue." [78]

Thomas Hearne contributed to Anglo-Saxon literary studies by saving the manuscript, since lost, of the *Battle of Maldon* (1726), and there were new editions of the Anglo-Saxon laws, of Bede and Asser's Latin *Life of Alfred*, the text containing a reprint of Alfred's Preface to Gregory. After the twenties of the century a lull seems to have come over Anglo-Saxon studies, during the very years when the revival of other English literature was gathering force. Only a popularization of some of Hickes's results has a curious interest, since it tries for the first time to make use of Anglo-Saxon poetry for purposes that can be called strictly literary. Campbell in his *Polite Correspondence* (1741) describes Leander, residing "in the Fens," with Miss Elstob's *English-Saxon Grammar* on his table, as an enthusiast for Anglo-Saxon poetry. In the letter Leander writes he reproduces Hickes's ideas on quantitative metre, praises the "sublime sentiment" and "furor poeticus" of the Anglo-Saxon poems and describes some prose writers. He complains of the difficulty of his study, "but still the *amor patriae* joined to a passion for poetry will spur me on to the utmost." He quotes the little poem on Durham from Hickes and even displays knowledge of an older printing in Twysden's *Historiae Anglicanae Scriptores Decem* (1652). He then speaks of *Athelstan's Victory*, which he knows from both Wheloc's and Gibson's editions of the *Anglo-Saxon Chronicle*, and reproduces from Hickes details on alliteration in ancient and modern poetry.

All this second-hand antiquarian knowledge is then suddenly turned to modern use. "Good translations from Saxon poetry would contribute not a little to restore the reputation of our poetry, if we returned to this Saxon manner of writing." Curiously enough, the author thinks that such imitations would resemble *Cooper's Hill* or *Windsor Forest*, poems "serving excellently to defend various passages in modern history from sinking into oblivion and affording a lasting picture of the places they are designed to represent." [79] The parallel between an Anglo-Saxon poem and *Windsor Forest* seems to us far-fetched indeed. Thus the purely bookish idea of a descriptive poem, useful as a vehicle of historical and topographical information, stands unrelated to the following description of Saxon poetry as inspired, enthusiastic, rhapsodical. Saxon "sonnets" join Welsh Odes, Pindarics, and Lapland Odes as examples of true original poetry. But the *Polite Correspondence* did not succeed in putting Anglo-Saxon poetry on the map of even primitive poetry. Edward Lye, the lexicographer, planned an edition of *Caedmon* in 1753, and in 1773 Daines Barrington published Alfred's *Orosius*. But this seems to have been the last book of any importance in Anglo-Saxon scholarship during the century.

Philology had, at least, established beyond doubt the Germanic character of the language, though as late as 1776 William Drake had to publish an elaborate refutation of the Celtic theory by parallels with the Gothic Bible.[80] But the political motive behind Anglo-Saxon studies which became so strong in the nineteenth century, mostly under German influence, was then almost non-existent. We see its germ, however, in Bishop Gibson's dedication of Camden's *Britannia* to King George I. He proclaims proudly that "the greatest part of his Majesty's subjects are of Saxon original." "If we enquire from whence our Saxon Ancestors came, we shall find that it was from his Majesty's Dominion in Germany," namely Hannover. This ingenious theory was directed against "those unnatural creatures, the Jacobites, who called the King a foreigner." [81] John Free, in a popular *Essay towards an History of the English Tongue* (1749), quotes this dedication and argues again at length for the Teutonic character of English. Anglo-Saxon is also firmly set into the linguistic tradition of English in Johnson's Preface to the *Dictionary* (1755) which reproduces Hickes on the derivation of English, quotes the Preface to Boethius and the Anglo-Saxon translation of Luke, and gives Hickes's account of Anglo-Saxon metre. Johnson remarks, with an unusual suspension of judgment, that "our ignorance of the laws of their metre and the quantities of their syllables excludes us from that pleasure which the old bards undoubtedly gave to their contemporaries." [82]

Only Gray recognized that "the poetry of our forefathers, the Saxons and Danes consisted of nothing else, than this alliteration and measure, without any rhyme." He studied Hickes in detail, and his list of Anglo-Saxon poems, meant apparently as an anthology to precede his "history of poetry," includes part of the "Dano-Saxon paraphrase of Genesis," which Hickes had quoted, the Gospel of Nicodemus as edited by Edward Thwaites, *Athelstan's Victory* and the *Death of Eadgar* from the *Anglo-Saxon Chronicle.* But Gray did not go beyond Hickes and probably could not understand Anglo-Saxon without the help of a translation, as is shown by his ignoring the Finnsburg fragment, which had been left untranslated by Hickes.[83] Percy did not even know "that there is anywhere extant an entire Saxon poem" all in alliterative verse, and Warton quotes *Athelstan's Victory* as the only pagan document he knows, though elsewhere he refers to *Beowulf* and the *Battle of Maldon.*[84] Thus the linguistic difficulties, then rarely overcome except by very few specialists, the ignorance of any large-scale poetical production that seemed to deserve the designation of primitive, and the general misconception of the nature of Old Germanic poetry, which made people look in vain for anything strikingly pagan and wild in Anglo-Saxon, led to a neglect that was not substantially remedied until much later, in the nineteenth century.

Anglo-Saxon poetry seemed too monkish and not primitive enough. The ideals of primitive poetry could be found realized only in the old ballads and in foreign literatures. Real old English popular ballads and songs were little known at that time and were seldom distinguished from much later broadsides or modern pastiches. But genuine ballads can be found, even before Percy, scattered in collections like those of James Watson, Allan Ramsay, William Thomson, and especially in the *Collection of Old Ballads* (1723) usually ascribed to Ambrose Philips.[85] But all the *Evergreens* cannot deprive Percy of the fame of having collected, for the first time, and commented on with a new emphasis, the Old English and Scottish ballads. However objectionable his methods of editing may be from a modern point of view, we must not forget that *Edward, Edward, Child Waters, Sir Patrick Spens*, and many other great poems were published by him for the first time, and with scarcely any "improvements." *Chevy Chase*, praised by Sidney and Addison, was frequently printed, for the first time critically by Hearne in 1719,[86] while the much later *Nut-Brown Maid* was carefully reprinted both by the *Muses' Mercury* in 1707 and by Capell in the *Prolusions* (1760). The editor of the *Muses' Mercury* attributed the poem to the time of Lydgate, and Prior, referring to the authority of Wanley, put it even earlier. But Capell correctly judged it to be an early sixteenth-century production, and the *Muses' Mercury* itself admitted that it is not a proper ballad, but rather an allegorical poem.

Between Percy and Warton the most important ballad publication was David Herd's *Ancient and Modern Scots Songs* (1769), an odd medley of good and bad, which was, however, edited with much greater reverence for the original folk-version than Percy displayed. In Scotland, where there was no great Renaissance tradition, respect for old airs and ballads was much deeper and the living oral tradition much more tenacious. Herd's book was only a selection of his MS collections, which were later used by Burns and Scott and were not exhausted till the labours of Child and Hans Hecht.[87]

"Sumer is icumen in" and many other early English lyrics were first quoted and discussed in Sir John Hawkins's *General History of the Science and Practice of Music* (1776).[88] Many of the popular ballads in Percy had to be rehashed and refurbished to be made palatable to "polite" taste, since early English poetry was still too near to fall completely under the category of "primitive." The natural voices of early men could be heard most clearly in the original poetry of other nations.

The nearest to Anglo-Saxon was, of course, Norse poetry.[89] Temple had been the first in England to show any literary interest in it, though antiquarians like Sheringham, Aylett Sammes and others had used the younger *Edda* for their purposes before. Temple quoted two stanzas from the *Death-Song of Ragnar Lodbrog* in Latin from Wormius' *Literatura Runica* (1651) and referred to the poem of Scallogrim *(Egil's Ransom)* as "truly poetical and in its kind Pindaric." [90] Hickes then reproduced the dialogue of Hervor with her father Angantyr, which he found in Olaus Verelius' edition of the *Hervarar Saga* (1672), in English prose and thus gave the first translation of any Icelandic poem into any modern language outside Scandinavian. These three poems remained the only bits of Old Norse poetry known to Englishmen for over half a century.[91] Hickes's translation was reprinted in the *Miscellany of Poems* (1716), usually called Dryden's, where Hickes's prose was simply printed as verse. The elder Warton, in his posthumous *Poems on Several Occasions* (1748), made two Runic odes out of the two stanzas quoted by Temple from *Ragnar Lodbrog*, and Husbands reproduced Temple on Scallogrim; Blair quotes the whole *Ragnar Lodbrog* in Latin from Wormius and even Goldsmith alludes to the prose *Edda*.[92]

A widening of this meagre knowledge came again only with Percy. His *Five Pieces of Runic Poetry* (1763, actually ready for publication in 1761) present a "treasure of native genius," showing "the workings of the human mind in its almost original state of nature." [93] The first poem, the *Incantation of Hervor*, is again merely a revision of Hickes's translation, though Percy looked into Olaus Verelius. The *Dying Ode of Ragnar Lodbrog* is again the poem from *Kráku-mál*, drawn from Wormius, which had been known to Temple. The third piece, the *Ransom of Egil*, had been alluded to as the ode of Scallogrim by Temple who found it in Wormius, where it came from the *Egil's Saga*. New are only two pieces: *The Funeral Song of Hacon*, ultimately derived from the *Hakonar-mál* which Percy found in Mallet, though he examined the original and Latin translations in Resenius and Bartholin. The last piece is the *Complaint of Harold*, again suggested almost certainly by the translation in Mallet, though Percy traced it to its earlier printing in Bartholin.[94]

All the poems are claimed to be translated from the Icelandic language and an appendix reprints the originals from the Danish antiquarians of the seventeenth century. But this need not to be taken quite literally. Percy himself points out that "every poem here produced has been already published accompanied with a Latin or Swedish version" and he acknowledges the help of Edward Lye, the lexicographer, who compared the versions "everywhere with the originals." [95] The Percy papers at Oxford show that, besides, Percy made two versions of the *Fatal Sisters* and translated several sets of verses from the *Heimskringla* apparently also with the help of Edward Lye.[96] Percy, it is fair to assume, could not read Icelandic without the help of a translation, but used the existing Latin and French handbooks with profit and gained some acquaintance of the original texts with the help of Lye.

The same is probably true of Thomas Gray. In 1768 appeared Gray's two odes from the Old Norse. One, the *Fatal Sisters,* a version of the *Darradarliod,* comes either from Torfaeus's *Oreades* or Bartholin, while the second, called the *Descent of Odin,* a version of *Baldr's Draumar,* is also in Bartholin, in Latin translation. These were the only fruits of Gray's Norse studies visible to his contemporaries. But Gray's manuscripts show that he had read Mallet as early as 1758 and compiled a full commentary on the *Fatal Sisters* and the *Descent of Odin* and a list of poems, which, with one exception, includes all the poems in Percy's *Five Pieces.* The dates seem to point to the fact that Gray's work suggested the whole selection to Percy, especially as the one poem not on his list, the *Ransom of Egil* can be found elsewhere in Gray's notes transliterated from the Runic characters in Wormius. Gray's list of Nordic poems, originally planned to precede a history of English poetry, includes also the *Voluspá* and *Havamal.* Though it has been argued that Gray knew Old Norse, it seems more plausible to assume that his knowledge did not go beyond a judicious use of Hickes, Mallet and the older Danish antiquarians.[97]

In 1770 Mallet's *Introduction à l'Histoire du Danemarck* was translated by Percy (or rather by some friends whose work he supervised) as *Northern Antiquities*. Percy wrote an introduction protesting against the confusion of Germanic and Celtic. Thus Mallet became accessible to the English public and as he reproduced the whole of the later and parts of the older *Edda* provided ample materials for information on Old Norse literature, though he himself was very lukewarm about its literary merits. Besides, Percy added parts of Göransson's new Latin translation of the prose *Edda*. Later William Mason versified Percy's *Complaint of Harold* as *The Song of Harold the Valiant*, and imitations, direct or indirect, became more numerous, until there was a whole spate of them towards the end of the century. But up to 1774, our present time-limit, knowledge was obviously restricted to a few set pieces known at second hand, and the translations show that neither the style nor the setting were understood. They were considered rude "effusions," on the same level as Indian or Ossianic poetry.

Celtic and Germanic traditions were often not clearly distinguished at that time, as bard and scald were terms almost interchangeable. Their idealization had begun very early. The Tudor antiquarians, in their patriotic fervour for everything "British," had already raised the status of the bard, who slowly assumed heroic proportions long before Gray's poem and Macpherson's sentimentalized version.[98] But actual Welsh poetry remained unknown for a long time, though there was a pretty full description of the prosody, with specimens, in John David Rhys' *Cambrobrytannicae Cymraecaeve Linguae Institutiones* (1592). Gildon and Husbands refer to Welsh Odes and Taliessin, and the *Polite Correspondence* (1741), remarkable in so many other ways, seems to have been the first to translate into English some of

Taliessin's odes from the Latin of Sir John Price's *Historiae Brytannicae Defensio* (1573).[99]

But the first direct translations from Welsh were those of Evan Evans in *Some Specimens of the Poetry of the Ancient Welsh Bards* (1764). Evans was one of a group of Welsh antiquarians whose most prominent member was actually Lewis Morris, who was also encouraged by Percy and Warton. Evans' book contains ten poems translated into English prose and a Latin dissertation on the Bards, with other Latin versions from Welsh. Gray saw the manuscript of the Dissertation and translated four fragments of two poems (Gwalchmai's *Awdl i Owain Gwynedd* and Aneurin's *Gododin*) which aroused much interest and became the starting point for many imitations from the Welsh. But Gray's studies were, as his manuscripts show, much more extensive than this outward result. Long before he knew Evans, he took interest in early Welsh history and had written the *Bard* based on an account in Thomas Carte's *History of England* (1747–1754), in its turn drawn from information supplied by Morris. Gray's Commonplace Books show that he copied from Rhys extensive analyses of intricate Welsh verse forms and rhyme schemes, and a note in his own copy of the *Odes* shows that he had this verse-structure in mind when he wrote certain lines of the *Bard*. Gray's interest in things Welsh extended to the language, though he can scarcely be said to have known it, and his list of Welsh poems, which was meant as a parallel to his lists of Anglo-Saxon and Norse poetry, includes some stanzas from Taliessin, the *Battle of Argoed Llyfain*, *Gwalchmai's Delights* and *Gruffud's Lamentations*. Thus Gray, who speculated also about Wales as the country of origin of rhyme, penetrated further into the mysteries of old Welsh poetry than any of his contemporaries, not Welsh themselves, largely owing to his usually judicious use of handbooks.[100]

Evans and Gray stimulated, however, further interest in Welsh. Even Dr. Johnson subscribed to a collection of Welsh poems which he could not read and recommended the reprinting of Rhys' *Institutiones* [101], and later in the century there were more translations like those by John Walters, Edward Jones and Charlotte Brooke. But Welsh poetry was completely overshadowed by the supposed ancient Gaelic poetry discovered by Macpherson. "Ossian" thus, for a long time, blocked the way to any knowledge of genuine Old Celtic poetry, though on the other hand he stimulated enormously all interest in these subjects. Both Evans and Percy recognized the encouragement given to them by the success of Ossian, though both were aware of the dubious evidence for the authenticity of the Gaelic poems.[102] The sham antique of Macpherson obscured the more genuine attempts to collect popular Gaelic poetry, made even before Macpherson by Jerome Stone and by the Rev. Alexander Pope.[103]

Early Romance poetry was also interpreted in the primitivist spirit. The Spanish verse romances were, as far as I know, first quoted by Blackwell in his book on Homer (1735) as examples of "passionate and metaphorical" discourse. He argues that in Greece "oracles, laws, spells, prophecies were first in verse." "Some vestiges of this poetical turn remain in the pictures of Eastern manners, that are preserved in the oldest accounts of the Moors and Spaniards, where the romances occur every other page, and the conversations upon passionate subjects run into a loose kind of verse." He quotes trochees from the *Historia de las Guerras Civiles de Granada* by Pérez de Hita.[104] The very same book was used by Percy, who included a translation of "Gentle River, Gentle River" in the *Reliques* as a specimen of the ancient Spanish manner, which "very much resembles that of our old English bards" and of "Alcanzor and Zayda," a Moorish tale.[105] Ten years later he prepared for print a little book with three other translations from the *Civil Wars*, a further very free composition in the Spanish style and a poem from *Don Quixote*. This collection was to form part of his general collection of folk-poetry of all nations, but was not published till 1932.[106] In Percy were, then, the beginnings of a tradition that led to Southey's *Cid* and Lockhart's *Spanish Ballads*.

Provençal poetry fell into this scheme. Since Rymer it had become known at least as a general type, and Gildon, among others, reproduces Rymer closely.[107] But Akenside's *Pleasures of Imagination* (1744) still shows complete ignorance of the Troubadours, whose "taste and composition" he calls "extremely barbarous." [108] A fuller account, in connection with King Richard I, can be found only in Horace Walpole's *Catalogue of Royal and Noble Authors* (1758), and more detailed knowledge came only after Warton's first volume. *The General Review of Foreign Literature* (1775) reproduced the main contents of de la Curne de Sainte Palaye's *Histoire littéraire des Troubadours*, translated in 1779, in an abridged version, by Mrs. Susan Dobson.[109]

Even knowledge of pre-Renaissance Italian poetry was very meagre. Dante, of course, had always been known by name and had been read by Milton and others. The earliest translation from Dante was, however, only the Ugolino passage, translated into blank verse by the elder Jonathan Richardson (1719). The same passage was turned into blank verse also by Gray and into couplets by Frederick Howard, fifth Earl of Carlisle (in *Poems*, 1772). It inspired a picture by Sir Joshua Reynolds, exhibited in 1773. Besides, there seems to have existed a complete translation of the *Divine*

Comedy into couplets by William Huggins but only a small fragment from the *Purgatory* has survived (1760). The wooden translation by Huggins of the *Orlando Furioso* does not promise well for this first English Dante. But critical comment was still largely unappreciative, in spite of the valiant efforts of an Italian, Guiseppe Baretti, writing in English, to impress the greatness of Dante on the minds of Englishmen.[110] The most enthusiastic comment from a reputable writer were the remarks of Joseph Warton in his *Essay on Pope* (1756), which praise the *Inferno* as "the next composition to the Iliad in point of originality and sublimity." [111] But Goldsmith represents the more general opinion in referring to the *Divine Comedy* as a "strange mixture of good sense and absurdity. . . . The truth is, Dante owes most of his reputation to the obscurity of the times in which he lived." [112] Even Petrarch was pressed somehow into the prevailing scheme of primitive poetry; Sir William Jones translated *canzone* in order to show that the "Italians have written in the true spirit of the Easterns."

This spirit was expounded by Sir William Jones himself, in his *Poems consisting Chiefly of Translations from the Asiatic Languages* (1772) in a curious essay *On the Poetry of the Eastern Nations*. He tries to deduce "a priori," as he says himself, from the wonderful climate of Arabia, and the richness of the Arab language, that the Arabs "must be naturally excellent poets." Persian poetry is similarly "deduced," and an "ode" by Hafiz is compared with the ninety-ninth sonnet of Shakespeare.[113] Hafiz was the Eastern poet who attracted most attention; he was also translated early by John Richardson, while Jones was the first to tell England something of Sadi and Ferdusi, as well as to translate *Sakuntala*.[114] As early as 1711 Lady Mary Montagu had sent a translation of a Turkish love-poem to Pope, which she thought "most wonderfully resembling the *Song of Solomon*." [115]

Interest in poetry travelled even further East, into China then made familiar through its gardening, porcelain and lacquer work. But Chinese literature remained far away and inaccessible. Still, through a French translation, a play *The Chinese Orphan* came to be known in England and was commented upon by Hurd, Kames, Brown, and Goldsmith and translated by Percy.[116] Percy fitted a Chinese novel and some lyrical pieces, known to him through a French source, into his world-wide scheme of primitive universal poetry.[117]

The primitive type of poetry was searched for and found even among the Red Indians and Laplanders. Montaigne's *Essays*, one of the earliest books to praise the "noble savage," printed an *American Love-ode*, which was twice imitated by Lady Winchelsea and the elder Warton. The same ode was later translated by Ritson and can be found as a "Snake-song" in Herder and Goethe. Montaigne had also added another little fragment of a song of an Indian prisoner singing in derision of his captors.

Other reports of Indians singing a song of defiance in the face of death were common in travellers' accounts and seized the imagination of the period. Thus Joseph Warton wrote a *Dying Indian*, and later Mrs. John Hunter wrote the *Death Song of a Cherokee Indian*, which was printed by Ritson and clearly shows, absurdly enough to our mind, the influence of *Ragnar Lodbrog*, mortally stung by a viper, "smiling in the embrace of death." But these were rather fantasies on themes brought by travellers than imitations of actual existing folk-poetry, though a later writer, William Preston, was very "confident that these Indian songs" are "irregular odes," and was "confirmed in this opinion by finding that several specimens of ancient poetry of uncivilized nations bear this form"—a curious vicious circle of argument which shows clearly how such conceptions arose from vague analogies taken from all over the world.[118]

Real Indian poetry, this time Peruvian, was, however, quoted by Daniel Webb in his *Observations on the Correspondence between Poetry and Music* (1769). This is a "sonnet" addressed to the Peruvian "Isis," quoted in Latin and translated into English, from Garcilaso de la Vega's *Commentarios Reales* (1609), which had been available since Purchas, particularly in a full translation by Sir Paul Ricaut, the historian of the Turkish Empire.[119]

The "wilder graces" [120] were seen also in the two Lapland songs that became familiar to every reader of the *Spectator*. They were drawn from Johan Scheffer's *Lapponia* (1673), a travel-book which was twice translated into English. Both versifications in the *Spectator*,[121] of the "Orra Moor" song and the "Reindeer" song, are much adapted to classicist taste, but they were felt as primitive. They were reprinted by Blair and also, in an older, more literal translation, by Kames, and were included by Ritson in the *Historical Essay on National Song*. They inspired, significantly, a third Lapland song, a hoax in the style of Ossian perpetrated by one George Pickering, which seemed, however, to have been successful to judge from the number of reprints and references.[122]

Thus mankind and its poetry was surveyed, quite literally "from China to Peru." The main materials for a history of English literature were assembled, the wide background of the poetic activities of other nations was sketched in, and all awaited only the shaping hand of the genuine historian.

CHAPTER FIVE

The Writing of Literary History

No SYSTEMATIC ATTEMPT to write the History of English Literature was made before Warton. But even Warton could not have conceived his plan, had not several incomplete attempts at the writing of literary history preceded him. Theories of literary history and its evolution on the one hand, and materials in editions, catalogues, etc., on the other, were accumulating throughout the century. There were also some attempts before Warton at a combination of these two approaches, though none of them fully exploited either the ideas or the materials at hand.

The old forms of literary history continued to flourish throughout the eighteenth century. Even the old verse-catalogue of English poets did not die out completely. Thus Samuel Cobb wrote a poem, *Of Poetry: Its Progress* (1700) which traces its history from Moses and Orpheus to Chaucer, the "English Ennius," Shakespeare and Roscommon.[1] Pope's *Essay on Criticism* (1711) contains a sketch of the history of criticism. There is a *Progress of Poetry* by Mrs. Julia Madan (1721)[2] and similar poems can be found in more obscure publications of verse. Three of the most important poets of the century, William Collins, Thomas Gray and Mark Akenside, kept up this tradition of writing literary history in verse. Collins' *Verses to Sir Thomas Hanmer* (1743) contrast the "slow gradations of the other arts" with the early flowering of poetry. Greece, Rome, Florence,

Provence, and Elizabethan England (which represents the "union of Tuscan fancy and Athenian strength") pass in review. Jonson, Fletcher and Shakespeare are distinguished in the style of Dryden's characterization, and finally French tragedy is hailed as "bright perfection." Collins apparently saw the chronological confusion in placing the bards of Provence after the Florentine poets, and in the 1755 edition he added lines on Goths, priests and Vandals as "learning's foes" and changed the relation between the Provençal and Florentine poets in accordance with history. But the coupling of Cosmo and Julius II with the Provençal poets shows how vague literary ideas were in the mind of a man who had himself planned a "History of the Revival of Learning under Leo X." [3]

Similar fantastic chronology and other misconceptions fill also the sketchy history of poetry in Mark Akenside's *Pleasures of Imagination* (1744). A note asserts that "about the age of Hugh Capet" the poets of Provence were in high reputation and their "vein of fable" is founded on "traditionary legends of the Saracen wars." [4] Only in Gray's *Progress of Poesy* (1754) has the new conception of literary history emerged. Gray starts with universal primitive poetry, the Laplanders and Indians, and then sketches the progress of poetry from Greece to Italy and hence to England. Obviously, no real contribution can be expected from a form that primarily served poetical purposes, though it is of some interest as indicating the condition of contemporary interest and knowledge. But the literary history in verse did not die with Gray; the *Essay on Epic Poetry* (1782) by William Haley is even more elaborate than anything that preceded it.

Another traditional form of literary history was collective biography. Every encyclopaedia and biographical dictionary theoretically falls under our review. But, as we are mainly interested in the changes of forms and methods, it will not be necessary to investigate too closely the respective merits or demerits of all such publications. The oldest type, the Latin catalogue in the style of Leland and Bale, persisted, too. Thomas Tanner wrote about 1710 his *Bibliotheca Britannica* (1748), a purely bibliographical and biographical compilation, originally planned as an edition of Leland, which was still pre-critical in such points as the inclusion of names like Boadicea. But he goes beyond Leland and Bale in including writers like Marlowe, Greene, and Peele.[5] Nearest to the old type is then George Mackenzie's *Lives and Characters of the Most Eminent Writers of The Scots Nation* (1708–1722). It gives full lives, abstracts and catalogues of works, quotations from judgments of the learned, etc., in a spirit far more critical than Tanner's. Even though Mackenzie's information is largely second-hand, his style and digressions show that his interests were not so exclusively antiquarian as Tanner's. He quotes Dryden's *Plutarch* to show his psychological interest in the "poor reasonable animal." [6]

But Mackenzie still largely confined himself to church-writers, though there are exceptions—he discusses Barbour, the Blind Harry, and Lindsay. The new type of collective biography, confined to English literature in the more narrow sense, as established by Winstanley, was taken up again by Giles Jacob, in the *Poetical Register* (1719). The first volume contains a list of English dramatic poets in alphabetical order, based on Langbaine and Gildon. The memoirs of Wycherley are new and so is information supplied by living authors like Congreve, Dennis, and Savage. The second volume (1720) called *An Historical Account of the Lives and Writings of our most considerable English Poets*, is actually an anthology of abstracts in alphabetical order, with an introductory essay on *The Rise, Progress, Beauty, etc. of Poetry*, which is merely a patchwork of quotations from Temple, Dryden, and others.

The great biographical encyclopaedias—of course not confined to literature—begin with the *General Dictionary, Historical and Critical* (1734–1741), edited by Thomas Birch and others and obviously based on Bayle, but adding some nine hundred English biographical articles, which are frequently valuable because they are first-hand.[7] The *Biographia Britannica* (1747–1766), edited by William Oldys and Joseph Towers, was confined to British biographies, and its seven folio volumes contain many scholarly lives by Oldys, including biographies of Drayton, Fulke Greville, Fuller and others. Dr. Johnson's *Lives* draw much biographical information from these two forerunners of the *Dictionary of National Biography*. But the fullest attempt at a collection of biographies, limited to English poets, was *The Lives of the Poets of Great Britain* (1753), which is known as Cibber's Lives, but was mainly written by Robert Sheils (who died in 1753), a Scotch Jacobite, whose political sentiments were suppressed or altered by the editor.[8] The book begins with Chaucer and ends with quite recent writers, like Aaron Hill and Ambrose Philips. As far as one can speak of any underlying historical conception, it is the old one of progress from the "morning star," Chaucer, to the "perfect consummation of Dryden." [9] Fairfax and Waller are stressed, in accordance with the old *fable convenue*, expounded by Dryden and Pope.

Other biographical collections of the time were on a less extensive plan; thus Horace Walpole's *Catalogue of the Royal and Noble Authors of England* (1758) is limited to "ten English princes and above fourscore peers." [10] Walpole is very critical of Tanner and writes most fully on Surrey and some later authors, but his whole principle of selection precluded any genuinely historical approach. David Erskine Baker's *Companion to the Play-House* (1764) reverts to the form established by Langbaine. It contains an alphabetical list of plays and authors with short biographies and bibliographies and an introductory sketch *Of the Rise and Progress of the English Stage*. James Granger's *Biographical History of England from Egbert the Great to the Revolution* (1769) is devised as a commentary on a "Methodical Catalogue of Engraved British Heads" and is a large collection of mainly anecdotical biographies, classified according to the social standing of the subjects, among whom poets, together with physicians, have only a very minor place.

The biographical collections of poets culminate in Johnson's *Lives of the Poets* (1779–1781). Though it appeared after Warton's first volumes, it must be included as it represents an early type and the finest fruit of a mind rooted in the neo-classical tradition. The *Lives* were originally urged on Johnson by a group of booksellers and were planned only as "little lives and little prefaces to a little edition of the English poets." [11] Their considerable elaboration and their later independent publication were obviously afterthoughts. The choice of lives was prescribed by the booksellers and Johnson was, from the outset, limited to the one living tradition from Cowley to Gray. He himself seems to have urged only the inclusion of minor poets like Blackmore, Watts, Pomfret and Yalden. Nothing came of a later suggestion, made by George III in an interview, that Spenser should have been included.[12]

The *Lives* are, of course, biography and criticism and only incidentally literary history. The whole scheme—a series of isolated biographies in chronological order—did not lend itself to literary history in the more narrow sense of the term.

But there is an historical outline in the very limitation to the neo-classicist movement. Johnson, in the "Life of Cowley," starts with a discussion of the metaphysicals as background and foil to the tradition he is about to treat in full and he stresses everywhere the anticipations and steps which led to its establishment. Only from incidental remarks can we reconstruct his view of the earlier course of English poetry. Johnson disparages what he knew of medieval English poetry. Chaucer's *Nun's Priest's Tale* seems to him "hardly worth revival" by Dryden's paraphrase, and Dryden is also censured for his "hyperbolical commendation" of the *Knight's Tale* because it contains "an action unsuitable to the times in which it is placed" and thus apparently violates decorum.[13] Medieval mysteries are dubbed "wild dramas" [14] and *Chevy Chase* is condemned for its "chill and lifeless imbecility," in accordance with his usual dislike of ballads.[15] But Johnson knows that the "poets of Elizabeth had attained an art of modulation, which was afterwards neglected and forgotten." [16] Still, the reform of English poetry begins with Waller, who himself acknowledged Fairfax as his model and "might have studied with advantage the poem of Davies." [17]

Like Waller, Denham is "deservedly considered as one of the fathers of English poetry"; [18] he is an "original author," who "traced a new scheme of poetry." [19] He improved our taste and advanced our language and "gained ground gradually upon the ruggedness of his age." [20] Also Cowley "sometimes attempted an improved and scientific versification," [21] but the actual founder of the new style is Dryden. "To him we owe the improvement, perhaps the completion of our metre, the refinement of our language, and much of the correctness of our sentiments." [22] Before the time of Dryden there was "no poetical diction, no system of words at once refined from the grossness of domestic use, and free from the harshness of terms appropriated to particular arts." [23] Johnson thought of the new system as a science which excludes all "casualty" and aspires to "constancy." [24] Thus, once established, it cannot and should not be changed. After Pope "to attempt any further improvement of versification will be dangerous." [25]

Johnson therefore always points out either relapses or approximations to this ideal norm. Though Addison was one of the earliest examples of correctness, he "debased rather than refined the versification which he had learned from Dryden." [26] Roscommon is declared "perhaps the only correct writer in verse before Addison" [27] and Prior was "amongst the most correct of the English poets; and he was one of the first that resolutely endeavoured at correctness." [28]

This view of a progress of English poetry towards an ideal scientific norm attained especially by Pope is curiously enough combined in Johnson with a constant recognition of the historical point of view and pleadings for a relativity of standards. He recognized that "wit has its changes and fashions and at different times, takes different forms." [29] He explicitly states that "to judge rightly of an author, we must transport ourselves to his time, and examine what were the wants of his contemporaries, and what were his means of supplying them." [30] However, he uses the historical argument largely as an apology for shortcomings and mistakes in older literature. Thus Dryden's *Threnodia Augustalis* has the "irregularity of metre, to which the ears of that age, however, were accustomed" [31] and Milton's verse was "harmonious, in proportion to the general state of our metre in Milton's age." [32] Waller's poem, on the danger of the Prince on the coast of Spain, "may be justly praised, without much allowance for the state of our poetry and language at that time." [33]

Once, in Johnson's defence of Pope's translation of Homer, the historical argument is prominent and effective. "Time and place will always enforce regard. In estimating this translation consideration must be had of the nature of our language, the form of our metre, and, above all, of the change which two thousand years have made in the modes of life and the habits of thought," as Pope wrote "for his own age and his own nation." [34] But the historical argument which seemed to Johnson valid in case of an adaptation of a work of remote antiquity, did not affect his main view of English literature as one continuous effort towards the establishment of one timeless norm, that of Pope and Dryden. Johnson certainly believes in progress (in spite of all personal pessimism as to human happiness). He rejects the view that the "world was in its decay and that souls partake of the general degeneracy." [35] "Every age," he thinks, "improves in elegance. One refinement always makes way for another." [36] But the new dispensation seems firmly established. Since Dryden, English poetry has had "no tendency to relapse to its former savageness." [37] This faith or hope may help us to explain Johnson's acrimonious remarks on Gray's and Collins's attempts to revive what he considered an obsolete and essentially superseded diction and versification. It explains in part, at least, the harshness of his comments on Milton's early poems, which he knew were not only highly valued by his contemporaries, but had also become the models of a new Miltonic school, of which he disapproved as of any archaism.

Besides this general scheme of the progress of English poetry which we can abstract from the *Lives*, the *Lives* contain also many digressions which can be called little exercises in literary history. Johnson sketches the history of pastoral poetry from Theocritus to Tasso,[38] mentions briefly the early English critics including Webbe and Puttenham, while acclaiming Dryden as the father of English criticism,[39] or traces the history of letter-writing in England from Howell to Pope.[40] Elsewhere he sketches the course of the Collier controversy [41] or enumerates the main practitioners before Pope of the art of "imitation" exhibited so powerfully in his own *London* and the *Vanity of Human Wishes*.[42]

In discussing Pope's translation of Homer, Johnson not only passes in review the older English translations, but surveys the history of verse-translation in general, though in practice he knows only Anguillara's Ovid and the *Iliad* of Salvini.[43] Johnson paid most attention to the history of versification, as metre loomed very large among the achievements of the neo-classical age. He sketches the history of blank verse since Surrey,[44] traces the triplet to Phaer, Hall and Chapman,[45] and points to the alexandrines in Spenser.[46] He knows that alliteration was used before Waller by Gascoigne and in Shakespeare's *Love's Labour's Lost*,[47] and he chides Dryden for his ignorance of the verse-form of either *Gorboduc* or Chapman's Homer.[48]

Johnson is sometimes also interested in tracing historical antecedents; he recognizes that the metaphysicals borrowed from Marino and his followers,[49] that Cowley's confusion of images could have been modelled on Sannazaro,[50] and he finds a parallel passage for a poem by Cowley in the Polish humanist, Casimir.[51] Once Johnson indulges in a somewhat disproportionate source-study when he demonstrates that some of Prior's epigrams are derived from the French or from a German humanist, Georgius Sabinus.[52] Johnson also shows that the design of *Windsor Forest* is derived from

Cooper's Hill with some attention to Waller's poem on the *Park*.[53]

The value of the genetic method for the study of an individual work of art is also recognized by Johnson. He quotes Milton's early plan for a drama on *Paradise Lost* from the Trinity College manuscript and reflects that "it is pleasant to see great works in their seminal state pregnant with latent possibilities of excellence." [54] He prints first versions of several passages from the manuscript of Pope's *Iliad* implying that he "delights to trace the mind from the rudeness of its first conceptions to the elegance of its last," [55] and quotes the changes made in different editions of Pope's *Essay on Man* and in the *Epistle to Arbuthnot*.[56]

All this could not be more than the casual remarks of a mind preoccupied with the analysis of human character and the pronouncement of critical verdicts. But Johnson was far more deeply steeped in historical lore and had a far wider knowledge of the history of English literature than is frequently assumed by those who think of him merely as the great oracle of neo-classicism. Many incidental pronouncements, the wealth of reading incorporated in the *Dictionary*, the preface with its sketch of the history of the English language, the editorial work on the *Harleian Miscellany*, the earlier lives of Ascham and Sir Thomas Browne and, of course, the edition of Shakespeare could prove this more than amply.[57] He also was touched by the rise of the historical sense and the general revival of older English literature.

Johnson's *Lives of the Poets* approach in size a compilation like Cibber's. But they grew out of a different type: an approach from the introductory biographical sketches to a series of extracts. *The Muses' Library, or a Series of English Poetry from the Saxons to the Reign of King Charles II* (1737) was planned exactly like Johnson's *Lives* though on a smaller scale and with a different chronological definition. It was compiled by Mrs. Elizabeth Cooper with the assistance of Oldys. The usual assertion that all the work was done by Oldys does not seem to be correct, as Oldys' diary shows that Mrs. Cooper borrowed books from Oldys for the preparation of a second volume. She must have been reading and selecting herself.[58] The vaguely worded preface does not point to Oldys either, though it is difficult to see whence some of her antiquarian information could have come if not from Oldys. The book begins rather as a continuous literary history with long extracts, but later separates into a series of biographies. The comments are more critical than in any of the older biographical collections, and the extracts are arranged not only chronologically, but also with obvious regard for representativeness. It is, in every way, the most valuable anthology of earlier English poetry before Percy and Headley.

Ramsay's *Evergreen, Being a Collection of Scots Poems* (1724) also showed historical considerations in the arrangement, but it includes no comments except in the brief introduction, though an account of the authors was promised in the third and fourth volumes, which were never published.[59] All the other anthologies of the time under consideration, like Bysshe's (1703) or Gildon's (1718), Hayward's (1738) or, later, Goldsmith's (1767), are innocent of any historical point of view or any intentions of this kind.

A historical point of view reappears only in Percy's *Reliques* (1765), where each volume is arranged in a roughly chronological order from early folk-ballads to very recent imitations. Percy wants to show "the gradations of our language, exhibit the progress of popular opinions, display the peculiar manners and customs of former ages, or throw light on our earlier classical poets." [60] Though the editing of the *Reliques* was, as was soon discovered, far from critical, the *Reliques* have scholarly pretensions in the little introductions prefixed to many poems; and the dissertations on the *Ancient English Minstrels*, on the *Origin of the English Stage*, on the *Ancient Metrical Romances* and on the *Metre of Pierce Plowman's Visions*, represent, in many ways, the best and most learned collection of essays on older English literary history that appeared before Warton. The anthology had become an important vehicle of literary history.

Another innovation in the forms of literary history was the separate publication of commentaries and notes. These grew out of marginalia, notes, and commonplace-books. We have mentioned Francis Thynne's polemical notes on Speght's edition of Chaucer (1598). Selden's notes on Drayton's *Poly-Olbion* (1613) are purely antiquarian and historical though they have their interest for English studies as they quote from Robert of Gloucester and Langland. Richard Brathwait's *Comment upon the two Tales of Chaucer* (*The Miller's Tale* and *The Wife of Bath's Tale*) (1665) is a quaint, moralizing paraphrase of no scholarly interest. Only Patrick Hume's elaborate commentary on Milton (1695) was the first more systematic literary annotation of an English poet. Lewis Theobald published his textual notes on Shakespeare independently in 1726 under the title of *Shakespeare Restored*, and similar more or less haphazard little books were common. Thus John Jortin in his *Remarks on Spenser's Poems* (1734) accumulated parallels (largely in Latin) to passages in Spenser, and the same type is preserved in the commentaries by Upton, Grey, Whalley, and, especially, Richardson. The Jonathan Richardsons, father and son, published *Explanatory Notes and Remarks on Milton's Paradise Lost* (1734), a book of notes introduced by a full life (a combination new at the time) and approaching a proper monograph on the poet. Out of such collections of notes grew Thomas Warton's *Observations on the Fairie Queene* (1754); Joseph Warton's book on Pope is also a monograph which is substantially a collection of notes covering the whole corpus of Pope's works.

But from the point of view of literary history, it is difficult to see that any of these forms could lead very far. The history in verse was obviously remote from the purposes of scholarship; the collective biography, by the isolation of the individual authors, was in its very nature antagonistic to a conception of the continuity of literature as an art; and the systematic elaborate commentary, valuable as it was for the interpretation of individual passages, blocked the way to general views and the use of historical criteria. But, in spite of this, some genuinely historical viewpoints permeated even these forms; in Johnson's *Lives* one can discern the outline of a history of English literature, and into their collections of notes on Spenser and Pope both Wartons managed by digressions to instill a good deal of historical matter.

Also political historiography began to take cognizance of literature and to incorporate some account of its development in the narration of national events. Already the sixteenth-century chronicles had noticed some authors like Chaucer, at least in passing, and his and other names occur in most histories of the seventeenth and early eighteenth centuries. A local history, Sir William Dugdale's *Antiquities of Warwickshire* (1656), contained one of the first accounts of Shakespeare in a description of Trinity Church at Stratford-upon-Avon. But even David Hume, who was the first to combine history with philosophy and whose sole program included a stress on the history of civilization in the Voltairian sense, in practice gives us only "chaotic catalogues of casually selected facts" in his sections on non-political events. These appendixes to chapters or concluding paragraphs oddly labelled as "miscellaneous transactions" during this or that reign have been rightly described by an admirer of eighteenth-century historiography as "little more than ragbags, specifically invented to receive whatever odds and ends cannot be utilized in the main body of the history." [61]

No name is mentioned in the medieval sections of Hume's *History* and, during the reign of Henry VIII only Sir Thomas More is exempted from general condemnation. Under Elizabeth, only Spenser is discussed at some length as a tedious writer, who in contrast to Homer was employed in drawing the "affectations and conceits and fopperies of chivalry." [62] The section listed under the reign of King James I contains some more systematic comments on English literature. We hear the usual commonplaces about the "lack of taste" and "want of judgment" of the Elizabethans, the "irregularities and absurdities of Shakespeare" and even his "total ignorance of all theatrical art and conduct." Then follow remarks on Jonson's learning, Fairfax's "ease and elegance" and Donne's satires. Even Elizabethan prose is disparaged for its "total disregard of the elegance and harmony of the period." Bacon, whose style is called "stiff and rigid," is considered inferior to Galileo and perhaps even to Kepler. But there is some praise for Raleigh's *History* and for Camden, and even King James is defended as a writer of "no mean genius." [63] A few pages at the end of the section on the Commonwealth add the customary praise for the "most wonderfully sublime of any poet in any language," who, however, prostituted his pen in the parliamentary cause. Waller is called "the first refiner of English poetry, at least in rhyme," though his beauties are "feeble and superficial." Cowley is disparaged as corrupted by the bad taste of his age and only Denham's *Cooper's Hill* is praised without reservation.

As to prose, Hume expresses his strong dislike for Hobbes, praises Harrington's *Oceana* and Clarendon and barely mentions Selden and Chillingworth.[64] Literary remarks conclude the whole work with a disparagement of the Restoration period which, in Hume's view, retarded the progress of polite literature in England. Even Dryden was a genius perverted by indecency and bad taste. Some praise is bestowed on Temple, and *Hudibras* receives commendation as "one of the most learned compositions in any language." [65] This string of loosely connected critical judgments, full of surprising omissions, contain scarcely one historical consideration and seem a disappointing performance to come from, unquestionably, one of the greatest minds of the eighteenth century.

But just before Warton's first volume was published, another large-scale *History of Great Britain* was getting into its stride. Robert Henry's five volumes were conceived on a new plan "different from any former history of this island, or indeed of any other country." [66] The novelty consists in a consistently carried out scheme of cultural history parallel to the political narrative. Each historical period is subdivided into seven chapters: the civil and military history; religious and ecclesiastical; a history of constitution, government and laws; a history of learning and learned men; a history of the arts; a history of commerce, shipping, money and coin, and finally a history of manners, virtues, vices, remarkable customs, etc. This plan is carried out so rigidly that one could read, for instance, all fifth chapters in every book as a continuous history of the arts. Thus the first volume (1771) contains an account of the origins of poetry and of poetry in the British Isles before the Anglo-Saxon invasion. Actually, it amounts to an account of the "humane and generous" Ossian, but Henry refers also to *Ragnar Lodbrog* in Percy's version, to Mallet and Wormius and accepts John Brown's views on the original unity of poetry and music.[67]

The second volume (1774) contains then a description of Anglo-Saxon literature; the accounts of Bede, Alfred the Great, etc., are arranged by centuries, while the picture of Old Germanic poetry is the current vaguely enthusiastic rebuttal of the climate theory. Poetry "burnt with as intense a flame under the arctic circle as under the equator. The truth is that the mountains of Germany, Sweden, Denmark (?), Norway, and even Iceland were the favourite seats of the Muses in this period." In detail, Henry knows only *Athelstan's Victory* and *Eadgar's Death*, two poems in the *Anglo-Saxon Chronicle*, and reproduces Hickes's views on Caedmon and the nature of Anglo-Saxon versification.[68] The third volume, published in 1777, could draw already heavily on Warton and thus must fall outside these considerations.

The narrative histories of individual genres were the most important preparatory steps to a general history of English literature. The drama lent itself first and most easily to a historical treatment, for reasons which are fairly obvious. No real history emerges from individual biographies. But the drama was a clearly established type of art, and inside this type there was striking evidence of great successive changes. Mysteries, moralities, Elizabethan "irregular" drama and modern "regular" drama were types so sharply distinguished that it was impossible to shut one's eyes to the problem of their succession. Besides, there was the model of a history of ancient drama with its succession of forms, like the three types of comedy. Thus an actual development of art could be traced fairly easily. Here the important conception of representativeness could be clarified early. Representativeness was inconceivable as long as there was no ideal point, no tendency towards which a genre was developing.

But Shakespeare was recognized soon as such a culminating point, and the ideal regular tragedy could serve as another. This process took a long time, and was by no means accomplished in the period under review. Gildon's *Essay on the Art, Rise and Progress of the Stage* (1710) is largely a patchwork from Rymer, which does not even use the information contained in Wright's *Historia Histrionica* (1699). Gildon begins only with Shakespeare, "who first ennobled the rude scene," [69] and otherwise does little more than enumerate names. The author of the preface to Dodsley's *Plays* (1744) has also to apologize for a "want of materials." He suggests, at least, the great similarity in the rise and progress of the modern stage in all the principal countries of Europe, and quotes Crescimbeni on Italian mysteries, mentions the Spanish autos and knows even Hans Sachs, whose name he spells quaintly as "Haanssacks." He concludes that "all the modern theatres in Europe began with singing, dancing and extempore dialogues or farces: from thence they proceeded to the mysteries of religion, and till the sixteenth century none of them attempted to exhibit either tragedy or comedy," [70] which is a substantially sound and genuinely historical conception. But the true drama is ascribed only to the miraculous creative genius of Shakespeare, Fletcher, and Jonson.

Warburton in one of his notes to his edition of Shakespeare (1747) tried to give another account of the "rise and progress of the modern stage." He quotes a French source [Goujet?] on the mysteries and ridicules them pompously. Gringoire, he says, added to them a farce called "*Sottié* with *un paysan* and *un sot commun*," and "we who borrowed all these delicacies from the French, blended the *Moralité* and *Sottié* together: so that the *paysan* and *sot commun*, the clown or fool, got a place in our serious moralities." Thus Warburton accounts for that "mongrel species, unknown to nature and antiquity, called tragicomedy." [71] However absurd the detail of this explanation may be, the whole approach to the question shows that a dim idea of an evolution of the genre was in his mind. D. E. Baker's *Brief View of the Rise and Progress of the English Stage* (1764) can be ignored as merely a reproduction of Dodsley.

A real advance in the history of the English drama was made only by Percy in his *Essay on the Origin of the English Stage* (1765); he rejects Warburton's account who "derives all his information from the French critics and his instances from the French stage," and is thus often "wide of the mark and generally superficial." [72] Percy tries to construe a logical sequence from "dumb shows," which grew into a regular series of connected dialogues, to the mysteries. These in turn required frequently the representation of some allegorical personage, such as Death, Sin, Charity, Faith and the like, and hence "the rude poets of these unlettered ages began to form complete dramatic pieces consisting entirely of such personifications." In the moralities he sees the seeds of tragedy and comedy. In *Hick Scorner* Percy recognizes the transition to the modern drama: "we need only to substitute other names to his personages" and "we have real characters and living manners." The writers of these moralities were "upon the very threshold of real tragedy and comedy," and acquaintance with Roman and Grecian models merely speeded up the process. "From the graver sort of moralities our modern tragedy appears to have derived its origin, as our comedy evidently took its rise from the lighter interludes and most of these pieces contain an absurd mixture of religion and buffoonery." Warburton has "well deduced from thence the origin of our unnatural tragicomedies." The Elizabethan histories are derived from the old mysteries, with which they share the disregard for the unities.[73] Though everything in Percy is very sketchy, the outline of a history of the English drama is there.

The last sketch of a history of the drama before Warton is Thomas Hawkins's introduction to *The Origin of the English Drama* (1773). Hawkins stresses the fact that the modern drama is not a revival of the ancient, but a completely different type, with its own laws. Therefore criticism of Shakespeare for his neglect of the rules is completely beside the point. The drama is as universal as poetry. He takes from Warburton's *Divine Legation* the idea that the Eleusinian mysteries were a kind of sacred drama and from Lowth the suggestion that there are traces of drama in the Bible. After describing the mysteries, Hawkins distinguishes "two different species of drama" at the beginning of the sixteenth century: one formed upon the ancient classic model, the other merely popular and of a "Gothic original," but capable of great improvement. The same distinction can be paralleled in the epic, if one contrasts Camoens with Ariosto or Spenser. Again comedy is derived from the comic interludes, tragedy was revived by classical scholars, tragicomedy is a concession to popular audiences. "Histories" were written in imitation of the composition of the old mysteries. Thus the "common theatres" performed plays "of the Gothic form, very much unlike the chaste and perfect models of antiquity." Hawkins's collection is thus designed to exhibit systematically "the rise and gradual improvement of our drama" before Shakespeare.[74]

In Hawkins the critical and antiquarian lines meet very clearly. The materials slowly accumulated or pointed out by others are here interpreted in the light of the new critical concept of Gothic versus Classical form, as we saw it elaborated first in Hurd. The infiltration of critical ideas, of conceptions of type, had definitely begun, though the materials were scanty and the ideas schematic. This process continued through Warton and Malone to Collier and later to Symonds' evolutionary history of *Shakspere's Predecessors*.[75]

The epic and romance were other literary genres round which historical ideas crystallized. Early in the century interest was still centred purely on epic poetry, and in practice on Homer, Virgil, Ariosto, Spenser and Milton. Thus Trapp's *Praelectiones Poeticae* (1711) discusses this series, though without any historical perspective; and Sir Richard Blackmore's *Essay on the Nature and Constitution of Epick Poetry* (1716)[76] defines the ideal epic, the nature of its machinery, of its sublime style, of its digressions, etc., in a rationalist spirit, opposed to traditional Aristotelianism. The discussions on Spenser all centre around the question of composition. Addison laboured to make *Paradise Lost* conform to Virgil and Homer, taking, for instance, great trouble to defend the fall of even perfect persons like Adam and Eve as permissible and tragic.[77] The epic genre remained in the early eighteenth century a discontinuous series of very few epical poems, which were constantly examined for their conformity to an ideal type. But, isolated as they were and scattered over many countries and centuries, this could not lead to anything like a history of epic poetry.

The novel was still something so new and considered so little worthy of serious critical attention that Hurd, for instance, is distinctly embarrassed in dealing with it.[78] He calls them "hasty, imperfect and abortive poems" and jokes about their "equivocal generation." The remarks by Smollett in the preface to *Roderick Random* (1748) refer only very sketchily to the origins of his own type of "picaresque novel" in Cervantes and *Gil Blas*. Kames contrasts the new novel of sentiments with that of wonderful adventures.[79] But anything like a history was attempted only after Warton, when Blair, Beattie, and Mrs. Clara Reeve connected the novel with the ancient romance.

Romance, however, was the topic that aroused most historical interest. Actual medieval romances were, as we have shown above, almost unknown up to Percy. Interest was rather aroused by the phenomenon of chivalry as a social institution, so curiously contrasted with those produced by the bourgeois mentality of the time. Strictly literary considerations were in the background and became more prominent only as poetry was necessarily used to provide sources for these social studies. Gildon suggested in 1718 that the Romances seem "a production of the Gothic genius," but that their writing goes back to Petronius, Lucian and Heliodorus.[80] But Warburton was apparently the first in England to consider seriously the question of the origin of romance. In a *Supplement to the Translator's Preface*, added to Charles Jarvis' *Don Quixote* (1742), he criticizes Huet severely for shirking the question, and decides to revive a theory voiced by Milton's foe, Salmasius—that romances had their origin in Eastern tales, brought thence by travellers from crusades and pilgrimages, apparently first to Spain. Turpin and Geoffrey of Monmouth were the two fountain-heads of romance, and the Spanish wars with the Saracens and the Crusades were their main topics. The chronological confusion and the ignorance of the actual contents of the romances strike us today as grotesque, and later Tyrwhitt trounced Warburton severely for them.[81]

But Spain was firmly established in the mind of antiquarians as the home of romance, and Spanish romances were early given a good deal of attention; certainly also the wide knowledge of *Don Quixote*, with its description of his library, was an added reason for studying them. Percy collected romances referred to in *Don Quixote*,[82] and even Dr. Johnson read through *Felixmarte of Hircania* when he stayed with Percy in 1764.[83] Richard Farmer had a copy of Munday's translation of *Amadis*,[84] and a sheet has been found among Thomas Gray's manuscripts which argues in detail that *Amadis* is of French origin and of a late date, as can be shown from its references to Britain.[85] The Spanish-Eastern theory was, however, defended by William Drake in a paper on the origin of the word "Romance" (1774). He shows that the term "Romance" originally meant Spanish, and propounds a theory, absurd to our minds, that the Saracens themselves translated their fictions into Spanish and carried them over the Pyrenees.[86]

But, in the meantime, the discussion had been put on another and wider basis with Hurd's *Letters on Chivalry and Romance* (1762). There is little in the book that can be described as historical; the *Letters* are a plea for the poetical use of Gothic manners and a defence of the composition of the *Fairie Queene*. On the question of origins Hurd more or less accepts Warburton, though he suggests a psychological explanation for the belief in giants. But he resolutely turns attention to the institutions and conventions of chivalry, while deploring the misfortune that romance did not find early great writers. He sees that romance was closely bound up with feudalism and that it declined when feudalism decayed.

Hurd's knowledge of the Middle Ages seems to come entirely from Sainte Palaye and some reading of Chaucer, while Percy was the first to inspect actual English medieval romances. He early planned their publication, first apparently as part of the *Reliques* and then as an independent volume. A letter to Dalrymple in 1763 suggests such a scheme and defends its interest, urging that the "romances are valuable as well upon account of their poetical merit, as the curious picture they give us of ancient manners. Tho' full of the wild romantic feats of chivalry they frequently display great descriptive and inventive powers." Percy censures the anti-quarians who have rejected poetical romances because they are founded on fictitious subjects, and thinks that Hurd's *Letters* may perhaps dispose the public to give a favourable reception to an anthology of the best of them.[87] In the *Reliques*, Percy takes the view that "the old romances of chivalry may be derived in a lineal descent from the ancient historical songs of the Gothic bards and scalds." The Oriental hypothesis is rejected because the "romances show no knowledge of Oriental manners or literature." Dragons were familiar to the Northern scalds. They may have brought them in their original migrations from the north of Asia, or might have borrowed them later from the Latin poets rather than from the Arabs.

Percy presumes that the Normans brought the romances from the North to France and hence to England. Though Percy recognized that many English romances must be translations from the French, he thinks that "the English had original pieces of their own." He repeats the contents of his letter to Dalrymple almost *verbatim* and recommends such a publication, as "it would throw new light on the rise and progress of English poetry, the history of which can be but imperfectly understood, if these are neglected." He stresses their value as a comment on innumerable passages in our ancient classic poets, meaning, of course, Spenser and Shake-speare. Percy, then, gives an abstract of *Libius Disconius* (or *Libaeus Desconus*), one of the worst examples from the

Gawain cycle, in order to show that the conduct of the fable is as regular as in any of the finest poems of classical antiquity. Unfortunately, the diction and the sentiments seem to him inferior, "but this is as might be expected in rude and ignorant times and in a barbarous unpolished language." [88] Percy cannot abandon the apologetic tone, the contempt for the "exploded" fictions of the Middle Ages, and those Procrustean theories about conformity with classical standards of composition which were modelled, of course, on Addison's *Chevy Chase* criticism. Percy's Northern theory, derived from Mallet, and ultimately from Temple and Bartholin, displays the same manner of thinking as Warburton's, the same preconception that there must be only one source of origin, the same preoccupation with the fabulous machinery and the same easy simplification of the ways of migration.

A third theory, the Celtic, has also its beginnings at that time, when Evans pleaded with Percy for the Welsh origin of the Arthurian romances.[89] How rationalist the approach to the origin of romance and chivalry long remained, can be best illustrated by William Robertson's famous first chapter in his *History of the Reign of Charles V* (1769). There the origin of chivalry is explained naïvely by the enforced idleness of those who had returned from the Crusades and who then, for want of better employment, turned to the rescuing of distressed damsels. The refinements of modern gallantry and the code of honour are then, reasonably enough, derived from this "whimsical institution." [90]

Thus even before Warton the main problem of the origin of romantic fiction had been recognized; something like the idea of a migration of *motifs* had emerged, and was later to lead to what, at the end of the nineteenth century, has been called rather inappropriately "comparative literature." The

attention devoted to "machinery" which was, in fact, nothing more than traditional folk-lore, also became later the
starting point for the study of popular beliefs and superstitions and thus finally of ethnography in the widest sense of
the term.

Even before Warton some attempts at a history of criticism were made, too. There were the muster-calls of names
in Pope's *Essay*, which ranges from Aristotle to Vida, Boileau, and Roscommon. "Critic-learning flourished most in
France" [91] is the leading thought of this outline. Sir Richard
Blackmore in his *Essay on the Nature and Constitution of
Epick Poetry* (1716) similarly surveys the history of criticism with special stress on Rapin and Bossu. Britain, till
about forty years ago, had no criticism; only Dryden, Rymer, his own Preface to *Prince Arthur*, Addison's papers on
Milton, Pope's Preface to his translation of the *Iliad*, and
Hughes's edition of Spenser have increased the understand-
ing of the "Nature and Constitution of Epick Poetry."

The only more ambitious attempt at a history of criticism
was, however, James Harris's *Upon the Rise and Progress of
Criticism* (1752). Harris here formulates the ideal of philology as "of a most comprehensive character, which should
include not only all accounts both of criticism and critics,
but of everything connected with letters, be it speculation
or historical." Harris distinguishes several species of criticism, following each other in temporal succession. The first
was philosophical, stimulated by Greek literature and represented by Aristotle; the second was historical, the race of
scholiasts, commentators and explainers of antiquity. These
two types of ancient criticism were revived, "after a long
and barbarous period," at the Renaissance. The philosophical type is represented by Vida, Scaliger, Rapin, Bouhours,
Boileau, Bossu, Shaftesbury, Pope and others. The second type

includes all the classical philologists and editors, among whom he mentions Thomas Stanley and Samuel Clarke as the only Englishmen. A new and modern type of criticism is "corrective," that is textual criticism, represented by the Scaligers, Casaubon, Heinsius, and in England by Bentley, Pearce, Markland and others. Harris ridicules the pretensions of textual criticism and especially Bentley's unfortunate *Paradise Lost*. A reprint of this sketch in 1781, the year after Harris' death, contains a new chapter on explanatory criticism, devoted to modern writers, and mentions the Wartons, Tyrwhitt, Upton, Addison and Mrs. Montagu, besides compilers of dictionaries, grammars and translators.[92]

Harris's attempt, though little more than a skeleton outline, is interesting considering its date, but cannot compensate us for the loss that literary history suffered when Dr. Johnson abandoned his own plan of a "History of Criticism, as it relates to judging of authors, from Aristotle to the present age." It was to include "an account of the rise and improvements of that art: and of the different opinions of authors, ancient and modern." [93] His plan has been carried out only very superficially and imperfectly, even today.

Historical concepts had their best chance of crystallizing around a history of poetry. On the whole, however, the old scheme of a uniform advance in the smoothness of versification towards Dryden and Pope held its sway without material change. But metrical history, though it underlay and determined this scheme, was never studied seriously at that time. A real extension, beyond the commonplace remarks on the continuous improvement from Fairfax to Pope, can be found only in Percy's *Essay on the Metre of Pierce Plowman's Visions* (1765). Percy was the first Englishman to demonstrate that alliteration was the principle of Anglo-Saxon and Germanic verse generally. In his correspondence with Evans he defended its Teutonic derivation against the Welshman's theory of the origin of alliteration with the Welsh bards.[94] He sees that Langland wrote in a metre "which probably never was wholly laid aside," and traces the continuation of alliteration down to the poem on Flodden Field. He knows also of cross-types between alliteration and rhyme, and tries to show that the metre of Robert of Gloucester was derived from alliterative verse. The metre of *Piers* seems to him related to the French alexandrine rather than to blank verse, with which it had been associated in earlier times.[95]

Among the many books on metre, only William Mitford's *Essay upon the Harmony of Language* (1774) sketches the "origin and progress of English versification." He accepts the results of Percy, tries to show that the extracts from *Cokaygne* in Johnson's *Preface* are of substantially the same metre as Milton's *L'Allegro* and *Il Penseroso*, and quotes the metres from Alfred's *Boethius* supplying them with accents. Chaucer and Gower introduced the heroic pentameter, while Surrey freed verse from the "shackles of rhyme." The metaphysical poets are condemned as inharmonious, while only Dryden "showed the full harmony of our language." [96]

But Gray was apparently the most indefatigable and systematic student of the history of versification at the time. None of his reflections saw the light then, and nothing was left actually in a final state. But his notes and commonplace books prove that he studied metre historically; he compiled a list of some fifty-nine measures, which shows the remarkable range of his reading. He discusses the metre of Lydgate and Chaucer in some detail, criticizing Urry and recognizing that *e* was pronounced and that several syllables came sometimes on one beat. He tabulates Welsh metres, and first borrowed from Crescimbeni the opinion that rhyme originated in Latin hymns: later he tried to show that it might have come rather from Welsh, while Welsh took alliteration from the Anglo-Saxons. Once he suggests that "perhaps rhyme might begin among the common people, and be applied only to the meaner species of poetry, adages, songs and vulgar histories passing by tradition from one to another," [97] an early expression of the romantic stress on the creativity of the "folk." But all Gray's studies remained in the form of disconnected notes. Consecutive narration, the telling of literary history as a series of events, was the important achievement of the time, and Gray's observations never reached that stage.

Such narrations before Warton were extremely rare and meagre; [98] astonishingly so, if one compares English with Continental activity on these lines. In the *Muses' Mercury* (1707) there was an essay *Of the Old English Poets and Poetry* which introduced a reprint of the *Nut-Brown Maid*, in black letter. [99] The unknown author—Oldmixon and Steele have been suggested [100]—speaks first of French literature, alluding to the *Roman de la Rose*, enumerates some medieval Latin poets and quotes from Robert of Gloucester and Langland, whom he supposes to have written in blank verse. He mentions two ballads, one of Robin Hood and another of Ralph, Earl of Chester. About seventy years after Langland came Chaucer and then Gower. They reformed our poetry, while Lydgate represented a further advance; he is more polished and regular. *Chevy Chase*, on which he quotes Sidney, is considered to be contemporary with Lydgate, and the *Nut-Brown Maid* is assigned to the same period. Under Henry VIII came the revival: Wyatt, Surrey, Henry Lord Morley, and Sir Francis Brian are mentioned. Sternhold and Hopkins came under Edward VI, but represent a relapse. Under Elizabeth followed Spenser, Fairfax, and Waller, and finally came Dryden, "who brought the harmony of English poetry to its present perfection." [101] Thus, except for the few remarks on the ballads, this first meagre sketch contains little more than a list of names and accepts the view of uniform advance towards Dryden.

The same sort of outline is then repeated in Charles Gildon's *Compleat Art of Poetry* (1718). After a few remarks on Italian and French literature, Gildon displays some faint knowledge of Gildas, digresses on the Provençal poets, borrowing from Rymer, and then mentions Chaucer, Gower, Lydgate, Wyatt, and Surrey as reformers of our metre and style. The smoothness of verse was, however, lost and not pursued by many great writers afterwards till Mr. Waller and Dryden "brought it to its last perfection." [102] Thus the whole Elizabethan age appears as a relapse from the point of view of correctness. The same list is repeated in Giles Jacob, and even Husbands thinks that "our poets scarce knew anything of the harmony of numbers till the days of Queen Elizabeth." [103]

The *Muses' Library* (1737) is an anthology, but the introduction tries to sketch "a sort of Poetical chronicle." The thesis is that "poetry and politeness grew up together." Langland, the first English poet, discloses, in the rudeness of his lines, the "rudeness of the age" he wrote in. After Chaucer, war and faction restored ignorance and dullness. Then Barclay and Skelton heralded a second dawn: Surrey naturalized Italian delicacy, Sackville introduced allegory [sic], and at last Spenser and Fairfax rose. The preface announces a consideration of Elizabethan criticism in the second volume, which was never published. Though the book is largely an anthology of Elizabethan poetry, Mrs. Cooper stresses that there were many writers before Chaucer and desires to show "from what low and almost contemptible original that happy genius raised his perfection at once." [104]

Another fragmentary attempt at a narrative history of English poetry can be found in that curious miscellany *The Polite Correspondence* (1741), apparently written by Dr. John Campbell.[105] The fine resolutions of the introduction, which even recognizes that the usual apologies for the barrenness of the times are a cover for idleness, are unfortunately not carried out in the body of the book. Very ambitious tasks are allotted to different correspondents, such as a "free Epistolary Dissertation on the Progress of Poetry from Chaucer to Dryden," but in practice nothing but miscellaneous remarks on primitive poetry and on Anglo-Saxon literature are accumulated. We hear little of poetry after the Conquest, which is supposed to be marked by a "greater air of libertinism, received from the Danes." Finally, it is quite properly decided that "the History of Poetry is a thing not to be written in a hurry," and, after some remarks on Shakespeare as a "very great scholar," the whole tails disappointingly off into translations from Alonzo de Ercilla and Quinault.[106] The author, though well informed on Anglo-Saxon for his time, has no scheme or plan in mind, and the epistolary form encouraged digressions and loose ends.

Just such skeleton schemes for a history of English poetry have been preserved from the hand of two of the greatest poets of the century: Pope and Gray. Pope's scheme, which was published first in 1769,[107] is merely a list of names, divided according to the schools of English poetry, a term derived from the current divisions of painters. The sketch is prefaced by a reference to Rymer's second part, or *A Short View of Tragedy*, which contains the passages on Provençal poetry. Pope labels the English poets according to their real or supposed foreign master. Thus

Chaucer belongs with Gower to the School of Provence; Surrey, Wyatt, Sidney, and Gascoigne to the School of Petrarch; and Sackville to the School of Dante. Spenser alone combines the school of Ariosto and Petrarch. This criterion of dependence on foreign models is crossed by a grouping of poets according to native masters: the schools of Chaucer, Spenser and Donne. Waller is then listed (with his predecessors) as head of a special group, not specifically labelled, obviously as the fountainhead of a new school to which Pope assigned himself.

This scheme as it stands has serious minor faults such as anachronism—Walter Mapes is put among the followers of Chaucer—and there are obviously merely vague memories of such names as Alabaster, who, as a purely Latin poet, seems ill at ease among the school of Spenser. The scheme, of course, suffers also from the all too simplified criterion of dependence either on a foreign or a native master, but it roughly points to the main historical divisions, and has the great merit of implying a break with the biographical tradition and a new attention to artistic families and schools.

Thomas Gray's scheme is known to us from a letter to Warton in 1770, first printed in 1783.[108] Gray's manuscripts show that he had planned and worked on a History of English poetry mainly for the years 1754–1757. He had studied the history of metres, penetrated into Welsh, Scandinavian, and to a less extent Anglo-Saxon poetry. He had compiled a catalogue of English poets from Tanner, Winstanley, and others and had written a paper on Lydgate and a smaller sketch of Samuel Daniel. The paper on Lydgate shows that Gray, if he could have finished his plan, would have given us a sober factual manual: biography, contents, comments on beauties, remarks on metre, comparisons with the chief models, but the dissipation of his energies into history and natural science, not to speak of the whole magnitude of the task, must have made him abandon his plan long before he had heard of Warton's. A note prefixed to the *Fatal Sisters* (1768) alludes to the scheme and says that in the introduction to the history he meant to have "produced some specimens of the style that reigned in ancient times among the neighbouring nations, or those who had subdued the greater part of this Island or were our progenitors," an obvious reference to his lists of Scandinavian, Welsh and Anglo-Saxon poems preserved in his notes.[109] When he sent his plan to Warton he had given up any thoughts of finishing, and probably reconstructed some of his earlier plans for the benefit of a friend and friendly rival.

Gray's scheme is a great advance on Pope's. It provides for a wide background of primitive poetry, and would have thus codified the dichotomy which we have discussed as central in all literary conceptions during the century. Gaelic (Welsh and possibly Erse) and Gothic (Scandinavian and Anglo-Saxon) were to be treated, and there was planned a sketch on the origin of rhyme among the Franks (Otfried apparently was in Gray's mind), the Saxons and the Provençaux. The pet theory about the origin of rhyme among the Welsh which had taken up much space has disappeared from the letter to Warton, probably because he had either abandoned it himself or did not wish to raise controversial matters. This dissertation he would have followed up with "some account of the Latin rhyming poetry from its early origin down to the fifteenth century."

Gray groups the English poets according to schools. Though he speaks like Pope of the school of Provence, he recognizes that it was first "improved" by the Italians, before Chaucer imitated it, and he speaks of Chaucer as belonging implicitly to the first Italian school. The second

Italian school is headed by Surrey, culminates in Spenser, and ends in Milton. It is inspired by Italian Renaissance poetry, though Spenser's subject matter (but not his manner) is "allegoric and romantic" and thus of "Provençal invention." The third Italian school is the metaphysical, which he derives apparently from Marino, though he mentions no Italian name. Donne is then (impossibly for chronological reasons) considered the head of these new Italianate Englishmen who, through Crashaw and Cleveland, lead up to Sprat. The fourth school, which has continued to Gray's own time, is the School of France, introduced after the Restoration. It begins (again in contradiction with chronology) with Waller and culminates in Pope.

The dividing lines between these schools actually correspond to the decisive turning-points in English poetical history, but obviously the exclusive derivation of English poetry from foreign models is misleading, and there is besides no attempt at linking these four schools into one continuous tradition. The remark on the contrast between Spenser's matter and manner draws a distinction much needed at a time which seemed to consider Spenser as "Gothic" in the extreme, but as the sketch is only a list of headings in a letter, criticism cannot be pressed too far. Besides, when Warton received the letter, he had already determined his own course and method. He alone had the perseverance to carry it out, and he determined, for good and ill, the future course of English literary history.

CHAPTER SIX

Thomas Warton

THE LAST CHAPTER tried to etch in a background for the figure of Thomas Warton, the author of the first great *History of English Poetry*. Against it he himself stands out more clearly. Warton did not merely inherit the body of opinions, materials, and methods described. He had actively collaborated in creating that body of scholarship with his first publication in literary history, the *Observations on the Fairie Queene of Spenser* (1754). There we find a first sketch for his *History of English Poetry*, and many features of the later *History* can be explained from its close connection with the earlier book. The *Observations* belongs to the tradition of collectanea, of independently published notes, and it actually grew out of marginalia. The British Museum owns a copy of Spenser with copious notes in Warton's hand.[1] The back of the title-page contains a first classification of his notes in the form of a sketch of the future book. Here are the main headings of the book: "Old Romances imitated—Classical Imitations—Chaucer is imitated—Allegories—Language—Falsification of Ancient Story and Mythology," etc. The published book has organized these random notes, and, disowning the idea of a commentary, attempts to "form a series of distinct essays on Spenser and exhibit a course of systematical criticism on the *Fairie Queene*."[2] More than traces of the collectanea origin have remained; the dissertations very frequently disintegrate into mere enumerations of passages under general headings like anachronisms and mistakes in costume, remarks on Upton's opinions and even a miscellaneous section which includes everything Warton could think of. But this scrapbook centre of the *Observations* is reinforced by a discussion of Spenser's composition and his allegory, which gives some historical perspective to the whole.

Warton, in his copy of Spenser, had already sketched his criticism of Spenser's composition. The manuscript notes point out "want of continuity and of general dependence." Warton thinks that "every book is too much a whole" and that Spenser would have done better to make "every book an entirely detached piece without reference to the rest." Similarly, the *Observations* express surprise that Spenser should have preferred the irregularities of Gothic romance to the propriety and uniformity of the Grecian and Roman models. But Warton "scarcely regrets the loss" of plan and exact arrangement of parts, as the *Fairie Queene* has graces "situated beyond the reach of art." He believes that "the faculties of creative imagination delight us, because they are unassisted and unrestrained by those of deliberate judgment. . . . Though in the *Fairie Queene* we are not satisfied as critics, we are transported as readers." [3] Warton thus accepts a criticism based on the classical canon of composition, and at the same time avoids it by pleading for an aesthetics of effect, regardless of the reprehensible cause, a conception which had already excited the anger of Rymer.

Only in the second edition of the *Observations* (1762) did Warton, obviously under the influence of Sainte Palaye and of Hurd's *Letters*, modify his attitude toward Spenser's composition; he now uses the argument, already put forward by Hughes and the Italian defenders of Ariosto, that it is "absurd to think of judging either Ariosto or Spenser by precepts which they did not attend to." [4] Today "critical taste is universally diffused, and we require the same order and design which every modern performance is expected to have, in poems where they never were regarded or intended. Spenser, and the same may be said of Ariosto, did not live in an age of planning." Spenser's poetry is without plan, is "the careless exuberance of a warm imagination and a strong sensibility," [5] and thus something primitive and spontaneous. Warton can be absolved from the contradiction or even confusion of mind often brought against him. [6] His attitude shows merely the common eighteenth-century dualism of classical propriety versus the flights of imagination, the first ideal being acknowledged by reason and tradition while the other was admired in the original geniuses of the past.

The second edition of the *Observations* contains evidence that Warton's interest in old literature had been newly fortified by the argument of "relativity." It shows the increase of historical tolerance in the age. In the 1754 edition, there was tolerance which was actually nothing new in itself. Warton merely echoes his contemporaries, especially Lowth's *Lectures*, published the year before, when he asks us to "look back upon the customs and manners which prevailed in his age," to "place ourselves in [the poet's] situation, and circumstances, that so we may be the better enabled to judge and discern how his turn of thinking, and manner of composing, were biased, influenced and, as it were, tinctured by very familiar objects and reigning appearances, which are utterly different from those with which we are at present surrounded." [7] The main drift of this argument is a defence of Spenser's use of chivalry, since "encounters of chivalry subsisted in our author's age" and "romances were then most eagerly and universally read." [8]

Similarly, allegory is shown to have been visible in pageants and fashionable in poetry. In a digression sketching the history of English poetry Warton went so far as to assert that English poetry "principally consisted in the allegorical species." [9] Before Chaucer and Gower there were merely chronicles in rhyme, like that of Robert of Gloucester. Gower and Chaucer introduced invention, but during the fifteenth century there was a relapse into primitive barbarism, exemplified by Hardyng's *Chronicle*. Stephen Hawes is then, rather unexpectedly, extolled as the "restorer of invention," who "made ample amends for this interval of darkness." [10] The *Mirror for Magistrates* and many poems of the Scottish Chaucerians are quoted as further examples of allegory, which culminated in Spenser and then rapidly declined, excepting only for Fletcher's *Purple Island*.

Warton saw later that this sketch of English poetry exaggerated the importance of allegory, and in the second edition he changed the sentence about English poetry as consisting "principally of the allegorical species" to "visions and antiquities." [11] The praise of Stephen Hawes is also toned down, though the general account of the history of English poetry remained the same. He now adds a sketch of the later history of English poetry. After the decline of allegory came a "species of poetry, whose images were of the metaphysical and abstract kind" and then an age of correctness followed, which Warton characterized unfavourably for the most part. "Imagination gave way to correctness, sublimity of description to delicacy of sentiment, and majestic imagery to conceit and epigrams. Poets began now to be more attentive to words, than to things and objects. The nicer beauties of happy expression were preferred to the daring strokes of great conception. Satire, that bane of the sublime, was introduced from France. The muses were debauched at court, and polite life, and familiar manners, became their only themes." [12] Here a division of English literature into three periods is hinted at: a sequence of allegorical, metaphysical, and correct satirical poetry.

While in the first edition Warton had justified Spenser's use of chivalry by the fact of its general vitality at the time, the new edition already attempts to stress the uses of chivalry in itself, obviously encouraged by Sainte Palaye's *Mémoirs*. Chivalry, adds Warton, "commonly looked upon as a barbarous sport, or extravagant amusement of the dark ages," had "no small influence on the manners, policies, and constitutions of ancient times, and served many public and important purposes" [13] Now, Warton more boldly justifies his own interest in chivalrous romances, "however monstrous and unnatural these compositions may appear to this age of reason and refinement." [14] They throw light on social history, on the nature of the feudal system, and preserve many curious historical facts. They are pictures of ancient usages and customs, and represent the manners, genius, and character of our ancestors. But further they stimulate imagination; "they store the fancy with those sublime and alarming images, which true poetry best delights to display." [15] Here true poetry is identified with imaginative, early poetry, but this genuine admiration does not prevent Warton from speaking about the "depths of Gothic ignorance and barbarity" of the Middle Ages and contrasting its "bad taste" [16] with the "new and more legitimate taste" [17] established since the Renaissance. We shall see how far conceptions underlying the *Observations* anticipate those behind the great *History*, and how far they were modified and revised.

The second edition of the *Observations* (1762) had already hinted that the subject of a "retrospect of English

poetry" before Spenser, "may, probably, be one day considered more at large, in a regular history." [18] Hurd, in a
letter dated October 10, 1762, speaks of Warton's "noble
design of giving a history, in form, of English poetry." [19]
Warton, in his answer on October 22, 1762, speaks of having been roused by Hurd's letter to think in earnest of what
he had hinted at in his *Observations,* a "formal History of
English Poetry." "I have long been laying in materials for
this work; and with regard to the influence of Chivalry and
Romance on modern poetry, I may now enlarge with some
freedom and confidence on this head as you have so nobly
ventured to speak out. I once had a scheme of publishing a
new edition of my favourite Chaucer with notes. But the
researches I made for that design will properly enough fall
in with my present intentions. The scheme of Chaucer I laid
aside as too laborious and extensive upon the whole, and as
attended with too many verbal minutiae." [20]

In 1763 Warton learned of Pope's scheme and saw a copy
sent to him by Mason. In a letter to Hurd he praises it as
"certainly a great curiosity, which is, indeed, for so short a
scheme, very ingenious and rational." [21] In 1764 he speaks
of materials collected for the History, and in 1765 he tells
Percy that "he is writing the *History of English Poetry*
which has never yet been done at large, and in form. My materials are almost ready." [22] But in 1766 he has to inform
both Hurd and Percy that the *History* is at present laid
aside for the publication of his edition of Theocritus, and
the same tale is repeated in 1768, with the promise to make
another "excursion into Fairy-land" as soon as he is released
from the other work.[23] Only in July 1769 does Warton
seem to have been able to "sit down in good earnest to
write the *History of English Poetry*. It will be a large work,

but as variety of materials have been long collected, it will be soon completed." [24]

His plan was now a conspectus from the Conquest to the Revolution of 1688. He inquired of Hurd about the scheme which he had heard Gray had drawn up, and, at Hurd's instance, Gray sent his sketch to Warton on April 15, 1770. Warton answered Gray on April 20, 1770, saying that he had not followed his plan, which was, however, of great service to him, and threw much light on many of his periods by giving connected views and details. He then states his own plan of a general dissertation on Northern poetry, followed by a history, beginning at the Conquest, "which I wrote chronologically in sections, and continue as matter successively offers itself, in a series of regular annals, down to and beyond the Restoration. . . . Though I proceed chronologically, yet I often stand still to give some general view, as perhaps a particular species of poetry, etc. and even anticipate sometimes for this purpose. These views often form one section, yet are interwoven with the tenor of the work, without interrupting my historical series." [25]

Warton excludes the drama and promises that the first volume (which includes Chaucer) will soon be in the press. Apparently only one volume, and that an obviously too condensed one, was planned to cover all the remaining matter. In September 1770 he writes to Percy that his *Opus Magnum* goes on swimmingly. We shall go to press in October." [26] But in January 1772 he has still to excuse his inability to finish his work, and says again that he "has fairly written out the first volume which is now in the press." [27] Only in August 1773 he was "sitting down to complete the first volume of the *History of English Poetry*." [28] But it was 1774 when the first volume saw the light. The second volume followed in 1778, and a third, bringing the story only to the beginning of the Elizabethan age, came out in 1781. Only a few sheets, discussing mainly Marston's and Hall's satires, were found after the death of the author and published in 1790. Thus the work remained unfinished, lacking even a new discussion of Spenser.[28a]

What had happened to mar the sanguine hopes of the early years? It was not only the general slowness of all scholars or an underestimation of the difficulties in his way. It was not even preoccupation with other tasks. Rather was it that a profound change of plan and method had obtruded itself on Warton in the course of his work. Miss Rinaker has printed an earlier plan of the *History*, which, though there seems to be no external criterion for its dating, must belong to a period some time soon after the publication of the second edition of the *Observations*.[29] It certainly shows no knowledge of the rich materials displayed in the first published volume.

In this outline, Warton asserts that the Saxons introduced the poetry of the Druids and that Hickes brought to light "many hymns." He thinks that the old British bards are somehow preserved in Robert of Gloucester. Nothing else seems to have been known to him before *Piers Plowman*, which is called "the first allegorical poem in our tongue." Then came Gower and Chaucer, who enriched the language, a process continued by Lydgate. Further, allegory declined and the "rudeness of Robert of Gloucester" was brought back by Hardyng. Stephen Hawes restored invention and "improved our versification to a surprising degree." The first classical age came under Henry VIII with the new turn poetry took in the writings of Surrey and Wyatt, "who were the very first to give us a sketch or shadow of any polished verse." An allusion to the "fine harvest of poetry under Elizabeth" concludes this surprisingly meagre summary, which combines the idea of English poetry as a series of allegories leading up to Spenser with the old scheme of a uniform progress of refinement in versification. Apparently it was only in the later sixties that Warton amassed new materials from manuscripts, and they swamped his original scheme and made him abandon the earlier plan. He now had recourse to the conception of "regular annals" and rejected expressly Pope's and Gray's schemes as destroying "that free exertion of research with which such a history ought to be executed, and not easily reconcilable with that complication, variety, and extent of materials, which it ought to comprehend." [30]

Thus it happened that Warton's *History* became less a work of history than, for instance, Gibbon's or Winckelmann's books, to mention only two of the great achievements of eighteenth-century historiography. It was, first of all, an accumulation of materials, a bibliography and anthology, and only secondarily a history. Warton knew practically everything that had been achieved by previous scholarship. If we would list his sources, we should have to copy the full bibliography of our preceding chapters. [31] He refers unmistakably to all the biographical dictionaries, from Bale to Cibber, the anthologies, editions, critical works, and partial histories we have surveyed above. They are supplemented by an independent inspection of hundreds of manuscripts and printed books, never before used by any author, except the compilers of catalogues. The great Cottonian and Oxford catalogues, Wanley's list in Hickes, the Catalogue of the Harleian manuscripts, the Catalogue of Bennet library and the bibliographies, especially Ames' *Typographical Antiquities*, were the guide-books which made Warton's search possible and comparatively easy.

Today it is obvious that Warton was not very well

equipped for this side of his great task. He apparently knew practically no Anglo-Saxon, and his knowledge of Middle English, though empirically large, was far from accurate or systematic. He was not a good palaeographer or philologist, and the extracts he quoted from manuscripts are marred by many misreadings, sometimes due to even less proficient amanuenses. His explanatory notes also frequently betray ignorance or carelessness, easily avoidable today when dictionaries and commentaries have systematized knowledge to an extent unimaginable in Warton's time. Warton and his helpers were unable to read manuscripts freely. When the handwriting or the language proved too difficult Warton gave up in despair and hurried on to some other easier task. It was thus surely not for lack of any sensibility but from sheer ignorance of the actual contents that Warton referred only briefly and slightingly to the *Owl and Nightingale*,[32] or quoted just a few random verses from Cotton Nero AX, the MS containing the *Pearl* (described as a "vision"), and *Gawain and the Green Knight*, the separate existence of which escaped Warton's hurried inspection.[33] It is easy to speak with Ritson of Warton's "indolence," [34] a charge manifestly unjust in view of the thousands of books and manuscripts he had actually investigated. One can rather speak of a lack of a sense of proportion, or a great ability for research wandering far afield and thus losing track of the great outlines of his task.

Though Warton frequently pulls himself back and asserts that he has "neither inclination nor intention to write a catalogue, or compile a miscellany," [35] he cannot resist the temptation to give long bibliographical lists with full titles or to quote pages and pages of extracts that make his books, in parts, look like an anthology. Warton thus combines practically all the older forms of literary history: the cata-

logue, the anthology with explanatory notes, the biography
(though there is least of this). All these are regularized and
arranged as a "chronological series," or "regular annals." [36]
In many sections, especially the early ones, the only general-
ization underlying his presentation of materials is the statement that between the years 1200 and 1300 the following
pieces of English poetry were written. This is as primitive a
stage of history-writing as any medieval chronicle's listing
of the main events under a calendar date without any attempt at selection or correlation. All this, however, is only
true of parts of Warton's book. There is more in it.

We cannot subscribe to Scott's dictum that Warton "presented the world with three huge volumes of mingled and
indigested quotations and remarks, in which the reader, like
the ancient alchymists in their researches, is sure to meet
everything but what he is seeking for." [37] Nor should we, of
course, accept Ritson's extreme view that the *History* is an
"injudicious farrago, a gallimaufry of things which both do
and do not belong to the subject, thrown and jumbled together, without system, arrangement, or perspicuity." [38]
Though these allegations are justified in part, Warton has
left not merely "a guide-book," a "report on the extant
work," [39] which would mean the negation of any history,
but a real, if loosely constructed, history with methods and
principles and a unified conception, though this is all too
frequently swamped by the mass of new materials. There is
some truth in Sir Egerton Brydges's view of the *History;* it
is at the opposite extreme from Ritson's. Brydges thought
that "to all the art of composition it joins so much original
research under the guidance of such exquisite and highly-
cultivated taste . . . that it at once delights by the charms of
genius and gratifies endless curiosity by its inexhaustible
mass of rich materials. No other work occurs to me, in

which these two opposite qualities are combined in any
eminent degree. Here they are united in the very highest
degree." [40] Though we must doubt the perfection of the
union, the combination of research with the historical
method is there.

Warton constantly makes excursions into neighbouring
fields, but he had a clear conception of the province of his
subject. Such a definition in itself means choice and thus
valuation. His book is called the *History of English Poetry*
and is really *English*, excluding Latin, Norman and even
Anglo-Saxon and Scottish, and it is limited to *poetry* to the
exclusion of drama and prose. Warton is not, as later historians were, obsessed with the idea of national character and
national tradition, which made the linguistic criterion supreme and isolated the literatures of Europe till their astonishingly uniform development becomes completely inex-
plicable. But still in Warton the purely English development
of verse from Robert of Gloucester to Pope is in the centre
of the picture, though he sketches incidentally some of the
background of Anglo-Saxon and Old French. The defect of
his comparative view is rather its excessive broadness and
sweep, and its limitation, on the other hand, to questions of
motifs and the derivation of "machinery," which in practice
meant folk-mythology. But Anglo-Saxon is excluded on the
ground that the Conquest represented a "signal change,"
with the other somewhat contradictory reason that Saxon
poems are "for the most part little more than religious
rhapsodies" [41] and thus have little which can be described
as "pagan" and native. Latin is excluded from the plan, as
is shown by a reference to a Latin poet who does "not
properly fall into our series" [42] and Scottish poetry is more
than once declared to be outside the scope of the work. He
leaves the history of dramatic poetry "to the examination of

those who are professedly making enquiries into the history of our stage from its rudest origin." [43]

But, in spite of these self-warnings, Warton tells us a great deal about the drama, much about prose, something about Latin and Norman poetry and even Anglo-Saxon, and gives the first fairly adequate history of Scottish poetry, going far beyond the detached lives of Dempster or Mackenzie. Moreover, inside the bounds of his *History of English Poetry* Warton recognizes necessary limits for that "free exertion of research" in the name of which he had rejected Pope's and Gray's schemes. He frequently apologizes for digressions. After enlarging on the popularity of the Alexander romance, he returns to the "main tenour of our argument." [44] Elsewhere he admits that "various matters suggested by the Prologue of *Richard Coeur de Lyon,* have betrayed us into a long digression and interrupted the regularity of our annals." [45] He tries to justify a long digression on the mendicant friars as "no digression," but as "connected with the general purport of this history." [46] He sometimes sees (though unhappily all too rarely) the distinction between historian and editor, and relegates, for example, the discussion of the intended number of the *Canterbury Tales* to an editor of Chaucer, "to whom it properly belongs." [47] He refuses to quote from a translation of Boethius, not only because it is no original but because it appears to "have contributed no degree of improvement to our poetry or our phraseology." [48] He once declines to enumerate the other writings of Rastell "as unconnected with the history of our poetry." [49] Though Warton violated his implied rules fairly frequently, he knew they existed.

He was also perfectly aware of the distinction between the critic and the antiquary, and sometimes realized that a principle of selection and evaluation must be used if anything like a history is to be the outcome. His criterion is not, of course, artistic value as such, but rather representativeness; he defends, for instance, his full treatment of the "mob of religious rhymers" during the Reformation by pointing out that "absurdities as well as excellencies, the weakness and the vigour of the human mind, must have their historian," [50] or apologizes "that every part of the subject" is not "equally splendid and interesting, in a work of this general and comprehensive nature, in which the fluctuations of genius are surveyed, and the dawnings or declensions of taste must alike be noticed." [51] In speaking about the metrical versions of the psalms by Sternhold and Hopkins, he even draws the distinction between a "monument of our ancient *literature*," and a monument of "our ancient *poetry*." [52] Warton might not have been a very great literary critic, but it is simply untrue that his standards were purely those of an antiquary or even an historian. In the correspondence with Hurd he distinguishes sharply between the critic and the antiquary, partly, it is true, in order to humour the violent prejudice of his correspondent against antiquarianism, and partly because of his own consciousness of difference from the older type of antiquarianism. "The antiquaries of older times," he says expressly, "overlooked or rejected" the romances, "which they despised as false and frivolous; and employed their industry in reviving obscure fragments of uninstructive morality or uninteresting history. But in the present age we are beginning to make ample amends: in which the curiosity of the antiquarian is connected with taste and genius." [53] In the *Observations* he had already ridiculed Hearne's "extreme thirst after ancient things" and his liking for black letters.[54] In the *History* he castigates Hearne's "conjectures as generally wrong," [55] though he pays tribute to his diligence. Hardyng's *Chronicle* is described as "almost beneath criticism, and fit only for the attention of the antiquary." [56] The life of one Bertram Walton, author of a satire on nuns, is "calmly resigned to the researches of some more laborious and patient antiquary," [57] while a reference to a conspiracy in a poem elicits a confession of reluctance to explore Holinshed for "this occult piece of history, which I leave to the curiosity and conjectures of some more laborious investigator." [58]

How little he himself shared the spirit of organized nineteenth-century research and how little he foresaw it, is obvious from such a remark as that on the *Prick of Conscience;* he prophesies, wrongly of course, that he would be "its last transcriber." [59] The most damning proofs of his unscholarly spirit are his vague references to books from the library of the late Mr. William Collins and the curious forgeries which he seems to have committed in his *Life of Sir Thomas Pope.*[60] Thus, at least in intention, Warton was not satisfied merely to collect materials for a history of poetry, but wanted to present them in a scheme of historical and literary values, based on "fundamental principles." [61]

His scheme is still largely the conception of a progress from "rudeness to elegance," the idea of a uniform advance from barbarism to refinement. The first page of the *Preface* enlarges on the conscious pride, on the "triumph of superiority" with which we "look back on the savage condition of our ancestors," and throughout the book Warton loves to indulge in the current metaphors of light and darkness. He seems complacently content with this age of "good sense, of politeness and philosophy," [62] with the "pure religion and those improved habits of life and manners which we, at present, so happily enjoy." [63] A long string of quotations could be adduced repeating endlessly the tag about the "barbarous ages," [64] the "ages of ignorance and superstition," [65] the "great picture of human follies which the un-polished ages of Europe hold up to our view." [66]

Obviously Warton had no sympathy for many of the most distinguished social and intellectual features of the Middle Ages. Catholicism is to him a mere "superstition," [67] "fooleries calculated only for Christians in a condition of barbarism." [68] He refers to the "barbarisms of the Catholic worship," [69] to the "specious and mechanical devotion of the times," [70] to "false religion" and "monastic igno-rance," [71] and modifies only slightly the opinion that monas-teries were "nurseries of illiterate indolence." [72] He shares the then current contempt for medieval philosophy, called "sophistry," [73] "scholastic cloud," [74] or "pedantries of the old barbarous philosophy," [75] and the thought of Thomas Aquinas is labelled "futile." [76] Warton's sympathy for chiv-alry as a social institution can be much overemphasized. He refers to tourneys as a "strange mixture of foppery and ferocity" [77] or to the "exaggerated ideas of gallantry" [78] current at the time. He sees in the whole system of ceremo-nies in the most refined courts of Europe of the fifteenth century a "mixture of barbarism, which rendered them ri-diculous. . . . Their luxury was inelegant, their pleasures indelicate, their pomp cumbersome and unwieldy." [79]

This condemnation of the medieval social scene is, after all, comprehensible in a High Churchman proud of his ra-tionality and politeness, his pacific manners, his bourgeois morality, and his preoccupation with the affairs of this world. But Warton's belief in progress extends far and wide into the field of literature. He professes to "pursue the prog-ress of our national poetry, from a rude origin and obscure beginnings, to its perfection in a polished age." [80] In the early stages this appears as the conception of linguistic prog-ress. Thus, as early as the thirteenth century, English was, in his view, "losing much of its ancient barbarism and obscurity," [81] meaning presumably obscurity to Warton and other modern readers. Robert de Brunne is described as having "contributed to form a style, to teach expression, and to polish his native tongue." [82] Chaucer, of course, appears as the great reformer who "polished the asperity, and enriched the sterility of native versification" [83] and "struggled with a barbarous language, and a national want of taste." [84]

But Warton also accepts the classicist idea of an advance of English versification towards the ideal regularity of Dryden and Pope. The alliterative metre in Langland appears to him not only a "singular, capricious affectation," [85] but also a clear retrogression. Warton, curiously overestimating, like most of his contemporaries, the possibility of deliberate choice, censures Langland gravely for "preferring and adopting the style of the Anglo-Saxon poets," "instead of availing himself of the rising and rapid improvements of the English language." [86] Chaucer is praised for his "harmony and perspicuity of versification," [87] and a couplet of Lydgate is singled out as indicating "dawnings of that poetical colouring of expression, and of that facility of versification, which mark the poetry of the present times." [88] In other verses by Lydgate "much harmony, strength, and dignity" [89] are found, presumably because of the regularity of the caesuras. Surrey is praised as the "first English classical poet," as "unquestionably the first polite writer of love-verses in our language," and his "correctness of style, justness of thought, and purity of expression" are extolled in contrast to Wyatt. Though Wyatt co-operates with Surrey in having "corrected the roughness of our poetic style," Warton considers him inferior to Surrey in "harmony of numbers, perspicuity of expression, and facility of phraseology." His style is "not intelligible," his versification even "negligent," [90] though he was the first "polished English satirist." [91]

Many of these judgments would be indorsed by modern scholarship. But through all of them shines the eighteenth-century standard of correctness. It becomes quite explicit when Warton praises a poem by Surrey for having "almost the ease and gallantry of Waller." [92] Similarily the "smoothness and facility of manner" of Lord Vaux's poems are contrasted with the rudeness of Skelton.[93] Nicholas Grimald's blank verse poems are praised for "approaching the legitimate structure of the improved blank verse," though they are "not entirely free from those dissonancies and asperities, which still adhered to the general character and state of our diction." Grimald is besides praised for his "chaste expression" and for couplets having "all the smartness which marks the modern style of sententious poetry, and would have done honour to Pope's *Ethic Epistles*." [94] Hall's satires are extolled for their "classical precision" and their "equally energetic and elegant" versification, in which "the fabric of the couplets approaches to the modern standard." [95]

This conception of progress in literature is by no means confined to questions of language and versification. Warton shares to the full the classicist dislike of extravagant metaphors, similes, and conceits. He agrees that they are definite defects in Shakespeare and he rebukes Marlowe for "indulgence of the florid style and accumulation of conceits" and "bombast." [96] Warton is also constantly on the watch for violations of classical ideas of composition and decorum. The *Edda* is coolly called an "extravagant tissue of unmeaning allegory, false philosophy, and false theology"; [97] medieval chronicles are censured for their lack of "connection of parts, and uniformity of subject." [98] Mysteries come in for criticism for "lack of decorum" and "monstrous and unnatural mixtures." [99] The "absurdities" [100] of romances are frequently pointed out, and he never passes by a mixture of Christian and heathen mythology that had offended him already in Spenser. In speaking of a panegyric to the Virgin Mary which compares her with Helen, Lucretia and Dido, he apologizes that "the common sense of mankind had not yet attained a just estimate of things." [101] The grotesque is censured as an "attribute of early poetry of all nations, before ideas of selection have taken place." [102] Warton also frequently admits that "our old English poets abound in unnatural conceptions, strange imaginations, and even the most ridiculous absurdities." These are frequently contrasted with modern compositions, written when "ideas of discrimination have taken place; when even common writers have begun to conceive, on most subjects, with precision and propriety." [103]

How little he was able to rise above the preconceptions of his times is most obvious from his pronouncements on Dante. He speaks of "grossest improprieties and absurdities," of Dante's "want of art and method," of his "childish and ludicrous excesses" and even "disgusting fooleries." A reference to Paolo and Francesca as "these distinguished victims of an unfortunate attachment" betrays his superior, ironical attitude.[104] Other statements show his whole-hearted acceptance of traditional humanistic standards. Petrarch was "too cultivated to relish the *Roman de la Rose*"; [105] he introduced a "more rational method of composition" [106] in comparison with the "barbarous beauties of the Provençal troubadours"; [107] he contributed to the attempt to "reclaim, at least for a time, the public taste, from love of Gothic manners and romantic imagery." [108] Warton refers to "the graces of genuine poetry and eloquence" [109] in classical authors, "the real models of style," [110] and regrets that during the Renaissance Englishmen did not "attend to their regularity of design and justness of sentiment." [111] Characterizing Elizabethan poetry in general, Warton emphasizes the lack of attention paid to the "canons of composition," to "niceties," "correctness," "selection and discrimination." [112] Genius was then not awed "by the consciousness of a future and final arraignment at the tribunal of taste." [113]

This list could be extended but is long enough to show that there was no insincerity or later conversion in Warton's *Verses on Sir Joshua's Painted Window at New College*, written in the year after publication of the third volume of the *History* (1782). It merely reasserts the principles implied in the *History*, though Warton, confronted with the singularly commonplace design of his friend, chose to make a recantation of his never whole-hearted Gothic taste. He sings of being brought "back to truth again,"

> "To truth, by no peculiar taste confined,
> Whose universal pattern strikes mankind;
> To truth, whose bold and unresisted aim
> Checks frail caprice, and fashion's fickle claim." [114]

Here Warton clearly thinks of the distinction made by Addison in his discussion of *Chevy Chase* between the "Gothic manner of writing," a "wrong artificial taste," and the "true taste" which "pleases all kinds of palates," an idea which comes apparently from Muratori.[115]

Taste for Gothic literature, architecture and painted glass appeared, like a taste for *Chinoiserie*, as a peculiar, special, capricious taste, a fashion, it was assumed, that would pass, while classical taste was certain of a universal appeal and would always return. Usually no sharp contradiction was felt between an acceptance of the eternal standards and a genuine interest and pleasure in the curious and wild, strange and imaginative. But Warton's interest in the Gothic goes, actually, beyond mere curiosity, or dilettantism, or even the indulgence of his antiquarian taste. He had some deeper sympathy and understanding, though he is prone to press medieval poems into a classicist pattern just as Addison did *Chevy Chase,* or Percy *Libius Disconius.* Warton quotes *Sir Degore* as an instance of "coincidence of events, and a uniformity of design," and endorses Percy's similar analysis.[116]

But elsewhere he begins to waver in his principles in favour of a new standard. Speaking of the *Knight's Tale,* he recognizes that "we are hardly disgusted with the mixture of manners, the confusion of times, and the like violations of propriety, which this poem, in common with all others of its age, presents in almost every page." [117] He sees the "great strokes of Gothic imagination yet bordering often on the most ideal and capricious extravagance" in Chaucer's *House of Fame.* [118] He recognizes that "extravagancies are essential to a poem of such structure, and even constitute its beauties," and censures Pope's imitation for "marring the character of the poem." He feels the self-contained character of the style and protests against its confusion or combination with the modern. "An attempt to unite order and exactness of imagery with a subject formed on principles so professedly romantic and anomalous, is like giving Corinthian pillars to a Gothic palace. When I read Pope's elegant imitation of this piece, I think I am walking among the modern monuments unsuitably placed in Westminster Abbey." [119] He also censures Prior's imitation of the *Nut-Brown Maid* as "misconceiving and essentially marring his poet's design." [120]

Warton's considerable sense of style and character and

his real, instinctive knowledge of the medieval genius come out most favourably in his able analysis of Chatterton. He does not detect many philological mistakes (he passes over the simple evidence available without noticing it), nor is he able to detect many historical anachronisms. But he proceeds to show the "air of modern poetry" in Chatterton, the "modern craft of thought," the "complexion of sentiments" and the "structure of composition." [121] It is unfortunate that Warton did not more freely exercise his sense of style in dealing with Ossian, though he was alert enough to complain that the "gentler set of manners" in these poems "disarranges all our established ideas concerning the savage stages of society," and that the absence of religion is a "perplexing and extraordinary circumstance." [122]

Warton's genuine feeling for medieval style was combined with a real liking for medieval poetry, which, though mingled with depreciation, cannot be denied to him. His love for Chaucer is deep, and he appreciates much in the Scottish Chaucerians, something in the romances and even in Stephen Hawes. He loves Froissart and, in spite of the many condescending remarks, he sees greatness in Dante. Much he did not know, or did not know properly, and his choice of medieval literature seems a little narrow today, limited as it is largely to picturesque allegory. His sympathy fails before Nordic poetry, "monkish rhymes," and mystical and speculative writings, and he shares with his time a violent condemnation of "that barbarous species of theatrical representation called mysteries." [123]

In Warton a recognition of classical standards and a (tempered) appreciation of Gothic picturesqueness or sublimity went hand in hand. We should not, as is frequently done, judge this state of mind simply as an intermediate transitional phase, a mere preparation for full-fledged romanticism. Nor should we minimize either of these two elements. Undoubtedly, if we look at Warton's book purely from a nineteenth-century perspective, it appears as a pioneer of romantic taste, and that a hesitating and lukewarm one. But in Warton's time, his view was a coherent conception, whose propounders had no feeling of contradiction. It was simply the result of the theory of the two sorts of poetry which has been described at length in a preceding chapter. This idea of a contrast between early imaginative and modern refined poetry was accepted by Warton, and, like many of his contemporaries, he also saw that the course of history that led to the modern type was not altogether happy from the point of view of absolute poetry.

Though Warton can scarcely be described as a primitivist, as the preceding quotations must have shown, he accepts, in the main, the picture of primitive man as a more imaginative and therefore more poetical being. He protests against the notion of a uniform "savage" state,[124] but he adopts, in practice, the naturalistic generalizations of his time. Warmth of fancy is with him a characteristic of all primitive nations, and warmth of fancy leads to figurative speech, partly, he thought with Warburton, because the limited vocabulary of primitive people "obliges them frequently to substitute similitudes and circumlocutions," [125] and partly because figurative speech and imaginative conceptions in European literature spread from the Orient to the West. Warton thus rejects Blair's view that figurative language and imaginative poetry are the product of a state of society, and accepts the view that imaginative poetry, and especially folk-mythology, could have arisen only in one single place: the East. Romantic fictions must have been imported into Europe by a "people whose modes of thinking, and habits of invention, are not natural to that country," as the Western climate gives birth only to "cold and barren conceptions." [126]

This curious assumption of a single point of radiation for all folk-mythology and romantic *motifs* is still far away from the later extravagant belief in the creative power of the "folk," and is essentially a rationalist dogma, closely connected with the belief in universal classical, rational taste as opposed to the mere capricious, and therefore local, Oriental or Gothic taste. On this assumption Warton builds his theory of the origin of romantic fiction. The Arabs in Spain handed romance to Brittany and hence to Wales, whence it penetrated through Geoffrey of Monmouth to England. The Crusades then reinforced the taste for romance, as "oriental expeditions established a taste for hyperbolical description, and propagated an infinity of marvellous tales." [127] Thus a "new cast of fiction" was acquired from the Crusades.[128]

Warton, however, tries to reconcile this Arabian theory, substantially derived from Warburton, whom he expressly praises for it,[129] with the Nordic theory as he had met it in Mallet and Percy. The supposedly "oriental," "extravagant," "imaginative" cast of Nordic imagination is accounted for again by the Eastern or "Georgian" origin of the Goths. The theory of the migration of Odin, conceived as a historical personage, from "that part of Asia which is connected with Phrygia" [130] was already familiar to seventeenth-century Danish antiquarians like Bartholin, and lent itself to exploitation by the theory of the Asiatic origin of all romantic fictions. Environment, climate, or rather the impressions of a new landscape on the minds of the poets—ideas familiar since Lowth and Wood—account easily enough for the "darker shade and more savage complexion" of the "fictions and superstitions of the North." "The formidable objects of nature to which they became familiarized in those northern solitudes, the piny precipices, the frozen mountains, and the gloomy forests, acted on their imaginations, and gave a tincture of horror to their imagery." [131]

As in Hurd, so in Warton, there is an easy transition from this early Germanic civilization to feudalism. Warton characterizes feudalism essentially in terms of primitivism, and derives its main features from the more primitive, pre-Christian society. He sees the germs of chivalry and of gallantry to women in the old Teutonic conceptions of fealty to a lord and respect for women. Like Percy and others he derives the minstrels straight from the scalds and Gothic romance from Arabian fable, fostered by existing superstitions of "dragons, dwarfs, fairies, giants and enchanters" [132] planted by the Gothic "scalders."

Warton did not see the difficulties of describing these supposed processes in detail and proving a theory arrived at either purely on speculative grounds or on the most meagre evidence. His only concrete attempt is the discussion of Chaucer's *Squire's Tale*, which is described as "Arabian fiction engrafted on Gothic chivalry." [133] The horse of brass, the glass mirror, the naked sword and the ring that taught the language of birds are all considered Arabian ideas, with some parade of parallels from Oriental sources. But otherwise Warton makes only such sweeping statements as that "dragons are a sure mark of Orientalism," [134] that Geoffrey of Monmouth's *Chronicle* consists "entirely of Arabian inventions," that the *Edda* shows "strokes of oriental imagination," [135] that the fanciful turns in the saints' legends are all from the East,[136] and even that Charlemagne "propagated" Arabian literature.[137] The remark on the dragons shows how far all these theories were built on vicious circles. It was simply assumed that dragons were of Oriental origin, and then any piece of writing in which dragons appeared was triumphantly flourished as a proof of the Oriental hypothesis. Not that there is no such problem as the influx of Oriental *motifs* during the Middle Ages; but Warton and his contemporaries made its solution impossible by the very extent of the questions they raised and by their inability to distinguish between universal elements in folk-mythology and more specifically, localized literary *motifs*. He did not see the contradiction in his own theory when elsewhere he asserted that the "genius of romance and popery was the same"; [138] nor was he apparently exercised about reconciling his taste for romance with the loathing he professed for Catholic "superstition."

Warton, on some points, approaches the primitivist view surprisingly. Speaking even of the time of Gower, he calls the minstrels "totally uneducated" and thinks that they "poured forth spontaneous rhymes in obedience to the workings of nature." [139] However, "they often exhibit more genuine strokes of passion and imagination than the professed poets" like the learned Gower.[140] Thus learning and education is seen in conflict with poetic creativeness, and the way is prepared for the adoption of the primitivist view that simple manners foster poetry. Warton accepts and repeats Hurd's main thesis that "the manners of romance are better calculated to serve the purposes of pure poetry, than the fictions of classical antiquity." [141] As knowledge and learning increase, poetry begins to deal less in imagination, and "these fantastic beings give way to real manners and living characters." [142]

The advance towards reason and inquiry, towards methodical composition, towards imitation of real life, judgment and rules of criticism, is seen, in spite of many contradictory assertions, as not entirely beneficial to the ultimate purposes of poetry. "The customs, institutions, traditions and religion of the Middle Ages, were favourable to poetry," and "ignorance and superstition, so opposite to the real interests of human society, are the parents of imagination." [143] Other passages elaborate this view, which presumes that, after all, pure poetry, true poetry may be found in the romantic imaginings of the "Gothic taste." Warton says in possibly the most often quoted passage of his book, "The lover of poetry will ask, what have we gained by this revolution? It may be answered, much good sense, good taste, and good criticism. But, in the mean time, we have lost a set of manners, and a system of machinery more suitable to the purposes of poetry, than those which have been adopted in their place. We have parted with extravagancies that are above propriety, with incredibilities that are more acceptable than truth, and with fictions that are more valuable than reality." [144] In isolation this passage sounds very "romantic," especially the last words, which seem to prefer fiction to reality, but in the light of all the evidence here presented, one feels that Warton did not quite mean as much as his words seem to imply. He certainly did not want to assert that fictions are more valuable than reality; merely that certain fictions are more valuable for the uses of poetry. But the passage clearly reveals a regret for the progress of poetry (seen elsewhere as a real progress) towards the second, more rational and more civilized type. He regrets the fact that chivalry (a set of manners) and folk-mythology (a system of machinery) cannot any more be used by poets, these fictions no longer carrying conviction with the modern reader.

This curious double point of view—acknowledgment of the progress of modern civilization and even of modern taste, and yet regret for the "world of fine fabling" [145]—had an interesting, logical consequence. The period of English literature which combined the advantages of both early and later poetry must have seemed to Warton the natural summit and the real ideal. He therefore adopts the view propounded by Hurd in the *Dialogue of the Age of Elizabeth* that the Elizabethan age was the golden age, the most "poetical" age, because it combined imagination and reason. There was then still alive, he argues, a "degree of superstition sufficient for the purposes of poetry, and the adoption of the machineries of romance." [146] Then, "the reformation had not yet destroyed every delusion, nor disenchanted all the strongholds of superstition," and "Reason suffered a few demons still to linger, which she chose to retain in her service under the guidance of poetry." [147] Also, "the national credulity, chastened by reason, had produced a sort of civilized superstition, and left a set of traditions, fanciful enough for poetical decorations, and yet not too violent and chimerical for common sense." [148] Criticism did not yet restrain imagination, satire did not yet exercise its pull on the flight of fancy, science had not yet blighted illusions. The period was "propitious to the operations of original and true poetry, when the coyness of fancy was not always proof against the approaches of reason, when genius was rather directed than governed by judgment, and when taste and learning had so far only disciplined imagination, as to suffer excesses to pass without censure or control for the sake of the beauties to which they were allied." [149] Hence the witches and fairies in Shakespeare and the chivalrous "set of manners" in Spenser found their new justification.

Ultimately, a conception of the development of English poetry in three stages emerges: a primitive, imaginative stage; a condition of synthesis between imagination and reason, realized by the Elizabethans; and a period of judgment and correctness which seemed final to Warton and ideal from the point of view of the social advance of humanity, even though it might spell death to imagination and poetry. Warton shares in the feeling of epigonism, of Alexandrianism, which unfortunately blighted so much literary history in later periods and made it frequently the ally of the most deadening, old-fashioned and conventional taste in opposition to any new literary movement. To a certain extent Warton anticipates Hegel's belief that the owl of Minerva flies in the dusk of a creative civilization, or—in agreement with his own metaphors—that the bright daylight of reason has dispelled the foul mists of superstition together with the golden haze of imagination.

But this view, developed here from Warton's casual pronouncements, lost, in actuality, much of its asperity, since the high valuation of old imaginative poetry worked as a leaven in a new poetical movement. Contrary to the rigid scheme which implies a belief in the further decline of imagination as a result of the further growth of reason, Warton and many of his contemporaries hoped to reverse the process, just as John Brown wanted to reunite poetry and music in the teeth of his theory. The Miltonic revival, in which Warton himself took part and which he was to describe in the Preface to his edition of Milton's minor poems (1785) as a "visible revolution," was such an attempt to reintroduce "fiction and fancy, picturesque description, and romantic imagery," without sacrificing "selection and discrimination, . . . address and judgment," which seemed to him the gains of modern poetry.[150]

Warton's conception of development is, fundamentally, a psychological one. It is based on the assumption that the growth of reasoning power dries up the sources of imagination, and, of course, on the fundamental assumption or observation that poetry (genuine poetry) is a product of the emotional forces of man. Thus a philosophy of history is implied rather than a strictly literary conception of the development of the art of literature. Concerning an evolution of genres, Warton is sceptical or indifferent and certainly behind the ideas of several of his contemporaries. Once he accepts the view of internal development in admitting (with Dr. Johnson and in the same context) that language changes "from reasons we cannot explain." [151] Several times he refers to the "necessary connection between literary composition and the arts of design," [152] an idea which would seem to imply either a synchronous development of different cultural activities or the all-pervading influence of a "spirit of the age." But Warton seems once to ascribe the rise of Renaissance arts simply to the influence of the Classics in literature, and elsewhere is content with an allusion to the mythological tradition that the "three Graces were produced at a birth." [153]

A pronouncement like "the English and French stages mutually throw light on each other's history" [154] seems also to presuppose some conception of necessary evolution, but actually Warton's account of the development of the English drama is far more loosely conceived than Percy's. Warton merely suggests that pageants "dictated ideas of a regular drama, much sooner than the mysteries" and that hence "a quick and easy transition to the representations of real life and rational action" [155] was possible. But in his account of the probable causes of the rise of mysteries he adopted (apparently from Tilliot's *Histoire de la Fête des Foux*) a pragmatist explanation, ascribing all steps in the process to conscious "changes of plan" on the part of the clergy who had "determined to take these (popular) recreations into their own hands." [156] With a similar unhistorical simplification he ascribes Calvin's supposed invention of psalmody to his conscious reflection that the "manufacturers of Germany were no judges of pictures," while his congregation "would be kept in good humour" by singing psalms.[157] The idea of the medieval clergy, after consultations, deciding to "turn actors," or of Calvin sitting down and planning the service, points to a rationalist conception of history similar to Voltaire's or Hume's, and obviously, by its extreme individualism, this excluded any evolutionary approach.

The idea of a progress of versification towards the ideal of Pope was old and narrow, but it was inherently literary. That of the three stages of poetry progressing from imagination to reason was psychological, with social implications. But both these conceptions were frequently overshadowed in Warton by a third: his belief that literature is merely a series of documents for the illustration of social history. The imagination-to-reason conception was a genuinely ideological conception of the evolution of society. But all too frequently Warton saw literature not as answering to this development towards reason or towards the present-day bourgeois society, but merely as a collection of *loci* illustrating isolated curiosities of ancient manners. Warton himself stresses the uses of literature for the illustration of ancient costumes and customs. Literature, he tells us, has the "peculiar merit of faithfully recording the features of the times, and of preserving the most picturesque and expressive representation of manners." [158] He stresses that the "manners and poetry of a country are so nearly connected that they mutually throw light on each other." [159] He pleads that the researches of the antiquary "tend to display the progress of human manners, and to illustrate the history of society." [160] In discussing individual poems he repeats over and over again that they present "pictures of ancient manners," "founded on truth and reality"; and actually "painted from the life." *King Horn*, Robert de Brunne, the romances in general, the *Canterbury Tales*, etc.,[161] all serve that purpose. He shows frequently how contemporary conditions, especially chivalry and the Catholic religion, are mirrored in literature, or more precisely are simply described or mentioned there, but he very rarely attempts to show concretely how society influences the course of English literature. He barely refers to the "national distractions" of the fifteenth century as "obstructing the exercise of those studies which delight in peace and repose." [162] Only the restoration of Popery under Mary is described as "highly pernicious to the growth of polite erudition," [163] though he has to modify this statement by alluding to the foundation of his own college, Trinity, at that very time. Early Elizabethan puritanism, too, is judged to have "retarded for some time the progress of ingenuous and useful knowledge." [164]

On the whole, Warton thinks that "all changes of rooted establishments, especially of a national religion, are attended with shocks and convulsions, unpropitious to the repose of science and study." [165] Among the causes of the Renaissance he lists the "felicities of long peace and public prosperity," [166] but these very rare and general references to the blessing of a stable society are outweighed by other passages asserting the independence of genius from society. "True genius," he says, "defies and neglects those events which destroy the peace of mankind, and often exerts its operations amidst the most violent commotions of a state." [167] As examples he quotes the early Italian writers living during the troubles of the Guelphs and Ghibellines, the age of Pericles as contemporary with the Peloponnesian war, the proscriptions of Augustus, "which did not prevent the progress of the Roman literature," and finally even the Marian persecutions, during which the *Mirror for Magistrates* was planned.

Thus social influences on literature are nowhere clearly analyzed. Warton's account amounts usually to nothing more than an assertion that religious liberty and the refinements of polite manners were favourable to literature. He frequently uses the conception of a dominant "age" merely in order to apologize for the lack of decorum in older literature. The manners in *King Horn* are "gross" and "absurd," but the "poet was only concerned with the justness and faithfulness of representation." [168] Chaucer selected the story of the *Miller's Tale* "in compliance with the prevailing manners of an unpolished age," [169] and his "obscenity is in great measure to be imputed to his age." [170] The indelicate expressions in Dame Berners' treatises on hunting are also ascribed to the "barbarism of the times." [171] This pressure of the "age" is a frequent concept in Warton. Thus John Heywood's comedies are defended for their "low incidents and ribaldry," as "perfection must not be expected before its time"; [172] and Latimer's sermons seem "barbarous beyond their age, in style, manner and argument." [173]

More concrete is Warton's theory that satire, irony, and especially burlesque is possible only in a refined and self-conscious society. "Satire is the poetry of a nation highly polished," [174] he declares, remembering Pope and forgetting the (otherwise) admired Langland. The "comic air of poetry" is due to "female society," [175] which in earlier times could not have been influential. Heywood's *Spider and the Fly* appeared in an age "not yet sufficiently refined, either to relish or to produce, burlesque poetry." [176] Such arguments are plausible only if we define these genres so narrowly as to make them conform only with later-day productions. Sometimes Warton hints at the idea of a harmony between an author and his age, when he alludes to Lord Berners' translations, "which co-operated with the romantic genius and the gallantry of the age" [177] or, in contrast, complains that poets like Andrew Borde "do not bear any mark of the character of the poetry which distinguishes this period." [178] But, otherwise, Warton still makes very scanty use of concepts adopted from political historiography, such as the Gothic times, the Reformation, and the Elizabethan age. Only at the beginning of his discussion of Elizabethan literature does he attempt a general characterization on the lines of the synthesis of imagination and reason described above.

Much more frequently Warton becomes simply descriptive and uses his materials as illustrations of "manners and customs, modes of life, and favourite amusements." [179] Picturesqueness is the bane of antiquarianism, and literary history, even in Warton, sometimes sinks to a mere inventory of pieces found in any museum of armour or costumes. How literally he sometimes interpreted this illustrative function is obvious from a remark disparaging the importance of allegory, because it "necessarily fails in that chief source of entertainment which we seek in ancient poetry, the representation of ancient manners." [180] There was much in this attitude that anticipated the future romantic interest in the mere trappings of medieval manners, and Warton exercised an influence on this point which was not altogether favourable to the future course of English literary history.

But it would be ungracious to conclude with a mere summary of Warton's negative features. We can stress his merits, though each time we have to temper our admiration with some reserves. Warton, above all, has this immense historical importance: he first produced a narrative *History of English Poetry* and thus introduced and established, at least in England, the whole conception and possibility of literary history, before then only very imperfectly realized. His main success was unfortunately not in the actual writing of a history, but rather in his ability to organize into an orderly scheme the materials accumulated by his predecessors and by his own researches. The weight of these materials was so great that it continually burst through the narrative form and made the *History* frequently a mere chronicle or anthology. But Warton continuously strove to write a proper history, and his book is permeated with the ideas current at his time. Warton was no innovator in this point; but he knew and used practically everything that had been achieved. The main conceptions and all the elements of a history are present in his volumes, though rarely integrated into a consistent whole.

Warton had some notion of selecting and evaluating his materials, according to fixed principle. He did not always apply it, but he saw the necessity of some criterion of "representativeness" in a scheme of values and this is a definite advance on the older, merely haphazard accumulation of materials. He thus helped to establish a tradition of English literary history focussed on the history of English poetry from the Conquest to Spenser. He sketched in a wide comparative background of Nordic, Anglo-Saxon, Old French, and Italian literature. He at least attempted a world-wide history of *motifs* and their migrations, without, however, clearly distinguishing between folk-lore and literary plots. He began to use some of the historical categories elaborated by a century, like the concepts of "age" and "period," of the "Middle Ages," the "Renaissance" and the "Elizabethan Age." On one point he was more conservative than several of his contemporaries; he had less comprehension for the evolutionary point of view and did not attempt to write a history of a genre. But he was not without his own conceptions of historical laws. He balanced, however, rather uneasily, between the old traditional acceptance of a regular "progress" towards the Age of Queen Anne and some psychological, and hence social, conception of the evolution of man's mind from imagination to reason. He saw literature in its social setting, though unfortunately he was too much preoccupied with the merely picturesque side of chivalry to understand the deeper social forces behind literature.

Thus, all the main problems of nineteenth-century literary history were formulated by Warton, even if his superstructure of ideas did not always properly control his materials. Warton was the first historian of English literature in the full sense of the term, and his title to credit is not lessened by the fact we have shown most of his ideas to have been common in his time. It was not entirely his fault, if his successors at first seized on only some isolated elements in his book and tended to ignore those pointing to real history. He showed the way, and his achievement, imperfect as it was, made genuine literary history in England possible.

NOTES

1. See the pedigree traced in Ludwig Traube, "Einleitung in die lateinische Philologie des Mittelalters," *Vorlesungen und Abhandlungen*, II, 162.
2. The English portions of the MS are printed in Thomas Tanner's *Bibliotheca Britannico-Hibernica* (1748), pp. xvii-xliii.
3. Modern edition by H. Knust, Tübingen, 1886.
4. A convenient collection of the passages is in Caroline S. Spurgeon's *Five Hundred Years of Chaucer Criticism*, I, 16 ff.
5. See Lydgate, quoted in Spurgeon, I, 37, 41.
6. Sir Philip Sidney, *An Apology for Poetry*, quoted from *Elizabethan Critical Essays*, ed. Gregory Smith, I, 156.
7. From John Coke's "The Debate betweene the Heraldes of Englande and Fraunce" (1550), Spurgeon, I, 90.
8. *Novum Organum* I, Aphorismus 84, *Works*, ed. J. Spedding, Ellis, et al., I, 190.
9. Gabriel Harvey, *Letter-Book, 1573-80*, ed. E. J. L. Scott. Fourth letter referring to Bodin, p. 86.
10. J. Leland, *Laboryouse Journey* (1549), p. F^r.
10a. Bale in his youth compiled lists of writers in the Carmelite order. The MSS are still extant. See J. M. Harris, *John Bale*, p. 137.
11. Abdias Assheton, "Vita Guilielmi Whitaker," prefixed to W. Whitaker's *Praelectiones* (1599).
12. *The Gospels . . . translated . . .* (1571), p. A^r.
13. K. Sisam, "The Authenticity of Certain Texts in Lombard's *Archaionomia* (1568)," *MLR*, XX (1925), 253. Robin Flower in *Lawrence Nowell and the Discovery of England* supports Sisam by a new argument: Nowell added passages to his transcript of Alfred's Bede which are obviously translated from Latin into Anglo-Saxon.
14. *Animadversions . . .* , ed. Furnivall, pp. 43, 55, 69 ff.
15. *The Arte of Rhetorique*, ed. by G. H. Mair, p. 203.

16. Gregory Smith's introduction to *Elizabethan Critical Essays*, I, lxvii.

17. See the quotations in Spurgeon, I, 102, 111.

18. See Gregory Smith, ed., *op. cit.*, I, 239, 240.

19. George Puttenham, *The Arte of English Poesie*, ed. G. D. Willcock and Alice Walker, p. 60.

20. *Ibid.*, p. 15.

21. *Ibid.*, p. 10.

22. Gregory Smith, ed., *op. cit.*, II, 362.

23. *Ibid.*, p. 383.

24. *Ibid.*, p. 384.

25. *Ibid.*, pp. 359, 368, 372.

26. *Ibid.*, p. 217.

27. *Ibid.*, Vol. I, pp. 294-295.

28. See *Works*, ed. J. Spedding, Ellis, et al., III (1857), 329; I, 502-4.

CHAPTER TWO

1. John Pits, *Relationes Historicae de Rebus Anglicis*, p. 9.
2. Thomas Fuller, *The History of the Worthies of England*, ed. John Nichols (1811), I, 414.
3. *Davidis Buchananis De Scriptoribus Scotis Libri Duo*, ed. David Irving (1837).
4. P. 245.
5. Thomas Fuller, *Worthies*, ed. J. Nichols (1811), I, 26.
6. *Ibid.*, p. 52.
7. Spingarn, ed., *Critical Essays of the Seventeenth Century*, II, 263.
8. *Ibid.*, p. 264.
9. Quotations in an annotated, interleaved copy in the British Museum (press-mark C. 45. d. 13.).
10. P. 195.
11. "The Life of Anthony Wood," *Athenae Oxonienses*, ed. Philip Bliss (1813), I, lx.
12. Harington's Preface to the second volume of the first edition, ed. P. Bliss, p. clxxv.
13. "Ad Lectorem," no pagination.
14. See A. Watkin-Jones, "Langbaine's *Account of the English Dramatick Poets* (1691)," *Essays and Studies*, XXI (1935), 75, for a description of the annotated copies preserved. Langbaine had published himself an *Exact Catalogue of all the Comedies* (1680) which, in its turn, was based on Francis Kirkman's list appended to *Tom Tyler* (1661). The title of Langbaine's book *Momus Triumphans* was given by London friends as a practical joke on the author. Langbaine angrily repudiated it and substituted the title *A New Catalogue of English Plays*. See J. M. Osborn, *John Dryden*, pp. 218-220.
15. Preface.
16. Spingarn, II, 129.
17. See Spingarn's introduction to his edition of the *Critical Essays of the Seventeenth Century* and his review of Saintsbury's *His-*

tory of Criticism, Modern Philology (hereafter cited as *MP*), I, (1903–1904), 477. For the later period see A. Bäumler, *Kants Kritik der Urteilskraft. Ihre Geschichte und Systematik*, Vol. I.

18. See G. M. Miller, *The Historical Point of View in English Literary Criticism from 1570–1770*. See also Odell Shepard's review of C. Rinaker's book on Warton, *Journal of English and Germanic Philology* (hereafter cited as *JEGP*), XVI (1917), 153.

19. In the growing literature on primitivism (e.g. Tinker, Fairchild) the series edited by A. O. Lovejoy, R. S. Crane, and others stands out. So far, *Primitivism and Related Ideas in Antiquity* by A. O. Lovejoy and G. Boas (1935), and a very valuable volume by L. Whitney, *Primitivism and the Idea of Progress in English Popular Literature of the Eighteenth Century* (1934), have been published.

20. Second edition (1692), p. 5. The first edition came out in the autumn of 1677. See Fred G. Walcott, "Dryden's Answer to Thomas Rymer's *Tragedies of the Last Age*," in *Philological Quarterly* (hereafter cited as *PQ*), XV (1936), 194.

21. See Walcott's paper, *loc. cit.*, which shows clearly that not only the *Heads of an Answer to Rymer's Remarks on the Tragedies of the Last Age* (*Works*, ed. W. Scott and G. Saintsbury, XV, 381), but the whole Preface to *Troilus and Cressida* (1678) was designed as such an answer.

22. *Works*, ed. W. Scott and G. Saintsbury, XV, 384.

23. See the list in Paul Spencer Wood, *The Opposition to Neoclassicism in England between 1660 and 1700*, Publications of the Modern Language Association (hereafter cited as *PMLA*), XLIII (1928), 182–97.

24. Dryden, *loc. cit.*, p. 385.

25. *The Impartial Critick* (1693), Spingarn, III, 148; also in Dennis, *Critical Works*, ed. Hooker, I, 11.

26. See Logan Pearsall Smith, *Four Words: Romantic, Originality, Creation, Genius*, Society for Pure English Tract, No. XVII; H. Thüme, *Beiträge zur Geschichte des Geniebegriffes in England;* P. Kaufman, "Heralds of Original Genius," *Essays in Memory of Barrett Wendell*, p. 191; E. Zilsel, *Die Entstehung des Geniebegriffes.*

27. For Bacon, see above. As to Bouhours, see Spingarn's introduction, p. cii.

28. Dryden, *Essays*, ed. W. P. Ker, I, 99.

29. *Ibid.*, p. 36.

30. *Works*, ed. Scott and Saintsbury, XV, 381.

31. Ker, I, 68.

32. Preface to *All for Love*. See Ker, I, 195.
33. Ker, *op. cit.*, II, 5. From the *Examen Poeticum* (1693).
34. William E. Bohn, "The Development of John Dryden's Literary Criticism," *PMLA*, XXXIX. (1903), 56 ff.
35. See Spingarn's "Introduction," p. lxvi, and Spingarn, II, 344. See also Scaliger, *Poetics*, Liber V, Chap. VI.
36. See Spingarn's Introduction, pp. ci–cii, and C. Marburg, *Sir William Temple*, pp. 30, 51. See especially Bodin's *Republic* 1577, Book V, Chap. 1 of which there is a summary in Hallam's *Introduction to the Literature of Europe*, II, 159.
37. See above. Dryden's Prologue to *Aureng-Zebe* (1676), *Works*, V, 201. Milton's *Paradise Lost*, Canto ix, lines 44-45.
38. Spingarn, III, 104-5.
39. Swift, *The Intelligencer*, No. 3 (1728). W. Congreve, *Concerning Humour in Comedy* (1695), Spingarn, III, 252. Farquhar, *Discourse upon Comedy* (1702), in Durham, *Critical Essays*, p. 275. Steele, The Guardian, No. 144 (1714). See also Hooker's edition of Dennis, *The Critical Works*, I, 436-37.
40. P. 1.
41. Ker, II, 87.
42. Spingarn, I, ci, and II, 334.
43. A. Cowley, Preface to *Poems* (1656), Spingarn, *op. cit.*, II, 80.
44. Spingarn, *op. cit.*, III, 45.
45. Longinus, Chap. XLIV. Milton, *Prose Works*, ed. J. A. St. John, I, 241.
46. W. Wotton, *Reflections upon Ancient and Modern Learning* (1694), Spingarn, III, 208-11.
47. See H. G. Paul, *John Dennis*. Paul goes so far as to distinguish a special patriotic tendency in criticism and quotes further instances.
48. See, e.g., A. O. Lovejoy, *The Great Chain of Being*. See also F. Meinecke, Troeltsch, and others on the rise of "historism."
49. See above, pp. 3, 9. There is a growing literature on the idea of progress: see, e.g., Delvaille, *Essai sur l'histoire de progrès;* R. H. Murray, *Erasmus and Luther;* J. B. Bury, *The Idea of Progress;* René Hubert, "Essai sur l'histoire de l'idée de progrès," *Revue d'Histoire de la Philosophie*, October, 1934, p. 289, and January, 1935, p. 1; R. F. Jones, *Ancients and Moderns*, and his paper "Science and Criticism in the Neo-Classical Age of English Literature," *Journal of the History of Ideas*, I (1940), 381.
50. See John D. Scheffer, "The Idea of Decline in Literature and Arts in 18th Century England," *MP*, XXXIV (1936), 155 ff. This concerns rather the biological parallel.

51. Spingarn, *op. cit.*, I, 144.
52. Spingarn, *op. cit.*, I, 16. See note on p. 241.
53 Addison, *Miscellaneous Works*, ed. A. C. Guthkelch, p. 31.
54. A. F. B. Clark, *Boileau and the French Classical Critics in England*, p. 132. See Dryden, *Works*, ed. Scott and Saintsbury XV, 223.
55. E. Waller, *Poems*, ed. C. Thorn Drury, p. xxii.
56. Rymer, p. 78-79.
57. Ker, I, 36-37, cf. 43-44.
58. *Ibid.*, II, 25.
59. Ker, II, 249.
60. *The Impartial Critick* (1693), Spingarn, III, p. 153.
61. Spingarn, III, 102-103.
62. Spingarn, II, 91.
63. Rymer, p. 84.
64. Ker, I, 83.
65. Wright, p. 29.
66. Ker, II, 42.
67. *Ibid.*, p. 99.
68. *English Works*, ed. W. A. Wright, 1904, p. 256. See also Velleius Paterculus, *Historiae Romanae*. "Naturaliter quod procedere non potest, recedit." (lib. 1.)
69. Spingarn, II, p. 6.
70. See Eduard Spranger, "Die Kulturzyklentheorie und das Problem des Kulturverfalls," *Sitzungsberichte der preussischen Akademie*, p. xxv, and C. Marburg, *Sir William Temple*, pp. 43 ff. See also F. J. Teggart, "A Problem in the History of Ideas," *Journal of the History of Ideas*, I (1940), 494.
71. Ker, II, 259.
72. Ker, I, 36.
73. William Temple, "Some Thoughts upon Reviewing the Essay of Ancient and Modern Learning," *Works*, III, 501.
74. *Ibid.*, p. 379.
75. Spingarn, III, 50. "Essay upon the Ancient and Modern Learning" (1690).
76. *Ibid.*, p. 60.
77. See Spranger, *loc. cit.*
78. "Of Poetry" (1690), Spingarn, III, 85.
79. "Essay upon the Ancient and Modern Learning," Spingarn, III, 55.
80. Spingarn, III, 108.
81. See Spingarn, and C. Marburg, *op. cit.*, pp. 64-65, and E. Seaton,

Literary Relations of England and Scandinavia in the Seventeenth Century, p. 134.

82. "Of Heroic Virtue," *Works*, III, 357.

83. *Ibid.*, p. 358.

84. Spingarn and especially C. Marburg give an excellent exposition of Temple and see the modernity of his mind. The essay by Macaulay and the pages in Taine should be dismissed from the mind.

85. Rymer, *Short View of Tragedy*, p. 67. For reference to Redi, in Rymer, p. 75, see Spingarn's introduction, p. lxxi.

86. A full account of Rymer's various sources is in Curt A. Zimansky's notes to his edition of Rymer's *Critical Works* (MS., Princeton doctoral dissertation, 1937).

CHAPTER THREE

1. Letter from Warton to Percy, June 15, 1765. See Leah Dennis, "The Text of the Percy-Warton Letters," *PMLA*, XLVI (1931), 1166.
2. E.g., in Clarissa Rinaker's *Thomas Warton.*
3. "Soliloquy," *Characteristics,* ed. Robertson, I, 137.
4. No. 160. Sept. 3, 1711, ed. Gregory Smith, II, 283.
5. L. Welsted, *Epistles, Odes . . .* (1724), p. xxxvii.
6. W. Sharpe's *Dissertation on Genius* (1755), W. Duff's *Essay on Original Genius* (1767), A. Gerard's *Esasy on Genius* (1774).
7. Young, in *English Critical Essays,* ed. E. D. Jones, p. 332.
8. *Ibid.,* p. 319.
9. See Shaftesbury, *Characteristics,* ed. Robertson, II, 257. "Taste or Judgment," and Welsted, *loc. cit.,* p. xxiii. The same identification in Pascal, Fraim du Tremblay, Muratori and Dubos.
10. "Of the Standard of Taste" (1757).
11. Harris, *Three Treatises* (1744). End of Chap. II.
12. Avison, *passim.*
13. "Of the Nature of that Imitation which takes place in what are called the Imitative arts," *Essays on Philosophical Subjects* (1795), p. 175.
14. *Works* (1799), IV, 549.
15. "Is Music an Imitative Art?" *Essays on Poetry and Music* (1776), Chap. VI, Sec. 1, p. 119.
16. On Reynolds see L. I. Bredvold, "The Tendency Towards Platonism in Neo-Classical Aesthetics," *ELH,* I (1934), 91. On D. Webb see Hans Hecht, *Daniel Webb.* Hamburg, 1920.
17. James Barry's lectures were given in 1784, but were not published until 1848.
18. *A Miscellany of Poems* (1731), Preface, p. d⁴.
19. See Nichol Smith, *Eighteenth Century Essays on Shakespeare,* p. 84.

20. "Miscellaneous Observations on the Tragedy of Macbeth" (1745), *Works* (1825), V, 55.
21. Lecture IV. Quotations from G. Gregory's translation (1787), I, 113.
22. Joseph Warton's *Essay on Pope*, I, (1756), 5.
23. "Of the Standard of Taste," *Essays and Treatises*, I, 255-256.
24. English translation (1764), p. 25.
25. *Works*, ed. R. Lynam, V, 116.
26. Wood's *Homer*, p. 7.
27. E.g., in G. M. Miller, *The Historical Point of View*. Heidelberg, 1913.
28. See O. Shepard's review of C. Rinaker's *Warton*, JEGP, XVI (1917), p. 153, and Victor M. Hamm's "A Seventeenth Century French Source for Hurd's *Letters on Chivalry and Romance*," *PMLA*, LII (1937), p. 820.
29. *An Essay on Criticism*, I. lines 120 -121.
30. *An Enquiry into the Present State of Learning* (1759), p. 95. This idea was elaborated by Goldsmith in the *Critical Review*, IX (1760), pp. 10-19, in course of an attack on the idolatry of Homer. See R. S. Crane, "A Neglected Eighteenth Century Plea for Originality and its Author," *PQ*, XIII (1934), p. 21.
31. *The Letters and Works of Lady Mary Montagu* (1886), I, 304. Pope's letter is dated June, 1717.
32. *Spectator*, No. 160, September 3, 1711.
33. *A Miscellany of Poems* (1731), Preface, p. e³.
34. Blackwell's *Homer*, p. 8 and *passim*.
35. *The History of the Rise and Progress of Poetry* (1764), p. 190-192. This passage is only in this abridgment and not in the *Dissertation* of 1763.
36. Wood's *Homer*, p. 84.
37. *New Essays* by O. Goldsmith (Chicago, 1927), pp. 10, 53-54. Identified by R. S. Crane. The essays were first published in 1760.
38. *Works*, ed. Guthkelch, II, 459.
39. See note 37.
40. *Poems consisting chiefly of translations from the Asiatick languages* (1772), Essay I, pp. 180-181.
41. "A Discourse Concerning E. Spenser," first printed in the Appendix of E. W. Bligh's *Sir K. Digby and his Venetia* (1932).
42. See note 32.
43. *Poems*, ed. A. L. Poole (Oxford, 1917), especially lines 86-87.
44. Letter to J. Brown, February 8, 1763, in *Correspondence*, ed. P. Toynbee and L. Whibley, II, 797.

45. *The Works of Mr. F. Beaumont and Mr. J. Fletcher*, ed. Theobald, Seward, Sympson, Preface, pp. xlii-iii.
46. "Of the National Character," *Essays*, I, 221-227.
47. Sterne, *Tristram Shandy*, Book I, Chap. XXI.
48. *Lives* (ed. Hill), I, 83.
49. *Ibid.*, I, 82.
50. *Sketches of a History of Man* (1774), I, 12.
51. See J. Dédieu, *Montesquieu et la tradition politique anglaise en France* (1909), p. 212. He refers to J. Arbuthnot's *Essay Concerning the Effects of Air on Human Bodies* (1733). See also Lester M. Beattie, *John Arbuthnot*, p. 366.
52. Wood's *Homer*, p. 15.
53. Shaftesbury, *Characteristics*, ed. Robertson, I, 142-143, 155.
54. "An Epistle to the Duke of Chandos," *Epistles, Odes . . .* (1724), p. 45. This use in referring to England is almost a century earlier than the oldest recorded instance (1819) in the *NED*.
55. Blackwell (1735), p. 61.
56. *Ibid.*, p. 24.
57. Upton (1746), pp. 33, 131.
58. *Enquiry into the Present State of Polite Learning* (1759), p. 14.
59. Kames, *Sketches* (1774), I, 109, 150.
60. "Of Civil Liberty" and "Of the Rise and Progress of the Arts and Sciences," *Essays*, (ed. 1777), I, 114, 118, 128.
61. *Letters*, ed. Dobrée, IV, 1308. Feb. 7, O.S. 1749.
62. *Lives of the Poets*, ed. Birkbeck Hill, III, 437. Refers to Gray, stanza II, l. 3.
63. *Advancement and Reformation of Modern Poetry* (1701), Chap. X-XIV in Hooker, I, 229-245.
64. Preface to *A Miscellany of Poems* (1731). Earlier passages referring to the Bible as literature are collected in R. S. Crane's paper on Husbands in *Modern Language Notes*, XXXVII (1922), pp. 27 ff.
65. *The Works of Mr. F. Beaumont and Mr. J. Fletcher*, Preface, lxii-xiii.
66. See especially Lois Whitney, *Primitivism and the Idea of Progress*.
67. 1735. Pp. 25, 55, 102, 113, etc.
68. Trans. G. Gregory (1787), I, 50.
69. Richard Hurd, *Letters on Chivalry and Romance*, ed. E. Morley, p. 71.
70. 1763 edition, pp. 3-5.
71. Duff, (1767), pp. viii-ix.
72. Hamm, Victor M., "A Seventeenth-Century French Source for

Hurd's *Letters on Chivalry and Romance*," *PMLA*, LII (1937), pp. 820-828.

73. Ed. E. Morley, pp. 95, 128.

74. "A Large Account of the Taste in Poetry," *The Comical Gallant* (1702), an adaptation of the *Merry Wives of Windsor*. Also in Hooker, I, 279.

75. "An Essay on the Art, Rise, and Progress of the Stage . . ." in Shakespeare's *Works* (1710), VII, lxvi.

76. E. Taylor (1774), quoted by R. W. Babcock, *The Genesis of Shakespeare Idolatry*, p. 187.

77. *Observations*, section X, pp. 74, 78, etc.

78. "The Poetical Balance," *Literary Magazine*, III (1758), 58. Goldsmith's authorship is doubted by R. W. Seitz in "Goldsmith and the *Literary Magazine*," *Review of English Studies* (hereafter cited as *RES*), V (1929), 410.

79. *Polite Correspondence*, p. 272.

80. The Lapland Songs are in No. 366, 406; *Chevy Chase* is in No. 70, 74.

81. Blair, p. 4.

82. *Ibid.*, pp. 21-23.

83. Letter to J. Brown, Feb. 8, 1763, in *Correspondence*, ed. P. Toynbee and L. Whibley, II, 798.

84. In Green and Grose's ed. of the *Essays*, 1875, II, 415.

85. *A Dissertation on the Rise, Union, and Power, the Progressions, Separations and Corruptions of Poetry and Music* (1763). See above, pp. 74-80.

86. *The Progress of Poesy* was sent to Warton on Dec. 26, 1754. It was published in 1757. The notes were not added until 1768.

87. Thomas Hawkins, *The Origin of the English Drama* (1773). Hawkins died in Feb., 1772.

88. Letter of Percy to E. Evans, July 23, 1764, quoted in Hans Hecht, *Thomas Percy und William Shenstone*, pp. xxii-xxiv.

89. *Ancient Songs Chiefly on Moorish Subjects*. Ed. D. Nichol Smith.

90. See note 88.

91. The quotation from the Preface to the *Reliques* (1765), I, x. The fullest account of Percy's plans is in Heinz Marwell, *Thomas Percy*. See also Cleanth Brooks, "The History of Percy's Edition of Surrey's Poems," *Englische Studien*, LXVIII (1934), 434, and V. H. Ogburn, "Thomas Percy's Unfinished Collection *Ancient English and Scottish Poems*," *ELH*, III (1936), 183.

92. "Of the Origin of Poetry in general," Introduction, p. ii.

93. "Of Poetry," *Poems on Several Occasions* (1700), p. 176.

94. *Characteristics*, ed. Robertson, I, 160.
95. *Praelectiones Poeticae* (1711), quoted from *Lectures on Poetry* (1742). Lect. II, pp. 27, 30, 173 ff., 203, etc.
96. Blair, p. 2.
97. Lowth, *loc. cit.*, p. 190.
98. The question of authorship is discussed by Caroline F. Tupper in *PMLA*, XXXIX (1924), 325 ff. Cf. R. S. Crane, *New Essays of Oliver Goldsmith*, Introduction, and O. Elton, *Survey of English Literature, 1730–1780*, I, 394.
99. *Works*, ed. P. Cunningham (1854), III, 302-307.
100. *A Poetical Dictionary of the Beauties of English Poetry* (1761), p. 1.
101. Duff (1767), p. 270.
102. In *Poems Consisting Chiefly of Translations from the Asiatick Languages* (Second ed., 1777), pp. 193, 194, 195, 200.
103. Blair, p. 3.
104. *Muses' Library* (1737), p. 1.
105. *Characteristics*, ed. Robertson, I, 161.
106. See above, pp. 39, 41-42.
107. *Essays and Treatises*, I, 139, 141.
108. Goldsmith, *Present State . . .* , pp. 10-11, 74-75, 77. Echoes of this view about the necessary decline of the arts can be found, e.g., in Joseph Priestley's *Lectures on History and General Policy.* (1826. First ed. 1788, based on lectures given in the sixties.)
109. Letter LXIII, *Works*, ed. Cunningham, II, 319-320.
110. Kames, *Sketches*, I, 155-156, 158, 162. Kames must have seen Winckelmann in the French translation of Sellius (1766).
111. Preface by Dugald Stewart to *Essays on Philosophical Subjects* (1795), pp. xli-xlii.
112. See John Rae, *Life of Adam Smith*, pp. 30-34. Blair in his *Lectures* (I, 381) refers to an unpublished MS by A. Smith, to which he is indebted for remarks on plain and simple style. Blair has been suspected of taking more from these lectures, but there is nothing in Blair's *Lectures* which would make such borrowing necessary or likely. A fuller description of Smith's lectures held later at Glasgow (though probably based on the early course), can be found in a recently published letter by J. Wodrow (see W. R. Scott, *A. Smith as Student and Professor*, pp. 51-52) which would confirm the view that these lectures were entirely rhetorical.
113. Two papers "Of the Nature of that Imitation which takes place in what are called the Imitative Arts" and "Of the Affinity be-

tween Music, Dancing and Poetry," in *Essays on Philosophical Subjects* (1795), pp. 133 ff., 179 ff. W. R. Scott in *Adam Smith* prints letters showing that the first and second parts of the "Essays on the Imitative Arts" were composed as lectures for the Literary Society of Glasgow, while the third (on Dancing) which was left unfinished, must have been written about 1776 or 1777. See pp. 283, 311-312.

114. See also Brown's *History of the Rise and Progress of Poetry through its several Species* (1764). This is an abridgment of the *Dissertation* for the "sake of such classical readers as are not particular conversant with music." There are, however, new chapters on the pastoral and the lesser kinds of poetry in ancient Greece. All the quotations in this text are from the *Dissertation*.

115. Cf. Konrad Burdach, "Schillers Chordrama," *Vorspiel, Gesammelte Schriften*, II, (1926), 116 ff.

116. *Essay on the Characteristics* (1751), especially pp. 375 ff.

117. Gregory, p. 126-163.

118. Webb, pp. 66, 70-1, 110, 130, 132.

119. *Some Specimens of the Poetry of the Ancient Welsh Bards* (1764) quotes a commission by Queen Elizabeth from Brown.

120. Percy, "Essay on the Ancient Metrical Romances," *Reliques* (1765), ed. H. B. Wheatley, p. 340.

121. The same idea before is in Abbé d'Aubigné's *Conjectures Académiques ou Dissertation sur l'Iliade* (1715).

122. Wood's *Homer*, pp. 167, 169.

123. 1767. Section VII, "Of the History of the Arts," p. 257, Section VIII, "Of the History of Literature," pp. 262-276, especially pp. 264-265.

124. W. C. Lehmann in *A. Ferguson and the Beginnings of Modern Sociology* seems to overrate him considerably, while Leslie Stephen's account in the *History of English Thought* (II, 214) is very inadequate.

125. *An Essay towards a Real Character and a Philosophical Language* (1668).

126. *A Treatise Concerning the Principles of Human Knowledge* (1710), in *Works*, ed. A. C. Fraser, I, p. 154.

127. *De Augmentis*, Liber VI, capitola I.

128. E. g., "French poetry is only pure prose in rhyme." Rev. P. Kilvert, *Memoirs . . . of . . . R. Hurd* (1860), p. 302. Earlier examples are in R. H. Wollstein's *English Opinions of French Poetry, 1660–1750*.

129. Gregory Smith, *Elizabethan Critical Essays*, II, 154.

130. Spingarn, *Seventeenth Century Critical Essays*, I, 41.

131. *The Literary Magazine*, II (1758), pp. 56, 102, 149, 197. The essays are probably by Goldsmith, as the later article "An Account of the Augustan Age in England" in the *Bee* (Nov. 24, 1759) simply transcribes long sections. See, however, R. W. Seitz, "Goldsmith and the *Literary Magazine*," *RES*, V (1929), 410.

132. Locke's *Essay of Human Understanding*, ed. A. C. Fraser, I, 384-385; II, 48-49.

133. *Hermes* (1751), Book II, Chap. V, pp. 407-408.

134. *Concerning Art to the Right Hon. the Earl of Shaftesbury*, pp. 4-5.

135. Diogenes Laertius, Liber X, section 24, paragraph 75. Lucretius, *De Rerum Natura*, Liber V, ll. 1026 ff.

136. *The Fable of the Bees* (second part, 1728), ed. Kaye, II, 286.

137. Blackwell, p. 38. He refers to Diodorus Siculus. See also pp. 40, 41, 42, 43, 57.

138. *The Divine Legation of Moses* (1741). Also in *Works*, ed. Hurd, 1811, IV, pp. 116, 133, 137-138, 170. He also refers to Diodorus Siculus, Liber II, and Vitruvius, Liber II, capitola 1.

139. *Hermes*, p. 410.

140. Lowth, *Lectures*, p. 101.

141. Blair, p. 2.

142. Duff, p. 267.

143. *Sketches of the History of Man* (1774), I, 107-108.

144. *Observations on the Correspondence between Poetry and Music* (1769), pp. 66, 70-71, 155.

145. *Spectator*, No. 411.

146. Welsted, *op. cit.*, p. x.

147. Preface to the *Dictionary* (1755, fourth ed. 1773), p. E.

148. 1762, Lecture XII, pp. 169, 176, 184, etc.

149. J. Swift, *A Proposal for Correcting, Improving and Ascertaining the English Tongue* (1712), in *Prose Works*, ed. Temple Scott, XI, 1.

150. *Works*, ed. R. Lynam, V, (1825), 48.

151. From Pope's *Essay on Criticism*, II, line 283.

152. First published appendix to the third edition of the *Theory of Moral Sentiments* (1767). W. R. Scott in *Adam Smith* argues that the essay could have been written only shortly before its publication, as it refers to Rousseau.

153. From seventh ed. (1792), II, 462.

154. Second ed., I, 443-444. On Monboddo, see especially A. O. Lovejoy, "Monboddo and Rousseau," *MP*, XXX (1933), 275.

CHAPTER FOUR

1. "Corrective" criticism in James Harris, *Upon the Rise and Progress of Criticism* (1752), Chap. V, reprinted in *Philological Inquiries* (1781).
2. I am aware that the Folios as well as Rowe's edition show some editorial care which could be described as textual criticism. (See M. W. Black and M. A. Shaaber, *Shakespeare's Seventeenth Century Editors.*) The novelty was in the collation of the quartos and not merely in the guesswork of an editor.
3. Quoted from Ronald B. McKerrow, *The Treatment of Shakespeare's Text by his Earlier Editors*, p. 21.
4. Morgann (1777), p. 16.
5. *Works*, ed. Lynam, V, 95.
6. Farmer (1767), p. 49.
7. Johnson's dedication to the Earl of Orrery of *Shakspear Illustrated* (1753), p. xi.
8. An exception could be made for Daniel Webb's comments on Shakespeare's verse and metaphor in his *Remarks on the Beauties of Poetry* (1762).
9. Kames, *Sketches of the History of Man* (1774), I, 113. See also *The Universal Magazine* (1776), quoted by R. W. Babcock, *The Genesis of Shakespeare Idolatry*, p. 188, who does not recognize the source.
10. J. Hughes on *Othello* in the *Guardian*, No. 37 (1713); Theobald on *Lear* in the *Censor*, No. 7-10 (1715). See D. Nichol Smith, *Shakespeare in the Eighteenth Century*, and Babcock, *loc. cit.*
11. *An Enquiry into the Learning of Shakespeare* (1748).
12. Jonson, I, iv.
13. Massinger, *Dramatic Works* (1761), I, 7.
14. See Austin Warren, "Pope's index to Beaumont and Fletcher," *Modern Language Notes* (hereafter cited as *MLN*), XLVI (1931), 515.
15. Nichols, *Literary Anecdotes*, I, 386. This may be Nichol's error.

16. *Works of Mr. F. Beaumont and Mr. J. Fletcher* (1750), I, lviii.
17. Bentley as quoted by J. Harris in *Upon the Rise and Progress of Criticism* (1752), p. 16.
18. Seward, *loc. cit.*, p. lix.
19. *A General History of the Stage*, pp. 17-18.
20. Spence, p. 21. Pope read *Gorboduc* in a copy lent to him by the elder Warton. See Pope's *Works*, ed. Elwin and Courthope, IX, 67-68.
21. See Beers, Phelps, De Maar, Cory, etc.
22. *Letters on Chivalry and Romance*, ed. E. Morley, p. 115.
23. *Ibid.*, p. 118.
24. *Ibid.*, p. 122.
25. *Ibid.*, p. 116.
26. Dryden and Pope, however, discussed the *Shepherd's Calendar* as a type of pastoral poetry. Dryden, *Works*, ed. Saintsbury and Scott, XIII, 324-325; Pope's *Discourse of Pastoral Poetry*.
27. "The True Picture of Love" and "A Receipt to Make a Cuckold." Neither of these poems is in Grosart's or Feuillerat's editions of Sidney's *Poems*.
28. *The Quintessence of English Poetry* (1740), praised, e.g., by H. Headley, *Select Beauties* (1787), is merely a reprint of the *British Muse*.
29. See R. H. Perkinson, "The Polemical Use of Davies's *Nosce Teipsum*," *SP*, XXXVI (1939), 597.
30. S. Daniel, *The Poetical Works* (1718), p. x.
31. *Amores Britannici* (1703), A 5ᵛ.
32. The "Essay" is not by Oldys as stated in the *DNB* (Oldys). The folio of 1748 was edited by Charles Coffey, as proved by John Mottley's "Compleat List of all the English Dramatick Poets" in Thomas Whincop's *Scanderbeg* (1747, p. 207). Oldys in his "Life of Drayton," in *Biographia Britannica*, III (1750), p. 1745, n. D., distinguishes between Drayton's "Late Editor" (Coffey died in 1745) and "The Author of the Preliminary Discourse." This seems to point to an unknown author of the "Essay"; it is unlikely that Oldys wrote it because it is completely different, both in style and content, from his later "Life of Drayton."
33. *The Polite Correspondence* (1741), p. 278. Letter to Warburton, Nov. 27, 1742, in *Works*, ed. Elwin and Courthope, IX, 225; *The Citizen of the World*, Letter XIII, in Cunningham's ed. of the *Works*, II, 133.
34. Tusser, 1710, Churchyard, 1776, W. Browne, ed. T. Davies, 1772, Fairfax, 1726, 1749. Hall, ed. W. Thompson, 1753. Marston's *Scourge of Villanie*, ed. J. Bowle in *Miscellaneous Pieces of An-*

cient English Poesie, 1764. Phineas Fletcher, ed. Lord Wood-houselee (1771).

35. See Earl R. Wasserman, "Elizabethan Poetry 'Improved,' " *MP,* XXXVII (1940), 357. Similar editorial practices were common. See M. D. Black and M. A. Shaaber, *Shakespeare's Seventeenth Century Editors* for evidence in anthologies.

35a. Cf. A. H. Nethercot, "The Reputation of the Metaphysical Poets during the Age of Pope," *PQ,* IV (1925), 163, "The Reputation of the Metaphysical Poets during the Age of Johnson and the Romantic Revival," *SP,* XXII (1925), 81, and "The Reputation of Donne as Metrist," *Sewanee Review,* XXX (1922), 463-474. The following details are derived from these articles.

35b. Warton, *History,* III, Appendix, p. 50. The imitation of "Go and catch a falling star" is in the *London Magazine,* X (June, 1741), 301. Cf. Hurd's Horace (1751), II, 97-99, and Warburton's edition of Pope (1751), IV, 241.

36. Cleanth Brooks, "The History of Percy's Edition of Surrey's Poems," *Englische Studien,* LVIII (1934), 424.

37. *Epistle to Augustus,* lines 37-38.

38. There is a Latin edition, Glasgow 1750, and Burnet's translation was reprinted in 1737, 1743, 1751, 1758, 1762, etc. Warner's *Memoirs* were printed with the 1758 ed.

39. Gibbon, *Miscellaneous Works* (1796), I, 107-108. The entry in Gibbon's journal is dated July 26, 1762.

40. Dodsley, p. xlvi. The *DNB* ascribes the Preface to Dodsley himself and to Sir Clement Cotterel Dormer, to whom the collection was dedicated. R. Straus, *Richard Dodsley,* pp. 63-64, considers it the work of Dodsley alone.

41. See list in W. B. C. Watkins, *Johnson and English Poetry before 1660.*

42. Quoted first in Sir John Hawkins's *Life of Dr. Johnson* (1787), p. 82.

43. Letter of Thomas Warton to Hurd, Oct. 22, 1762, *Bodleian Quarterly Record,* VI (1932), 303 ff.

44. The passages on Chaucer, praised by C. Spurgeon (in *Chaucer devant la critique*), from George Sewell and others seem singularly unimpressive.

44a. Thynne, *Animadversions,* p. 43. The arguments in favor of Thomas Warton as the discoverer of Chaucer's source given by Miss Rinaker (*Thomas Warton,* p. 88n) are unconvincing.

45. One of the authors of the French *Roman de la Rose,* Jean de Meung, was considered an Englishman by Bale (*Catalogus* 1557, Second part, p. 58, "Joannes Mone: Anglus Natione").

This view was repeated as late as 1707 by the author of the "Old English Poets and Poetry," who calls him "John Moon."

46. Spence, *Anecdotes*, ed. Singer (1820), p. 20.

47. *The Muses' Library* (1737), p. 19.

48. *The Dictionary* (4th ed., 1773), I, F^r. This error originated in Leland who misinterpreted a passage in Gower's *Confessio Amantis*. It was already pointed out and corrected by F. Thynne in his *Animadversions*, ed. Furnivall, p. 19.

49. *Muses' Library*, p. 7.

50. *Ibid.*, p. 8.

51. Cibber, I, p. 18.

52. Percy, *Reliques* (1765), III, 261.

53. 1725, 1727. Reprinted by David Caskey from the Cotton MS (Titus CXVII).

54. The transcripts are now in possession of Mr. James M. Osborn, New Haven, Conn.

55. Leah Dennis, "Percy's Essay on the Ancient Metrical Romances," *PMLA*, XLIX (1934), 81-97.

56. Cf. E. Hammond, *Chaucer: A Bibliographical Manual*, pp. 406 ff.

57. *Muses' Library*, p. 30.

58. Preface to the *Dictionary* (4th ed. 1773), I, G.

59. *Muses' Library*, p. 31.

60. Cibber, I, 26.

61. Edited by John Fortescue-Aland (1714). Cf. *The British Librarian* (ed. W. Oldys, 1738), No. 4, and Johnson's Preface to the *Dictionary*.

62. Ames, p. 43. The Prologue and the titles of the books are quoted with the conclusion mentioning Sir Thomas Maleore (sic).

63. See W. Geddie, *A Bibliography of Middle Scots Poets*, p. lix. The MS is in the Advocates' Library, Edinburgh. Some materials are in *Catalogues of Scotish Writers*, ed. J. Maidment, (1833).

64. Geddie, p. lx.

65. *A Description of May* was published separately in 1752, *A Description of Winter* in 1754. Both are in *Original Poems and Translations* (1761). There is another very free paraphrase of the May prologue by Jerome Stone in *Scots Magazine*, XVII (1756), 294.

66. *Polite Correspondence*, pp. 301-302.

67. Thomas Gray, *Works*, (1843), V, 36, from *Reminiscences of Gray by the Rev. Norton Nicholls*, and William P. Jones, "Thomas Gray's Library," *MP*, XXXV (1938), 257.

68. Warton recommends to Dalrymple "a task, for which he is well qualified, The History of Scottish Poetry." *History of English Poetry*, II, 278.

69. Dodsley's Preface, p. xiii.

70. Oct., 1762, quoted in Hans Hecht, *Thomas Percy und William Shenstone*, p. 86.

71. *Muses' Library*, p. 1.

72. Joseph Ritson, in *Bibliographia Poetica*, pp. 54-55, notes that the poem is a translation, apparently by Robert Fabian, from a Latin poem, preserved and possibly written by Henry, Archdeacon of Huntingdon, inserted in Fabian's history. Substantially the same information can be found in Ritson's letter to J. C. Walker (June 24, 1794), first quoted in B. H. Bronson's *Joseph Ritson*, I, 237-238.

73. S. Johnson, Preface to the *Dictionary* (4th ed., 1773), I, E 2.

74. Warton, *History of English Poetry*, I, 209.

75. *Ibid.*, I, vi.

76. Hickes, *Thesaurus*, II, 218-219.

77. A pamphlet, *Testimonies of Learned Men in favour of the Intended Edition of Saxon Homilies* (1713), and some proofs of the edition are in the British Museum (Press-mark 695 1.8). The MS is in the Landsdown Collection (370-374).

78. Quotations from Margaret Ashdown, "Elizabeth Elstob, the learned Saxonist," *Modern Language Review* (hereafter cited as *MLR*), XX (1925), 125.

79. *Polite Correspondence*, pp. 235, 261, 268-273, 277-278.

80. *Archeologia*, Vol. V (1779), Vol. IX (1789).

81. Camden's *Britannia* (Second ed. of Gibson's translation. 1722), Dedication.

82. Preface to the *Dictionary* (4th ed., 1773), I, E.

83. See Thomas Gray, *Essays and Criticisms*, ed. E. S. Northup, p. 85, and see especially William Powell Jones, *Thomas Gray, Scholar*.

84. Thomas Percy, *Reliques* (1765), III, 261. See Warton's "Of the Origin of Romantic Fiction," *History*, I, e3ᵛ-e4ᵛ, 2.

85. For a discussion of the merits of these collections see Sigurd B. Hustvedt, *Ballad Criticism in Scandinavia and Great Britain During the 18th Century*. Hustvedt suggests that Ambrose Philips who had been to Denmark (in 1709) had seen the Danish collections of ballads. But Lillian de la Torre-Bueno has brought forward telling arguments against Philips's connection with that publication. (See *Anglia*, LIX (1935), 252.) See also Grace R.

Tennery, "Ballad Collections of the 18th century," in *MLR*, V (1915), 283.

86. At the end of Preface to *Gulielmi Newbrigiensis Historia* (1719).

87. See introduction to *Songs from David Herd's Manuscripts*, ed. H. Hecht. Percy had access to Herd's MS collections and wanted to utilize them in his projected *Ancient English and Scottish Poems*. See V. H. Ogburn, "Thomas Percy's Unfinished Collection," *ELH*, III (1936), 183.

88. Hawkins, II, 93, with the music.

89. See Paul Van Tieghem, *Le Préromantisme*, Vol. 1. See also F. E. Farley, *Scandinavian Influences in the English Romantic Movement*, and J. A. W. Bennett, "The Beginnings of Norse Studies in England," *Saga-book of the Viking Society for Northern Research*, XII (1937), 35-42.

90. "Of Heroic Virtue," *Works*, III (1757), 358.

91. However, two "ancient Danish Odes" in the *Polite Correspondence* (1741), pp. 293-295, should be added. Though they claim to be translations from Wormius and Saxo Grammaticus respectively, they seem free improvisations in eighteenth-century style which have only very remote connection with any actual Icelandic poetry. These two pieces were reprinted, with only slight changes, by John Logan, in that curious production called Michael Bruce's *Poems on Several Occasions* (1770). As neither Logan nor Bruce was yet born when the *Polite Correspondence* was published, one cannot help suspecting Logan of appropriating Campbell's work to swell the number of poems ascribed to his dead friend Bruce.

92. Hickes, I, 193-195; Husbands, *op. cit.*, Preface, sig. *c*ᵛ.; Blair in the *Dissertation on Ossian*, and Goldsmith on the *Present State of Polite Learning*.

93. Percy, "Preface," sig. *A 8* and *A 8*ᵛ.

94. The poems can be best identified by referring to their places in Vigfusson and York Powell's *Corpus Poeticum Boreale*, "Ragnar Lodbrok," II, 341; "Egil's Ransom," I, 267; "The Incantation of Hervor," I, 164; "The Funeral of Hacon," I, 262; "The Complaint of Harold," II, 228.

95. Percy, "Preface," sig. *A 4*ᵛ, *A 8*.

96. See J. A. W. Bennett, *loc. cit.*

97. See W. P. Jones, *Thomas Gray, Scholar*. See also G. L. Kittredge's "Gray's Knowledge of Old Norse," in W. L. Phelps' *Selections from Gray*, pp. 90-99.

98. See Jones, *op. cit.*, and E. B. Howe, "The Idealised Bard of the

18th Century," *Abstracts of Theses*, University of Chicago, Humanistic Series, VI (1927–1928).

99. *Polite Correspondence*, p. 248. One of these poems was reprinted in the *European Magazine*, VII (1785), 382, as the work of John Campbell.

100. See again Jones on Gray, and Edward D. Snyder, *The Celtic Revival in English Literature, 1760–1800*. See also Saunders Lewis, *A School of Welsh Antiquarians*, and W. J. Hughes, *Wales and the Welsh in English Literature*.

101. John J. Parry, "Dr. Johnson's Interest in Welsh," *MLN* (1921), 374.

102. See Heinz Marwell, "Percy und die Ossian-kontroverse," *Anglia*, VIII (1934), 392, and W. J. Hughes, *op. cit.*, pp. 165 ff.

103. See O. Jiriczek, "Jerome Stone's Ballade Albion and the Daughter of May, published in 1756," *Englische Studien*, XLIV (1912), 193 ff. Stone wrote a Letter in praise of Gavin Douglas (1755). On A. Pope, see L. C. Stern, "Die ossianischen Heldenlieder," *Zeitschrift für vergleichende Literaturgeschichte*, NF, VIII, 82 ff.

104. Blackwell, *Homer*, p. 41, n.

105. *Reliques*, I, 318.

106. See Introduction to the ed. by David Nichol Smith.

107. *The Compleat Art of Poetry* (1718), I, 74-75, etc.

108. *Pleasures of Imagination* (First ed., 1744), p. 48, n.

109. *The General Review of Foreign Literature* (1775), pp. 6-7. The editor was Thomas Winstanley (1749–1823), see *DNB*.

110. See Roderick Marshall, *Italy in English Literature*; Paget Toynbee, *Dante in English Literature*. See also L. F. Powell, "W. Huggins, and Tobias Smollet," *MP*, XXXIV (1936–1937), 179.

111. Joseph Warton, *Essay on Pope* (4th ed., 1783), I, 266.

112. *Present State*, p. 45. The Earl of Chesterfield wrote to his son that he was fully convinced that "Dante was not worth the pains necessary to understand him." (Feb. 8, O. S. 1750, *Letters*, ed. Dobrée, IV, 1504). Horace Walpole found Dante "extravagant, absurd, disgusting, in short a Methodist parson in Bedlam." (Letter to W. Mason, June 25, 1782, *Letters*, ed. P. Toynbee, XII, 274).

113. *Poems consisting chiefly of translations from the Asiatick Languages*. Second ed., 1777, Preface, p. xi.

114. *Ibid.*, pp. 176-188.

115. *A Specimen of Persian Poetry or Odes of Hafez* (1774).

116. Lady Mary Montagu, *Letters and Works*, I, 180.

117. Shan Yi Chan, "The Influence of China on English Culture during the 18th Century," *Abstracts of Theses,* University of Chicago, Humanistic Series, VII (1928–1929), 537. Percy's translation of the *Chinese Orphan* from Du Halde is in *Miscellaneous Pieces* (1762). Goldsmith reviewed Murphy's translation of the play from Voltaire's adaptation, in the *Critical Review,* May, 1759. Hurd in his *Discourse on Poetical Imitation* (1751) sees resemblances of the plot to the *Electra* of Sophocles and an unconscious following of Aristotle's rules. See also Kames, not noticed by Shan Yi Chan, in *Sketches of the History of Man* (1774), I, 108-109. Here the *Chinese Orphan* is disparaged as "languid" and this character ascribed to the peaceful and stagnant nature of Chinese society.

118. *Hau Kiou Choaan* (1761), and *Miscellaneous Pieces Relating to the Chinese* (1762). On the sources see Alda Milner-Barry and L. F. Powell, "A Further Note on Hau Kiou Choaan," *RES,* III (1927), 218. The novel was translated into English by James Wilkinson. A part in Portuguese was translated by Percy. The poetry comes from Du Halde's *Description . . . de la Chine* (1735).

119. F. E. Farley, "The Dying Indian," *Anniversary Papers by Colleagues and Pupils of G. L. Kittredge,* p. 251. See also note on p. 137 of Farley's *Scandinavian Influences;* H. B. Jones, "The Death Song of the Noble Savage," *Abstracts of Theses,* University of Chicago, Humanistic Series, III (1924–1925), and William Preston, *Poetical Works* (1793), II, 14.

120. Webb's *Observations,* pp. 95-98. An abridgment is in Purchas (1625).

121. *Spectator,* No. 366, April 30, 1712.

122. F. E. Farley, "Three Lapland Songs," *PMLA,* XXI, N. S. XIV (1906), 1 ff.

CHAPTER FIVE

1. *Poems on Several Occasions* (1700).
2. In *The Flower Piece. A Collection of Miscellany Poems by Several Hands* (1731).
3. Cf. first edition (1743) with version in Dodsley's *Collection* (1755), IV, 64. For Collins' plan of a "History of the Revival of Learning" see Warton's *History*, II, 350.
4. Note to Book II, p. 48 of first edition.
5. These names derived from Wood. See William T. Davies, "Thomas Tanner and his *Bibliotheca*," *TLS* (Dec., 1935), p. 856.
6. (1708), I, xiii.
7. See J. M. Osborn, "Thomas Birch and the *General Dictionary*, (1734-41)," *MP*, XXXVI (1938), 25.
8. See note in Sir W. Raleigh's *Six Essays on Johnson*, p. 125, furnished by David Nichol Smith.
9. I, 16-17.
10. Advertisement.
11. Letter to Boswell, May 3, 1777. *Life*, ed. Hill, III, 124.
12. Boswell's *Life*, ed. Hill, IV, 473 and II, 48 n.
13. *Lives of the English Poets*, ed. B. Hill, I, 455.
14. *Ibid.*, I, 121.
15. *Ibid.*, II, 148. Johnson condemns *Hardyknute* (Boswell II, 91) and ridiculed an antiquarian proudly displaying "a copy of the *Children in the Wood*, which he firmly believed to be of the first edition." (Rambler, 177.)
16. *Ibid.*, I, 293.
17. *Ibid.*
18. *Ibid.*, I, 75.
19. *Ibid.*, I, 77.
20. *Ibid.*, I, 251.
21. *Ibid.*, I, 61.
22. *Ibid.*, I, 469.
23. *Ibid.*, I, 420.

24. *Ibid.*, I, 468.
25. *Ibid.*, II, 251.
26. *Ibid.*, II, 145.
27. *Ibid.*, I, 235.
28. *Ibid.*, II, 208.
29. *Ibid.*, I, 18.
30. *Ibid.*, I, 411.
31. *Ibid.*, I, 438.
32. *Ibid.*, I, 318.
33. *Ibid.*, I, 288.
34. *Ibid.*, III, 238 and 240.
35. *Ibid.*, I, 137.
36. *Ibid.*, III, 239.
37. *Ibid.*, I, 421.
38. *Ibid.*, III, 316-18.
39. *Ibid.*, I, 410.
40. *Ibid.*, III, 159.
41. *Ibid.*, II, 219-21.
42. *Ibid.*, III, 176.
43. *Ibid.*, III, 114-5 and III, 236-7.
44. *Ibid.*, I, 192.
45. *Ibid.*, I, 466.
46. *Ibid.*
47. *Ibid.*, I, 295.
48. *Ibid.*, I, 415-6.
49. *Ibid.*, I, 22.
50. *Ibid.*, I, 41-42.
51. *Ibid.*, I, 46.
52. *Ibid.*, II, 207-8.
53. *Ibid.*, III, 225.
54. *Ibid.*, I, 124.
55. *Ibid.*, III, 125-6.
56. *Ibid.*, III, 162 and III, 177-78.
57. For a fuller discussion of Johnson's acquaintance with older English poetry see W. B. C. Watkins, *Johnson and English Poetry before 1660* (Princeton, 1936) and consult the useful compilation of passages in J. E. Brown's *The Critical Opinions of Samuel Johnson* (Princeton, 1926).
58. See Oldys' Diary quoted by James Yeowell in *A Literary Antiquary: Memoir of W. O., Esq.* London. 1862. p. 1. One circumstance speaks also against the exclusive authorship of Oldys. Mrs. Cooper (p. 31) complains that she was never able to attain a sight of Occleve's *De Regimine Principis*. Oldys' diary mentions that a

friend (James West) had shown him this very book in 1735. (See Oldys' notes in his copy of Winstanley, printed in *Notes and Queries*, 2nd series, XI, 181.)

59. Preface, p. ix.
60. Vol. I, Preface, p. ix.
61. Both quotations from J. B. Black, *The Art of History*, p. 115.
62. *The History of England* (1879), IV, Appendix III, 233-234.
63. *Ibid.*, pp. 397 ff.
64. *Ibid.*, V, 462 ff.
65. *Ibid.*, VI, 345 ff.
66. Henry, *History of Great Britain* I (1771), iii.
67. *Ibid.*, pp. 352-367.
68. *Ibid.*, II (1774), 425-432.
69. Vol. VII of Shakespeare's *Works* (1710), p. lxvi.
70. Preface, I, iii, viii, etc.
71. Shakespeare's *Works,* ed. Warburton (1747), V, 265, a note to *Richard III*, Act III, Scene 1.
72. Letter to E. Evans, March 20, 1764 quoted in H. Marwell, *Thomas Percy*, p. 56.
73. I, 118 ff.
74. Preface, pp. i-xvi.
75. Other ostensible histories of the drama can be described. The *History of the English Stage* (1741), ascribed to Thomas Betterton, is a collection of biographies and anecdotes on post-Restoration actors and actresses. "An Essay on the Antient and Modern Drama" in William Hawkins's *Dramatic and other Poems, Letters, Essays* (Oxford, 1758) contains no historical matter. "The British Theatre" in the *London Magazine* of 1767 (XXXVI, 265) contains a sketch of the older drama, largely compiled from Dodsley's introduction, and the "History of the English Drama, Till the Time of Shakespeare" in the same periodical (1773, XCII, 632), is an abridgment of Thomas Hawkins, without any acknowledgment to its source.
76. In *Essays upon Several Subjects* (1716).
77. *Spectator*, No. 273, Jan. 12, 1712.
78. Richard Hurd, *Works* (1811), II, 19, from the "Idea of Universal Poetry."
79. *Sketches of the History of Man* (1774), I, 107-108.
80. *The Compleat Art of Poetry* (1718), I, 75.
81. Vol. I, "communicated by a learned writer well known in the literary world." See Pope's delighted letter in John Selby Watson's *Life of William Warburton* (1863), p. 209. Warburton's article is reprinted in *Works* of Shakespeare (1747), Vol. II,

after p. 288, as note to *Love's Labour's Lost*, Act I, Scene 1. Tyrwhitt, *Supplement to the Edition of Shakespeare's Plays.* . . . (1780), I, 373.

82. Warton's letter to Percy, September 4, 1762, in Leah Dennis, "The Text of the Percy-Warton Letters," *PMLA*, XLVI (1931), 1166 ff.

83. Boswell, *Life of Johnson*, ed. Birckbeck Hill, I, 57, 562.

84. A copy of Munday's translation (1590) in the British Museum contains a note in Farmer's hand pointing to its omission in Ames and to a note on Munday by Hearne. (Press-mark C. 57. e. 30).

85. P. Toynbee, "Gray on the origin and date of *Amadis de Gaul*," in *MLR*, XXVIII (1932), 60-61.

86. *Archeologia*, Vol. IV (1786), paper XII (read Dec. 1, 1774).

87. Letter to Dalrymple, September 8, 1763; see Leah Dennis, "Percy's *Essay On the Ancient Metrical Romances*," *PMLA*, XLIX (1934), 81-97.

88. III, 1.

89. H. Marwell, *Thomas Percy*, pp. 60-61.

90. I, 70-71.

91. III, line 153.

92. "Printed in the year 1752, from the MSS. of J. H. of S. in the County of W." Also in *Philological Inquiries* (1781).

93. See Sir John Hawkins, *Life of Samuel Johnson* (1787), pp. 81-82.

94. See H. Marwell, *Thomas Percy*. The correspondence has not been printed.

95. II, 260-268.

96. Section X, pp. 168 ff.

97. Commonplace Book, II, 805, quoted in W. P. Jones, *Thomas Gray, Scholar*, pp. 94-95.

98. Among the papers of Joseph Spence, now in the possession of James M. Osborn of Yale University, is the MS of a short history of English poetry. It is written in French, presumably by Spence for the instruction of one of the young noblemen whom he accompanied on the grand tour in the 1730's. The "History of English Poetry" in the *Court Magazine* (1761) was inaccessible.

99. Vol. I, No. 6 (June, 1707), p. 127.

100. E. K. Broadus in "Addison's Influence on the Development of Interest in Folk-poetry in the Eighteenth Century," *MP*, VIII (July, 1910), 123-134, suggests Steele. R. P. McCutcheon, "Addison and the *Muses' Mercury*," *SP*, XX (1923), 17, pleads more convincingly for Oldmixon.

101. *Loc. cit.*, p. 133.

102. Gildon, I, 83.

103. *A Miscellany of Poems by Several Hands* (1731), Preface, p. d2ᵛ.

104. *The Muses' Library*, pp. ix, xi, xvi, 1.

105. See A. D. McKillop, "A Critic of 1741 on Early Poetry," *SP*, XXX (1933), 504. Mr. McKillop establishes the date and assigns the book to John Campbell (1708–1775), a prolific miscellaneous writer. The ascription becomes certain if we note the title-page of a new edition in 1754, *The Rational Amusement, with a preface by the Author of the Memoirs of the Duke de Ripperda.* (See *DNB* under Campbell.) The preface clearly speaks of its author as the writer of the whole book. The text is reprinted unchanged. The book had been pointed out by D. Nichol Smith in *Warton's History of English Poetry*, pp. 14–15.

106. *Polite Correspondence*, pp. 235, 236, 292, 311, 313.

107. In Owen Ruffhead, *Life of A. Pope* (1769), p. 425.

108. Letter, dated April 15, 1770, in the *Gentleman's Magazine*, Feb., 1783, pp. 100–101, or in *Correspondence*, ed. P. Toynbee and L. Whibley, III, 1122–1125.

109. Cf. W. P. Jones, *Thomas Gray, Scholar*, 1937. For Warton's answer to Gray, April 20, 1770, see the following chapter on Warton, above, p. 172.

CHAPTER SIX

1. A copy of the 1617 folio (Press-mark C. 28. 4.7.).
2. *Observations* (2nd ed., 1762), II, 262. There is a slightly different text in 1st ed. (1754), p. 310.
3. First ed., p. 13.
4. Second ed., I, 15.
5. *Ibid.*
6. See R. D. Havens, "Thomas Warton and the Eighteenth Century Dilemma," *SP*, XXV (1928), pp. 36 ff.
7. *Observations,* 1st ed., p. 217.
8. *Ibid.*
9. *Ibid.*, p. 227.
10. *Ibid.*, p. 233.
11. Second ed., II, 101.
12. *Ibid.*, p. 111.
13. *Ibid.*, p. 267.
14. *Ibid.*, pp. 267-268.
15. *Ibid.*, p. 268.
16. First ed., p. 3.
17. Second ed., I, 1.
18. *Ibid.*, II, 101, note.
19. "Correspondence between Warton and Hurd," *Bodleian Quarterly Record*, VI (1929–1931), 303 ff.
20. *Ibid.*
21. *Ibid.*, dated Dec. 25, 1763.
22. See Leah Dennis, "The Text of the Percy-Warton Letters," *PMLA*, XLVI (Dec., 1931), 1166. Letter dated June 15, 1765.
23. *Ibid.*, Oct. 24, 1768.
24. *Ibid.*, p. 1192, letter dated July 4, 1769.
25. See, e.g., Thomas Gray's *Correspondence*, ed. P. Toynbee and L. Whibley, pp. 1128-1130. Letter dated April 20, 1770.
26. Dennis, *op. cit.*, letter dated Sept. 13, 1770.

27. Letter to Hurd in the *Bodleian Quarterly*, *loc. cit.*, dated Jan. 17, 1772.
28. A letter to Price, August 16, 1773, quoted by C. Rinaker, *Thomas Warton*, p. 82.
28a. Thomas Caldecott sent the "unpublished part" of Warton's *History* to Thomas Percy in 1803 (Nichols, *Illustrations*, VIII, 372). There are no means to ascertain what the MS contained.
29. *Ibid.*, p. 83.
30. *The History of English Poetry*, (1st ed.), Preface, p. v.
31. Miss Rinaker, *op. cit.*, gives a valuable list of the sources to which Warton refers.
32. *History*, I, p. 25.
33. *Ibid.*, III, 107-108. Thus Ker (*Essays*, I, 92) is mistaken when he says that Warton never found the *Pearl*.
34. *Observations on the Three First Volumes of the History of English Poetry* (1782), p. 47. Also, the Preface to the new ed. of the *History* by W. C. Hazlitt (1871) calls Warton "excessively indolent, equally careless . . . in many essential respects incompetent for his self-appointed task." (p. viii.)
35. *History*, I, 208.
36. *Ibid.*, Preface, p. v.
37. *Miscellaneous Prose Works*, XVII (1835), 96. Article on Todd's ed. of Spenser originally in *Edinburgh Review*, 1805.
38. Ritson, *Observations*, p. 48.
39. Quotations from Ker's lecture on Warton (*Essays*, I, 92). Ker, in practice, was, of course, not content with this "guide-book" ideal. The whole point of view which denies the need and even possibility of literary history proper strikes me as absurd. One might just as well tell historians of art that there should be only collectors, curators of museums, guide-lecturers in museums and compilers of guide-books. But the view is common.
40. *The Anti-Critic*, (1822), article XXV, "Th. Warton," p. 92.
41. *The History*, Preface, p. vi.
42. *Ibid.*, I, 232.
43. *Ibid.*, I, 239. See C. Rinaker, "Warton's Correspondence with Malone," *JEGP*, XIV (1915), 107-118.
44. *Ibid.*, I, 133.
45. *Ibid.*, I, 150.
46. *Ibid.*, I, 288.
47. *Ibid.*, I, 454, note.
48. *Ibid.*, II, 35.
49. *Ibid.*, II, 365, note.
50. *Ibid.*, III, 194-195.

51. *Ibid.*, II, 366.
52. *Ibid.*, III, 178.
53. *Ibid.*, I, 209.
54. *Observations* (1st ed.), pp. 227-228; (2nd ed.), II, 102, note.
55. *History*, I, 87.
56. *Ibid.*, II, 127.
57. *Ibid.*, II, 165.
58. *Ibid.*, II, 47.
59. *Ibid.*, I, 256.
60. See D. N. Smith's Warton Lecture, and H. E. D. Blakiston, "Thomas Warton and Machyn's Diary," *English Historical Review*, XI (1896), 282-300. For a defence of Warton see Rinaker, *op. cit.*, pp. 71-73.
61. *History*, Preface, p. vii.
62. *Ibid.*, II, 196.
63. *Ibid.*, II, 430, note.
64. *Ibid.*, II, 167.
65. *Ibid.*, I, 137.
66. *Ibid.*, II, 373.
67. *Ibid.*, I, 339.
68. *Ibid.*, III, Dissertation (hereafter cited as Diss.) III, p. xvii.
69. *Ibid.*, III, 495.
70. *Ibid.*, I, 237.
71. *Ibid.*, II, 408.
72. *Ibid.*, II, 443-444.
73. *Ibid.*, I, 339.
74. *Ibid.*, II, 421.
75. *Ibid.*, III, 3.
76. *Ibid.*, II, 420.
77. *Ibid.*, I, 332.
78. *Ibid.*, II, 97.
79. *Ibid.*, I, 339.
80. *Ibid.*, Preface.
81. *Ibid.*, I, 43.
82. *Ibid.*, I, 77.
83. *Ibid.*, I, 342.
84. *Ibid.*, I, 457.
85. *Ibid.*, I, 312, 314.
86. *Ibid.*, I, 266.
87. *Ibid.*, I, 457.
88. *Ibid.*, II, 66.
89. *Ibid.*
90. *Ibid.*, III, 27, 29.

91. *Ibid.*, III, 38.
92. *Ibid.*, III, 16.
93. *Ibid.*, III, 44.
94. *Ibid.*, III, 62, 67.
95. *Ibid.*, III, Appendix, 5. (Section XLIV.)
96. *Ibid.*, III, 439 and Appendix, p. 11.
97. *Ibid.*, Diss. I, p. h 4ᵛ.
98. *Ibid.*, I, 137.
99. *Ibid.*, I, 243.
100. *Ibid.*, I, 433.
101. *Ibid.*, II, 60.
102. *Ibid.*, II, 64.
103. *Ibid.*, "Emendations and Additions," II, 156.
104. *Ibid.*, III, 241, 243, 247.
105. *Ibid.*, I, 383.
106. *Ibid.*, "Emendations and Additions," II, 458.
107. *Ibid.*, II, 409-410.
108. *Ibid.*
109. *Ibid.*, II, 410.
110. *Ibid.*, II, 420.
111. *Ibid.*, III, 494.
112. *Ibid.*, III, 499.
113. *Ibid.*
114. "Verses," *Works*, (5th ed., 1802), I, lines 64-68.
115. *Spectator* No. 70, 74. See J. C. Robertson, *Studies in the Genesis of Romantic Theory*, p. 70. Robertson does not notice Addison's indebtedness on this point.
116. *History*, I, 182.
117. *Ibid.*, I, 367. It should be noted that the word "disgust" had much milder connotations in the eighteenth century than today.
118. *Ibid.*, I, 389-90.
119. *Ibid.*, I, 396.
120. *Ibid.*, III, 140.
121. *Ibid.*, II, 156.
122. *Ibid.*, Diss. I, g 3.
123. *Ibid.*, II, 369.
124. *Ibid.*, Diss. I, "those strong and undistinguishing notions of barbarism," etc., p. d3.
125. *Ibid.*, Diss. I, p. d3.
126. *Ibid.*, Diss. I, p. a.
127. *Ibid.*, I, 109-110.
128. *Ibid.*, I, 150.
129. *Ibid.*, I, 111.

130. *Ibid.,* I, 127, note.
131. *Ibid.,* Diss. I, p. d4.
132. *Ibid.,* I, 110.
133. *Ibid.,* I, 398.
134. *Ibid.,* Diss. I, p. c.
135. *Ibid.,* p. h4ᵛ.
136. *Ibid.,* Diss. III, III, xv.
137. *Ibid.,* Diss. II, p. c2.
138. *Ibid.,* Diss. III, III, xvi.
139. *Ibid.,* II, 31.
140. *Ibid.*
141. *Ibid.,* I, 434.
142. *Ibid.,* I, 468.
143. *Ibid.,* II, 462.
144. *Ibid.,* II, 463.
145. Hurd, *Letters on Chivalry and Romance,* ed. Morley, p. 154.
146. *History,* III, 490-491.
147. *Ibid.,* III, 496.
148. *Ibid.,* p. 497.
149. *Ibid.,* p. 501.
150. Preface to Milton's *Poems* (1785), p. xii. See also III, 497, 499.
151. *History,* I, 7.
152. *Ibid.,* II, 412.
153. *Ibid.,* III, 160.
154. *Ibid.,* I, 249.
155. *Ibid.,* II, 202.
156. *Ibid.,* p. 367.
157. *Ibid.,* III, 165.
158. *Ibid.,* Preface, p. ii.
159. *Ibid.,* III, 159.
160. *Ibid.,* I, 209.
161. *Ibid.,* 42, I, 97, I, 117, 209, I, 435, etc.
162. *Ibid.,* II, 51.
163. *Ibid.,* 454.
164. *Ibid.,* p. 457.
165. *Ibid.,* p. 461.
166. *Ibid.,* III, Appendix, 1.
167. *Ibid.,* III, 209.
168. *Ibid.,* I, 42.
169. *Ibid.,* I, 423.
170. *Ibid.,* I, 431.
171. *Ibid.,* II, 171 note.
172. *Ibid.,* III, 87.

173. *Ibid.*, II, 450.
174. *Ibid.*, III, 500.
175. *Ibid.*
176. *Ibid.*, III, 92-93.
177. *Ibid.*, II, 58.
178. *Ibid.*, III, 70.
179. *Ibid.*, I, 117.
180. *Ibid.*, II, 264.

BIBLIOGRAPHY

I. PRIMARY SOURCES

This Bibliography attempts to list all publications up to 1774, which can be called English literary scholarship or history. The place of publication is London, unless otherwise indicated.

Addison, Joseph (?). *A Discourse on Ancient and Modern Learning.* 1739.

Addison, Joseph, and Steele, Richard. *The Spectator.* Ed. by Gregory Smith. 4 vols. 1897.

Akenside, Mark. *The Pleasures of Imagination.* 1744.

Ames, Joseph. *Typographical Antiquities: being an Historical Account of Printing in England, 1471–1600.* 1749.

Archeologia or Miscellaneous Tracts relating to Antiquity. 12 vols. 1770–1796.

Ascham, Roger. *English Works.* Ed. by James Bennet, with *Life* by Samuel Johnson. 1761.

Ascham, Roger. *Epistolarum Libri quattuor.* Ed. by William Elstob, with *Life* by E. Grant. 1703.

Ascham, Roger, *The Scholemaster.* Ed. by James Upton. 1711. New ed. 1743.

Avison, Charles. *An Essay on Musical Expression.* 1752.

Aubrey, John. *Brief Lives.* Ed. by A. Clark. 2 vols. Oxford, 1898.

Aubrey, John. *Letters written by eminent persons . . . and Lives of eminent men.* Ed. by John Walker. 2 vols. in 3. 1813.

Bacon, Francis. *The Complete Works.* Ed. by Thomas Birch, with *Life* by David Mallet. 4 vols. 1740.

Bacon, Francis. *Letters and Remains.* Collected by Robert Stephens, ed. by John Locker. 1734.

Bacon, Francis. *Letters, Speeches, Charges.* Ed. by Thomas Birch. 1763.

Bacon, Francis. *Opera Omnia.* Ed. by John Blackbourne. 4 vols. 1730.

Bacon, Francis. *The Philosophical Works . . . methodized, and made English by Peter Shaw.* 3 vols. 1733.

Bacon, Francis. *Resuscitatio.* With *Life* by William Rawley. 1657.

Bacon, Francis. *The Works.* Revised by J. Gambold and W. Bowyer. 5 vols. 1765.

Bacon, Francis. *The Works.* Ed. by J. Spedding, R. L. Ellis, and D. D. Heath. 7 vols. 1857–1874.

Baker, David Erskine. *The Companion to the Playhouse.* 2 vols. 1764.

Bale, John. *Illustrium majoris Britanniae scriptorum . . . Summarium.* Ipswich, 1548. (Fictitious imprint. Probably printed at Wesel.)

Bale, John. *Index Britanniae Scriptorum.* Ed. by Reginald L. Poole and Mary Bateson. Oxford, 1902.

Bale, John. *Scriptorum illustrium majoris Brytannie . . . Catalogus.* 2 vols. Basle, 1557–1559.

Barrington, Daines, ed. *The Anglo-Saxon Version, from the Historian Orosius by Alfred the Great.* 1773.

Bates, William. *Vitae selectorum aliquot virorum qui doctrina, dignitate, aut pietate inclaruere.* 1681.

Bayly, Thomas (Hall, Richard). *The Life and Death of John Fisher.* Ed. by Th(omas) C(oxeter). 1739.

Beattie, James. *Essays on Poetry and Music as they affect the mind.* 1776.

Beaumont and Fletcher. *The Works.* Ed. by Colman. 7 vols. 1711.

Beaumont and Fletcher. *The Works.* Ed. by Lewis Theobald, T. Seward, and J. Sympson. 10 vols. 1750.

Berkeley, Bishop. *The Works.* Ed. by A. C. Fraser. 4 vols. 1871.

Bernard, Edward. *Catalogi Librorum Manuscriptorum Angliae et Hiberniae in unum collecti.* Oxford, 1697.

Biographia Britannica. 7 vols. 1747–66.

Blackmore, Sir Richard. *Essays upon Several Subjects.* 1716.

Blackwell, Thomas. *An Enquiry into the Life and Writings of Homer.* 1735.

Blair, Hugh. *A Critical Dissertation on the Poems of Ossian.* 1763.

Blair, Hugh. *Lectures on Rhetoric and Belles Lettres.* 2 vols. 1783.

Blount, Sir Thomas Pope. *Censura Celebriorum Authorum.* 1690.

Blount, Sir Thomas Pope. *De Re Poetica: or Remarks upon Poetry.* 1694.

Blount, Sir Thomas Pope. *Essays.* 1691.

Boileau, Nicolas. *The Works . . . made English by several hands.* 3 vols. 1711–1713.

Boswell, James. *The Life of Samuel Johnson.* Ed. by G. Birkbeck Hill. 6 vols. Oxford, 1887.

Bourne, Henry. *The History of Newcastle-upon-Tyne.* Newcastle, 1736.

Bowle, John, ed. *Miscellaneous Pieces of Antient English Poesie.* 1764.

Brathwait, Richard. *Comment upon the two tales of . . . Chaucer.* Ed. by C. S. Spurgeon. 1901.

Brown, John. *A Dissertation on the Rise, Union, and Power, the Progressions, Separations, and Corruptions of Poetry and Music.* 1763.

Brown, John. *An Essay on the Characteristics.* 1751.

Brown, John. *The History of the Rise and Progress of Poetry, through its several Species.* Newcastle, 1764.

Browne, William. *Works.* Ed. by W. Thompson and T. Davies. 3 vols. 1772.

Brydges, Sir Egerton. *The Anti-Critic.* Geneva, 1822.

Buchanan, David. *De Scriptoribus Scotis Libri Duo.* Ed. by D. Irving. Edinburgh, 1837.

Burley, Walter (Burlaeus Gualterus). *Liber de vita et moribus philosophorum.* Ed. by H. Knust. Tübingen, 1886.

Burnet, Gilbert. *Some Passages of the Life and Death of John, Earl of Rochester.* 1680.

Burney, Charles. *A History of Music.* 4 vols., 1776–1789.

Camden, William. *Britannia.* Translated by Edmund Gibson. Second ed., 1722.

Camden, William. *Remaines of a greater worke concerning Britain.* 1605.

(Campbell, John). *The Polite Correspondence, or Rational Amusement.* (1741).

(Campbell, John). *The Rational Amusement.* 1754.

Capell, Edward. *Notes and Various Readings to Shakespeare.* 3 vols. 1779–1783.

Capell, Edward, ed. *Prolusions or Select Pieces of Antient Poetry.* 1760.

(Casley, David). *A Catalogue of the Harleian Collection of Manuscripts.* 2 vols. 1759 (actually published in 1762).

(Casley, David). *A Catalogue of the Manuscripts of the King's Library.* 1734.

Cave, William. *Scriptorum Ecclesiasticorum Historia Literaria.* 1688.

Chaucer, Geoffrey. *The Workes of our antient and lerned English poet . . . ,* ed. by Thomas Speght. 1598.

Chaucer, Geoffrey. *The Works.* Ed. by J. Urry with *Life* by John Dart. 1721.

Chesterfield, Lord. *Letters.* Ed. by B. Dobrée. 6 vols. 1932.

Chetwood, W. R. *A General History of the Stage.* 1749.

Chetwood, W. R. *Memoirs of the Life and Writings of Ben Jonson.* Dublin, 1756.

Chetwood, W. R., ed. *A Select Collection of Old Plays.* Dublin, 1750.

Churchyard, Thomas. *The Worthiness of Wales.* 1774.

Cibber, Colley. *An Apology for the Life of Colley Cibber, Comedian.* 1740.

Cibber, Theophil (actually Robert Sheils). *The Lives of the Poets of Great Britain and Ireland.* . . . 5 vols. 1753.

Cobb, Samuel. *Poems on Several Occasions.* Second ed., 1710.

Collins, William. *Poems.* Ed. by A. L. Poole. Oxford, 1917.

Cooper, Mrs. Elizabeth, ed. *The Muses' Library or a Series of English Poetry.* Vol. 1. 1737.

Crusius, Lewis. *The Lives of the Roman Poets.* 2 vols. 1726.

Dalrymple, Sir David (later Lord Hailes), ed. *Ancient Scottish Poems, published from the MS of George Bannatyne* (1568). Edinburgh, 1770.

Daniel, Samuel. *Poetical Works . . . to which is prefix'd Memoirs of his Life and Writings.* 2 vols. 1718.

Davies, Sir John. *The Original Nature and Immortality of the Soul.* 1716.

Davies, Myles. *Athenae Britannicae: Or a Critical History of the Oxford and Cambridge Writers and Writings.* 6 vols. 1716–1719.

Dempster, John. *Scotorum Scriptorum Nomenclatura.* Bononiae. 1620.

Dempster, Thomas. *Historia Ecclesiastica Gentis Scotorum.* Bononiae, 1627.

Dennis, John. *The Advancement and Reformation of Modern Poetry.* 1701.

Dennis, John. *The Comical Gallant: or the Amours of Sir John Falstaffe.* 1702.

Dennis, John. *The Critical Works.* Ed. Edward Niles Hooker. Vol. I. (1692–1711). Baltimore, 1939.

Dennis, John. *The Grounds of Criticism in Poetry.* 1704.

Dennis, John. *The Impartial Critick: or Some Observations.* . . . 1693.

Dodsley, Robert, ed. *A Select Collection of Old Plays.* 12 vols. 1744.

Donne, John. *The Poetical Works.* 3 vols. Edinburgh, 1779.

Douglas, Gavin. *A Description of May.* Modernized by F. Fawkes. 1752.

Douglas, Gavin. *A Description of Winter.* Modernized by F. Fawkes. 1754.

Douglas, Gavin. *Virgil's Aeneis.* Ed. by Thomas Ruddiman, with *Life* by John Sage. Edinburgh, 1710.

Drayton, Michael. *Amores Britannici. Epistles, Historical and Gallant.* Ed. by John Oldmixon. 1703.

Drayton, Michael. *England's Heroick Epistles.* 1737.

Drayton, Michael. *The History of Queen Mab, or the Court of Fairy.* 1751.

Drayton, Michael. *Poly-Olbion.* (With notes by John Selden.) 1613.

Drayton, Michael. *Works.* Ed. by Charles Coffey. 1748.

Drayton, Michael. *Works.* 4 vols. 1753.

Drummond, William. *Works.* Ed. by J. Sage and T. Ruddiman. Edinburgh, 1711.

Dryden, John. *Essays.* Selected and edited by W. P. Ker. 2 vols. Oxford, 1899.

Dryden, John. *Works.* Ed. by Sir Walter Scott. Revised by G. Saintsbury, 18 vols. Edinburgh, 1882–1893.

Duff, William. *Critical Observations on the Writings of the Most Celebrated Original Geniuses in Poetry.* Edinburgh, 1770.

Duff, William. *Essay on Original Genius.* 1767.

Dugdale, Sir William. *The Antiquities of Warwickshire Illustrated.* 1656.

Durham, W. H., ed. *Critical Essays of the Eighteenth Century, 1700–1725.* New Haven, 1915.

Elstob, Elizabeth, ed. *An English-Saxon Homily on the Birth-day of St. Gregory.* 1709.

Elstob, Elizabeth. *The Rudiments of Grammar for the English-Saxon Tongue.* 1715.

Elstob, William, ed. *Sermo Lupi ad Anglos.* Oxford, 1701.

Evans, Evan. *Some Specimens of the Poetry of the Ancient Welsh Bards.* 1764.

Fairfax, Edward. *Godfrey of Bulloigne.* 1726. Later ed., 1749.

Farmer, Richard. *An Essay on the Learning of Shakespeare.* 1767.

Fawkes, Francis. *Original Poems and Translations.* 1761.

Ferguson, Adam. *An Essay on the History of Civil Society.* Edinburgh, 1767.

Flecknoe, Richard. *A Short Discourse of the English Stage.* 1664.

Fletcher, Phineas. *Piscatory Eclogues.* Ed. by Lord Woodhouselee (Alexander Fraser Tytler). Edinburgh, 1771.

Flower Piece, The. A Collection of Miscellany Poems by Several Hands. 1731.

Fortescue, Sir John. *The Difference between an Absolute and a Limited Monarchy.* Ed. by J. Fortescue-Aland. 1714.

Foxe, John. *Actes and Monuments of these latter . . . days.* Second ed., 1570.

Free, John. *An Essay towards an History of the English Tongue.* Fourth ed., 1788.

Fuller, Thomas. *Abel Redivivus.* 1651.

Fuller, Thomas. *The Church History of Britain.* 1655.

Fuller, Thomas. *The History of the Worthies of England.* Ed. by J. Nichols. 2 vols. 1811.

General Dictionary. Ed. by Thomas Birch *et al.* 10 vols. 1734–1741.

Geoffrey of Monmouth. *The British History.* Translated by Aaron Thompson, "with a large Preface." 1718.

Gerard, Alexander. *Essay on Genius.* 1774.

Gerard, Alexander. *Essay on Taste.* Edinburgh, 1758.

Gibbon, Edward. *An Essay on the Study of Literature.* 1764.

Gibbon, Edward. *Miscellaneous Works.* Ed. by Lord John Sheffield. 2 vols. 1796.

Gibson, Edmund, ed. *Chronicon Saxonicum seu Annales.* Oxford, 1692.

Gibson, Edmund, ed. *Polemo-Middinia. Carmen Macaronicum.* Oxford, 1691.

Gildon, Charles. *The Compleat Art of Poetry.* 2 vols. 1718.

Gildon, Charles. *The Laws of Poetry.* 1721.

Gildon, Charles. *Miscellaneous Letters and Essays.* 1694.

Goldsmith, Oliver. *An Enquiry into the Present State of Polite Learning.* 1759.

Goldsmith, Oliver. *New Essays.* Ed. by Ronald S. Crane. Chicago, 1927.

Goldsmith, Oliver (?). *A Poetical Dictionary, or the Beauties of the English Poets.* 1761.

Goldsmith, Oliver. *Works.* Ed. by J. W. M. Gibbs. 5 vols. 1884–1886.

Goldsmith, Oliver. *Works.* Ed. by P. Cunningham. 4 vols. 1854.

Granger, James. *A Biographical History of England from Egbert the Great to the Revolution.* 3 vols. 1769–1774.

Gray, Thomas. *The Correspondence.* Ed. by Paget Toynbee and L. Whibley. 3 vols. Oxford, 1935.

Gray, Thomas. *Essays and Criticisms.* Ed. by C. S. Northup. Boston, 1909.

Gray, Thomas. *Poems.* Ed. by A. L. Poole. Oxford, 1917.

Gray, Thomas. *Selections from the Poetry and Prose.* Ed. by W. L. Phelps. Boston, 1894.

Gray, Thomas. *Works.* Ed. by J. Mitford. 5 vols. 1835–43.

Gregory, John. *A Comparative View of the State and Faculties of Man with those of the Animal World.* Third ed. 1766.

Greville, Sir Fulke. *The Life of Sir Philip Sidney.* 1652.

Grey, Zachary. *Critical, Historical and Explanatory Notes on Shakespeare.* 2 vols. 1754.

Hakluyt, Richard. *The Principal Navigations, Voiages, Trafficks and Discoveries.* 1589.

Hall, John. *Satires.* Ed. by W. Thompson. 1753.

Hallam, Henry. *Introduction to the Literature of Europe, in the fifteenth, sixteenth and seventeenth centuries.* 4 vols. 1878.

The Harleian Miscellany. Ed. by William Oldys, S. Johnson, *et al.* 8 vols. 1744–1746.

Harris, James. *Hermes.* 1751.

Harris, James. *Philological Inquiries.* 3 parts. 1781.

Harris, James. *Three Treatises.* 1744.

Harris, James. *Upon the Rise and Progress of Criticism.* Privately printed. 1752.

Harvey, Gabriel. *The Letter Book.* Ed. by E. J. Scott. 1884.

Hawkins, Sir John. *A General History of the Science and Practice of Music.* 3 vols. 1776.

Hawkins, Sir John. *The Life of Samuel Johnson.* 1787.

Hawkins, Thomas. *The Origin of the English Drama.* 3 vols. Oxford, 1773.

Hayward, Thomas, ed. *The British Muse.* 1738.

Hayward, Thomas, ed. *The Quintessence of English Poetry.* 1740.

Hearne, Thomas, ed. *Guilelmi Newbrigensis Historia.* 3 vols. Oxford, 1719.

Hearne, Thomas, ed. *Joannis Glastoniensis Confratris et Monachi Chronica.* 2 vols. Oxford, 1726.

Hearne, Thomas, ed. *Peter Langtoft's Chronicle.* . . . 2 vols. Oxford, 1725.

Hearne, Thomas, ed. *Robert of Glocester's Chronicle.* . . . 2 vols. Oxford, 1724.

Henry, Robert. *A History of Great Britain on a New Plan.* 5 vols. Edinburgh, 1771–1793.

Herd, David. *Ancient and Modern Scotish Songs.* 1769. 2 vols., 1776.

Herd, David. *Songs from David Herd's Manuscripts.* Ed. by H. Hecht. Edinburgh, 1904.

Heywood, Thomas. *The Hierarchy of the Blessed Angels.* 1635.

Hickes, George. *Institutiones Grammaticae Anglo-Saxonicae et Moeso-Gothicae.* Oxford, 1688–1689.

Hickes, George. *Linguarum Veterum Septentrionalium Thesaurus*

Grammatico-Criticus et Archeologicus. 2 vols. Oxford, 1703–1705.

Hooker, Richard. *The Laws of Ecclesiastical Polity.* With *Life* by John Gauden. 1662.

Hume, David. *Essays.* Ed. by T. H. Green and T. H. Grose. 2 vols. 1875.

Hume, David. *Essays and Treatises on Several Subjects.* 2 vols. 1777.

Hume, David. *The History of England.* 4 vols. New York, 1873.

Hume, Patrick, ed. *The Poetical Works of John Milton.* 1695.

Hurd, Richard. *The Correspondence of Richard Hurd and William Mason and Letters of Richard Hurd to Thomas Gray.* Ed. by E. H. Pearce and L. Whibley. Cambridge, 1932.

Hurd, Richard. *Letters on Chivalry and Romance.* Ed. by E. Morley. Oxford, 1911.

Hurd, Richard. *Moral and Political Dialogues.* 1759.

Hurd, Richard. *Works.* 8 vols. 1811.

Husbands, John. *A Miscellany of Poems by Several Hands.* Oxford, 1731.

Jacob, Edward, ed. *The Lamentable and True Tragedy of M. Arden, of Feversham.* Feversham, 1770.

Jacob, Giles. *An Historical Account of the Lives and Writings of Our Most Considerable English Poets.* 1720.

Jacob, Giles. *The Poetical Register, or the Lives and Characters of the English Dramatick Poets.* 1719.

James, Thomas. *Catalogus librorum bibliothecae quam Thomas Bodleius . . . instituit.* Oxford, 1605.

Johnson, Samuel. *A Dictionary of the English Language.* Fourth ed. 2 vols. 1773.

Johnson, Samuel. *The Lives of the English Poets.* Ed. by G. Birkbeck Hill. 3 vols. Oxford, 1905.

Johnson, Samuel. *Observations on the Tragedy of Macbeth.* 1745.

Johnson, Samuel. *Proposals for Printing by Subscription the Dramatick Works of William Shakespeare.* 1756.

Johnson, Samuel. *The Works.* Ed. by R. Lynam. 11 vols. 1825.

Jones, Sir William. *Poems consisting chiefly of translations from the Asiatick Languages.* 1772.

Jones, Sir William. *Works.* 4 vols. 1799.

Jonson, Ben. *Timber or Discoveries.* Ed. by Felix Schelling. Boston, 1892.

Jonson, Ben. *The Works.* Ed. by Peter Whalley. 7 vols. 1756.

Jortin, John. *Miscellaneous Observations upon Authors.* 2 vols, 1731–1732.

Jortin, John. *Remarks on Spenser's Poems.* 1734.

Joscelyn, John, ed. *The Gospels of the fower Evangelistes, translated in the olde Saxon tyme . . . into the vulgare toung of the Saxons.* 1571.

Kames, Lord (Henry Home). *Elements of Criticism.* 3 vols. Edinburgh, 1762.

Kames, Lord. *Sketches of the History of Man.* 2 vols. Edinburgh, 1774.

Knight, Samuel. *The Life of Dr. John Colet.* 1724.

Lambard, William, ed. *Archaionomia, sive de priscis Anglorum legibus libri.* 1568. New ed. Cambridge, 1644.

Langbaine, Gerard. *An Account of the English Dramatick Poets.* 4 vols. Oxford, 1691.

Langbaine, Gerard. *Momus Triumphans: or the Plagiaries of the English Stage.* 1688.

Langbaine, Gerard, and Gildon, Charles. *The Lives and Characters of the English Dramatick Poets.* 1699.

Leland, John. *Commentarii de scriptoribus Britannicis.* Ed. by Antonius Hall. 2 vols. Oxford, 1709.

Leland, John. *A Laboryouse Journey and Serche for England's Antiquities.* 1549.

Lennox, Charlotte. *Shakespear Illustrated.* 3 vols. 1753.

Lewis, John. *A Complete History of the Several Translations of the Holy Bible.* Second ed., 1739.

Lewis, John. *The History of the Life and Sufferings of Dr. John Wickliffe.* 1720.

Lewis, John. *The Life of Dr. John Fisher.* Ed. by T. Hudson Turner. 2 vols. 1855.

Lewis, John. *The Life of Mayster Wyllyam Caxton.* 1747.

Lewis, John. *The Life of Reynold Pecock.* 1744.

Lily, George. "Virorum aliquot in Britannia Elogia," Paulo Giovo, *Descriptio Britanniae.* Venice, 1548.

L'Isle, William. *A Saxon Treatise concerning the Old and New Testament Written by Aelfricus Abbas.* 1623.

L'Isle, William. *Divers Ancient Monuments. . . .* 1638.

Locke, John. *An Essay of Human Understanding.* Ed. by A. C. Fraser. 2 vols. Oxford, 1894.

Lowth, Robert. *Lectures on the Sacred Poetry of the Hebrews.* Translated by G. Gregory. 2 vols. 1787.

Mackenzie, George. *Lives and Characters of the Most Eminent Writers of the Scots Nation.* 3 vols. 1708–1722.

Maidment, John, ed. *Catalogues of Scotish Writers.* Edinburgh, 1833.

Mallet, David. *The Life of Francis Bacon.* 1740.

Mallet, Paul Henri. *Northern Antiquities, or Description . . . with a translation of the Edda.* 2 vols. 1770.

Mandeville, Bernard. *The Fable of the Bees.* Ed. by F. N. Kaye. 2 vols. Oxford, 1924.

Mandeville, Sir John. *The Voyages and Travels.* Ed. by David Casley. 1725.

Marshall, Thomas (Mareschallus). *Quatuor D. N. Jesu Christi Evangeliorum Versiones perantique duae Gothice scil. et Anglo-Saxonice.* Dordrecht, 1665.

Massinger, Philip. *The Dramatick Works.* Ed. by Thomas Coxeter. 4 vols. 1761.

Middleton, Conyers. *A Dissertation Concerning the Origin of Printing in England.* 1735.

Milton, John. *See* Hume, Patrick; St. John, J. A.; and Warton, Thomas.

Mitford, William. *An Essay on the Harmony of Language.* 1774.

Monboddo, Lord (James Burnet). *The Origin and Progress of Language.* 6 vols. 1773.

Montagu, Lady Mary. *Letters and Works.* Ed. by M. M. Thomas. 2 vols. 1886.

More, Thomas. *Utopia.* Glasgow, 1750 (in Latin).

More, Thomas. *Utopia.* Translated by Bishop Burnet. 1737.

Morgann, Maurice. *An Essay on the Character of Falstaff.* 1777.

Mottley, John. "A Compleat List of all the English Dramatick Poets." Thomas Whincop, *Scanderbeg.* 1747.

The Muses' Mercury, or Monthly Miscellany. Vol. I. 1707.

Nicolson, William. *The English, Scotch and Irish Historical Libraries.* 1736.

Oldys, William. *The British Librarian.* 1737. Re-issue, 1738.

Oldys, William; Johnson, Samuel; and Mattaire, M. *Catalogus Bibliothecae Harleianae.* 5 vols. 1743.

Parker, Matthew, ed. *A Testimonie of Antiquitie.* 1567 (?).

Peacham, Henry. *The Compleat Gentleman.* 1622.

Percy, Thomas. *Ancient Songs chiefly on Moorish Subjects.* Ed. by David Nichol Smith. Oxford, 1932.

Percy, Thomas. *Five Pieces of Runic Poetry.* 1763.

Percy, Thomas. *Hau Kiou Choaan.* 4 vols. 1761.

Percy, Thomas. *Miscellaneous Pieces Relating to the Chinese.* 2 vols. 1762.

Percy, Thomas. *Reliques of Ancient English Poetry.* 3 vols. 1765.

Percy, Thomas. *Reliques of Ancient English Poetry.* Ed. by H. B. Wheatley. 3 vols. 1891.

Percy, Thomas. "The Text of the Percy-Warton Letters," (ed. Leah Dennis) *PMLA,* XLVI (1931), 1166.

Phillips, Edward. *Theatrum Poetarum: or a Compleat Collection of the Poets.* 1675.

Phillips, Edward. "Tractatulus de Carmine Dramatico Poetarum Veterum," J. Buchler *Sacrarum Phrasium . . . Poeticarum Thesaurus.* 1669.

Pits, John. *Relationum historicarum de Rebus Anglicis Tomus I.* Paris, 1619.

Pope, Alexander. *The Works.* Ed. by W. Elwin and W. J. Courthope. 10 vols. 1871–1889.

Preston, William. *Poetical Works.* 2 vols. 1793.

Price, Sir John. *Historiae Britannicae Defensio.* 1573.

Priestley, Joseph. *A Course of Lectures on the Theory of Language and Universal Grammar.* Warrington, 1762.

Priestley, Joseph. *Lectures on History and General Policy.* Ed. by J. T. Rutt. 1826.

Puttenham, George (?). *The Arte of English Poesie.* Ed. by G. D. Willcock and A. Walker. Cambridge, 1936.

Raleigh, Sir Walter. *The History of the World.* Ed. by William Oldys. 2 vols. 1736.

Raleigh, Sir Walter. *The Works.* Ed. by Thomas Birch. 2 vols. 1751.

Ramsay, Allan, ed. *The Evergreen, Being a Collection of Scots Poems, Wrote by the Ingenious before 1600.* 2 vols. Edinburgh, 1724.

Rawlinson, Christopher, ed. *An. Manl. Sever. Boethi Consolationis Philosophiae Libri V.* Oxford, 1698.

Rhys, David. *Cambrobrytannicae Cymraecaeve Linguae Institutiones.* 1592.

Richardson, Jonathan. *Explanatory Notes and Remarks on Milton's Paradise Lost.* 1734.

Richardson, John, translator. *A Specimen of Persian Poetry or Odes of Hafez.* 1774.

Ritson, Joseph. *Bibliographia Poetica.* 1802.

Ritson, Joseph. *Observations on the Three First Volumes of the History of English Poetry.* 1782.

Robertson, William. *A History of America.* 1777.

Robertson, William. *The History of the Reign of the Emperor Charles V.* 3 vols. 1769.

Roper, William. *The Life of Sir Thomas More.* Ed. by John Lewis. 1729.

Ruffhead, Owen. *The Life of Alexander Pope.* 1769.

Rymer, Thomas. *A Short View of Tragedy.* 1693.

Rymer, Thomas. *The Tragedies of the Last Age.* 1678.

Sackville, Thomas, and Norton, Thomas. *Gorboduc.* Ed. by Joseph Spence. 1736.

St. John, J. A., ed. *Milton's Prose Works.* 5 vols. 1848–1853.

Scott, Sir Walter. *Miscellaneous Prose Works.* Vol. XVII. 1835.

Shaftesbury, Earl of. *Characteristics of Men, Manners, Opinions and Times.* Ed. by J. M. Robertson. 2 vols. 1900.

Shakespeare. William. *Hamlet.* Ed. by Charles Jennens. 1773.

Shakespeare, William. *His Comedies, Histories and Tragedies.* Ed. by E. Capell. 10 vols. 1768–1769.

Shakespeare, William. *Julius Caesar.* Ed. by Charles Jennens. 1774.

Shakespeare, William. *King Lear.* Ed. by Charles Jennens. 1770.

Shakespeare, William. *Macbeth.* Ed. by Charles Jennens. 1773.

Shakespeare, William. *Othello.* Ed. by Charles Jennens. 1773.

Shakespeare, William. *The Plays.* Ed. by S. Johnson. 8 vols. 1765.

Shakespeare, William. *The Plays.* Ed. by S. Johnson and G. Steevens. 10 vols. 1773.

Shakespeare, William. *Twenty Plays.* Ed. by G. Steevens. 4 vols. 1766.

Shakespeare, William. *The Works.* Ed. by Alexander Pope. 7 vols. 1723–1725.

Shakespeare, William. *The Works.* Ed. by N. Rowe. 9 vols. 1714.

Shakespeare, William. *The Works.* Ed. by L. Theobald. 7 vols. 1734.

Shakespeare, William. *The Works.* Ed. by W. Warburton. 8 vols. 1747.

Sharpe, William. *A Dissertation on Genius.* 1755.

Sidney, Sir Philip. *The Defense of Poesy.* Glasgow, 1752.

Sidney, Sir Philip. *The Defence of Poetry and Observations on Poetry and Eloquence from the Discoveries of Ben Jonson.* Ed. by Joseph Warton. 1787.

Sidney, Sir Philip. *The Works.* Ed. by Mrs. Stanley. 3 vols. 1724–1725.

Skelton, John. *Pithy, Pleasaunt and Profitable Workes of Maister. . . .* 1736.

Skelton, John. *The Tunnyng of Elynour Runnyng.* 1719.

Smith, Adam. *Essays on Philosophical Subjects*. Ed. by D. Stewart. 1795.

Smith, Adam. *The Theory of Moral Sentiments*. Third edition. 1767.

Smith, Gregory G., ed. *Elizabethan Critical Essays*. 2 vols. Oxford, 1904.

Smith, Thomas, ed. *Catalogus librorum manuscriptorum bibliothecae Cottonionae*. Oxford, 1696.

Spelman, Sir John. *Aelfredi Magni Anglorum Invictissimi Regis Vita*. Oxford, 1678.

Spelman, Sir John. *The Life of Alfred the Great*. Ed. by Thomas Hearne. Oxford, 1709.

Spence, Joseph. *Anecdotes, Observations, and Characters of Books and Men*. Ed. S. W. Singer. 1820.

Spencer, John. *Catalogus Universalis Librorum . . . in Bibliotheca collegii Sionii*. 1650.

Spenser, Edmund. *The Fairie Queene*. Ed. by Thomas Birch. 3 vols. 1751.

Spenser, Edmund. *The Fairie Queene*. Ed. by John Upton. 2 vols. 1758.

Spenser, Edmund. *The Fairie Queene*. Ed. by Ralph Church. 4 vols. 1758–1759.

Spenser, Edmund. *The Works*. Ed. by John Hughes. 6 vols. 1715.

Spingarn, J. E., ed. *Critical Essays of the Seventeenth Century*. 3 vols. Oxford, 1908–1909.

Sprat, Thomas. *An Account of the Life and Writings of Mr. Abraham Cowley*. 1668.

Sterne, Laurence. *The Life and Opinions of Tristram Shandy*. 9 vols. 1760–1766.

Strype, John. *The Life and Acts of Matthew Parker*. 1711.

Surrey, The Earl of. *The Poems of Henry Howard . . . with the Poems of Sir Thomas Wiat*. Ed. by G. Sewell. 1717.

Swift, Jonathan. *The Prose Works*. 12 vols. Ed. by Temple Scott. 1907.

Tanner, Thomas. *Bibliotheca Britannico-Hibernica*. Ed. by David Wilkins. 1748.

Temple, Sir William. *Works*. 4 vols. 1757.

Theobald, Lewis. *Memoirs of Sir Walter Raleigh*. 1719.

Theobald, Lewis. *Shakespeare Restored*. 1726.

Thynne, Francis. *Animadversions uppon Annotacions. . . . Ed. by F. J. Furnivall. 1875.

Thwaites, Edward, ed. *Heptateuchus, Liber Job, et Evangelium Nicodemi*. Oxford, 1698.

Trapp, Joseph. *Lectures on Poetry* . . . translated from the Latin. 1742.

Trapp, Joseph. *Praelectiones Poeticae.* 1711.

Tusser, Thomas. *Tusser Redivivus.* 1710.

Twysden, Roger, ed. *Historiae Anglicanae Scriptores Decem.* 1652–1653.

Tyrwhitt, Thomas. *Observations and Conjectures upon some Passages of Shakespeare.* Oxford, 1766.

Upton, James. *Remarks on Three Plays of Benjamin Johnson* (sic). 1749.

Upton, John. *Critical Observations on Shakespeare.* 1746.

Upton, John. *A Letter Concerning a new Edition of the Fairie Queene to Gilbert West.* . . . 1751.

Verstegan, Richard (Rowlands, Richard). *A Restitution of Decayed Intelligence.* 1605.

Vigfusson, G., and Powell, F. York. *Corpus Poeticum Boreale.* 2 vols. Oxford, 1883.

Waller, Edmund. *Poems.* Ed. by G. Thorn Drury. 1893.

Walpole, Horace. *A Catalogue of the Royal and Noble Authors of England.* Second ed. 2 vols. 1759.

Walpole, Horace. *Letters.* Ed. by Mrs. Paget Toynbee. 16 vols. Oxford, 1903–5.

Walton, Izaak. *The Lives of John Donne, Sir Henry Wotton, Richard Hooker, George Herbert, and Robert Sanderson.* Ed. by G. Saintsbury. Oxford, 1927.

Warburton, William. *The Divine Legation of Moses Demonstrated.* 2 vols. 1738–41.

Warburton, William. "Supplement to the Translator's Preface" in Cervantes, *Don Quixote,* translated by Charles Jarvis. Third ed. 1756.

Warburton, William. *Works.* Ed. by R. Hurd. 8 vols. 1811.

Ware, Sir James. *De scriptoribus Hiberniae.* Dublin, 1639.

Warner, Ferdinando. *Memoirs of the Life of Sir Thomas More.* 1758.

Warton, Joseph. *Essay on Pope.* Vol. 1. 1756.

Warton, Thomas. "The Correspondence between Warton and Hurd," *Bodleian Quarterly Record,* VI (1932), 303.

Warton, Thomas. *The History of English Poetry.* 3 vols. 1774–1781. Fragment of Vol. IV with new ed. of Vol. III in 1790.

Warton, Thomas, ed. *Milton's Poems upon Several Occasions.* 1785. New ed. 1791.

Warton, Thomas. *Observations on the Fairie Queene of Spenser.* 1754. Second ed. 1762.

Warton, Thomas. *The Poetical Works.* 2 vols. Oxford, 1802.

Warton, Thomas, ed. *The Union or Select Scots and English Poems.* 1753.

Watson, James, ed. *A Choice Collection of Comic and Serious Scots Poems.* 3 vols. 1706–1711.

Webb, Daniel. *Observations on the Correspondence between Poetry and Music.* 1769.

Webb, Daniel. *Remarks on the Beauties of Poetry.* 1762.

Welsted, Leonard. *Epistles, Odes.* 1724.

Whalley, Peter. *An Enquiry into the Learning of Shakespeare.* 1748.

Wheloc, Abraham, ed. *Historiae Ecclesiasticae Gentis Anglorum Libri V.* Cambridge, 1644.

Whitaker, William. *Praelectiones.* With "Vita Guilelmi Whitaker" by Abdias Assheton. 1599.

Wilkins, John. *An Essay towards a real Character and a Philosophical Language.* 1668.

Wilson, Thomas. *The Arte of Rhetorique.* Ed. by G. Mair. Oxford, 1909.

Winstanley, William. *Lives of the Most Famous English Poets.* 1687.

Wood, Anthony à. *Athenae Oxonienses, An Exact History of All the Writers. . . .* Ed. by P. Bliss. 4 vols. 1820.

Wood, Robert. *An Essay on the Original Genius and Writings of Homer.* A new ed., 1775 (privately printed in 1769).

Wright, James. *Country Conversations.* 1694.

Wright, James. *Historia Histrionica.* 1699.

Young, Edward. "Conjectures on Original Composition," *English Critical Essays (Sixteenth, seventeenth, and eighteenth centuries).* Selected and edited by Edmund D. Jones. Oxford, 1922. (First ed. 1759.)

II. SECONDARY SOURCES

Obvious reference books, like the *Dictionary of National Biography*, are not listed. The usual abbreviations are used for the titles of periodicals, *SP* for *Studies in Philology*, *MP* for *Modern Philology*, etc. The place of publication is London, unless otherwise indicated.

Adams, Eleanor, F. *Old English Scholarship from 1566–1800*. New Haven, 1917.

Albrecht, Walter. *Ueber des Theatrum Poetarum von Miltons Neffen Edward Phillips*. Leipzig, 1928.

Allen, B. Sprague. *Tides in English Taste*. 2 vols. Cambridge, Mass., 1937.

Ashdown, Margaret. "Elizabeth Elstob, the Learned Saxonist," *MLR*, XX (1925), 125.

Babcock, R. W. *The Genesis of Shakespeare Idolatry*. Chapel Hill, N. C., 1931.

Bäumler, Alfred. *Kants Kritik der Urteilskraft: ihre Geschichte und Systematik*. Vol. I. München, 1923.

Bateson, F. W. *English Poetry and the English Language*. Oxford, 1934.

Bennett, J. A. W. "The Beginnings of Norse Studies in England," *Saga-book of the Viking Society for Northern Research*, XII (1937), 35.

Besterman, Theodore. *The Beginnings of Systematic Bibliography*. Second ed. Oxford, 1936.

Black, J. B. *The Art of History. A Study of Four Great Historians of the Eighteenth Century*. 1926.

Black, Matthew W., and Shaaber, Matthias A. *Shakespeare's Seventeenth Century Editors (1632–1685)*. New York, 1937.

Blakiston, H. E. D. "Thomas Warton and Machyn's Diary," *English Historical Review*, XI (1896), p. 282.

Bligh, E. W. *Sir Kenelm Digby and his Venetia.* 1932.

Bohn, W. E. "The Development of John Dryden's Literary Criticism," *PMLA*, XXXIX (1907), p. 56.

Bosker, A. *Literary Criticism in the Age of Johnson.* Groningen, 1930.

Bredvold, L. I. "The Tendency towards Platonism in Neo-Classical Aesthetics," *ELH*, I (1934), 91.

Broadus, E. K. "Addison's Influence on the Development of Interest in Folk-Poetry in the Eighteenth Century," *MP*, VIII (1910), 123.

Bronson, B. H. *Joseph Ritson: Scholar-at-Arms.* 2 vols. Berkeley, Calif., 1938.

Brooke, C. F. Tucker. "The Renascence of Germanic Studies in England, 1559–1689," *PMLA*, XXIX (1914), 135.

Brooks, Cleanth. "The History of Percy's Edition of Surrey's Poems," *Englische Studien*, LVIII (1934), 424.

Brown, Joseph Epes. *The Critical Opinions of Samuel Johnson.* Princeton, 1926.

Burdach, Konrad. *Vorspiel. Gesammelte Schriften.* Vol. II. Berlin, 1926.

Bury, J. B. *The Idea of Progress: An Enquiry into its Origin and Growth.* 1920.

Carlson, C. Lennart. *The First Magazine: A History of the Gentleman's Magazine.* Providence, R. I., 1939.

Cassirer, Ernst. *Die Philosophie der symbolischen Formen.* 3 vols. Berlin, 1923.

Chan, Shan Yi. "The Influence of China on English Culture during the Eighteenth Century," *Abstracts of Theses.* University of Chicago. Humanistic Series, VII (1928–1929), 537.

Chapman, R. W. "Bennet's *Ascham*," *RES*, V (1929), 69.

Christie, Richard Copley. "Biographical Dictionaries," *Selected Essays and Papers.* 1902, p. 1.

Clark, A. F. B. *Boileau and the French Classical Critics in England* (1660–1830). Paris, 1925.

Collins, J. Churton. *Essays and Studies.* 1895.

Corney, Bolton. *Facts relating to William Oldys, Esq.* Greenwich, 1837.

Cory, Herbert. *The Critics of Edmund Spenser.* Berkeley, Calif., 1911.

Crane, Ronald S. "An Early Eighteenth Century Enthusiast for Primitive Poetry—John Husbands," *MLN*, XXXVII (1922), 27.

Crane, Ronald S. "A Neglected Mid-eighteenth Century Plea for Originality and its Author," *PQ*, XIII (1934), 21.

Davies, W. T. "Thomas Tanner and his *Bibliotheca*," *TLS* (December, 1935), 856.

Dédieu, J. *Montesquieu et la tradition politique anglaise en France.* Paris, 1909.

De La Torre-Bueno, Lillian. "Was Ambrose Philips a Ballad Editor?" *Anglia*, LIX (1935), 252.

Dennis, Leah. "Percy's *Essay On Ancient Metrical Romances*," *PMLA*, XLIX (1934), 81.

Douglas, David C. *English Scholars.* 1939.

Dowling, C. M. *Sir William Davenant's Gondibert: Its Preface and Hobbes's Answer.* Philadelphia, 1934.

Draper, J. W. "Aristotelian Mimesis in Eighteenth Century England," *PMLA*, XXXVI (1921), 372.

Draper, J. W. *Eighteenth Century Aesthetics: A Bibliography.* Heidelberg, 1931.

Draper, J. W. "Poetry and music in eighteenth century aesthetics," *Englische Studien*, LXVII (1932), 70.

Dutton, G. B. "Thomas Rymer and French Aristotelian Formalism," *PMLA*, XXIX (1910), 152.

Elton, Oliver. *A Survey of English Literature, 1730–1780.* 2 vols. 1928.

Fairchild, H. N. *The Noble Savage.* New York, 1928.

Farley, F. E. "The Dying Indian," *Anniversary Papers by Colleagues and Pupils of G. L. Kittredge.* Boston, 1913.

Farley, F. E. "Three Lapland Songs," *PMLA*, XXI, N. S. XIV (1906), 1.

Farley, F. E. *Scandinavian Influences in the English Romantic Movement.* Boston, 1903.

Flasdieck, Hermann M. *John Brown (1715–1766) und seine Dissertation on Poetry and Music.* Halle, 1924.

Flower, Robin. *Laurence Nowell and the Discovery of England.* Oxford, 1934.

Flügel, Ewald. "Bacon's *Historia Literaria*," *Anglia*, XXI (1899), 259.

Folkierski, Wladyslaw. *Entre le classicisme et le romantisme.* Paris, 1925.

Fueter, Eduard. *Geschichte der neueren Historiographie.* München, 1911.

Funke, Otto. *Englische Sprachphilosophie im späteren achzehnten Jahrhundert.* Bern, 1934.

Funke, Otto. *Studien zur Geschichte der Sprachphilosophie.* Bern, 1927.

Geddie, William. *A Bibliography of Middle Scots Poetry*. Edinburgh, 1912.

Good, John Walter. *Studies in the Milton Tradition*. Urbana, Ill., 1915.

Gordon, E. V. *An Introduction to Old Norse*. Oxford, 1927.

Graham, Walter. *The Beginnings of English Literary Periodicals: A Study of Periodical Literature, 1665–1715*. New York, 1926.

Graham, Walter. *English Literary Periodicals*. New York, 1930.

Green, C. C. *The Neo-Classic Theory of Tragedy in England during the Eighteenth Century*. Cambridge, Mass., 1934.

Green, F. C. *Minuet: A Critical Survey of French and English Literary Ideas in the Eighteenth Century*. 1935.

Hadley, Frances W. "The Theory of Milieu in English Criticism from 1600 to 1801," *Abstracts of Theses*. University of Chicago. Humanistic Series, IV (1928), 321.

Hamm, Victor M. "A Seventeenth Century French Source for Hurd's *Letters on Chivalry and Romance*," *PMLA*, LII (1937), 820.

Hammond, E. *Chaucer: A Bibliographical Manual*. New York, 1908.

Harris, Jesse M. *John Bale*. Urbana, Ill., 1940.

Havens, Raymond D. *The Influence of Milton on English Poetry*. Cambridge, Mass., 1922.

Havens, Raymond D. "Thomas Warton and the Eighteenth Century Dilemma," *SP*, XXIV (1928), 36.

Hecht, Hans. *Daniel Webb*. Hamburg, 1920.

Hecht, Hans. "Kleine Studien zu Graves, Shenstone und Percy," *Anglia*, LVIII (1934), 139.

Hecht, Hans. *Thomas Percy, Robert Wood und J. D. Michaelis*. Stuttgart, 1933.

Hecht, Hans, ed. *Thomas Percy und William Shenstone: Ein Briefwechsel*. Strassburg, 1909.

Heidler, Joseph B. *The History, from 1700 to 1800, of English Criticism of Prose Fiction*. Urbana, Ill., 1926.

Hooker, E. N. "The Discussion of Taste from 1750 to 1770, and the New Trends in Literary Criticism," *PMLA*, XLIX (1934), 577.

Howe, Earle Barton. "The Idealised Bard of the Eighteenth Century," *University of Chicago Abstracts of Theses*, Humanistic Series, VI (1929), 367.

Hubert, René. "Essais sur l'histoire de l'idée de Progrès," *Revue de l'histoire de la philosophie*, Oct., 1934, p. 289, and Jan., 1935, p. 1.

Hughes, W. J. *Wales and the Welsh in English Literature from Shakespeare to Scott*. Wrexham, 1924.

Hustvedt, Sigurd B. *Ballad Criticism in Scandinavia and Great Britain during the Eighteenth Century.* New York, 1916.

Jiriczek, Otto. "Jerome Stone's Ballade Albion and the Daughter of May," *Englische Studien,* XLI (1912), 193.

Jones, H. B. "The Death Song of the Noble Savage," *Abstracts of Theses.* University of Chicago. Humanistic Series, III (1924–5).

Jones, Richard Foster. *Ancients and Moderns: A Study of the Background of the Battle of Books.* "Washington University Studies." St. Louis, Mo., 1936.

Jones, Richard Foster. *Lewis Theobald: His Contribution to English Scholarship.* New York, 1919.

Jones, Richard Foster. "Science and Criticism in the Neo-classical Age of English Literature," *Journal of the History of Ideas,* I (1940), 381.

Jones, William P. "Gray's Library," *MP,* XXXV (1938), 257.

Jones, William P. *Thomas Gray, Scholar.* Cambridge, Mass., 1937.

Kaufman, Paul. "Heralds of Original Genius," *Essays in Memory of Barrett Wendell.* Cambridge, Mass., 1926, p. 191.

Kaye, F. B. "Mandeville on the Origin of Language," *MLN,* XXXIX (1924), 136.

Ker, W. P. *Thomas Warton.* Oxford, 1910.

Kilvert, P. *Memoirs . . . of Richard Hurd.* 1860.

Lehmann, W. C. *Adam Ferguson and the Beginnings of Modern Sociology.* New York, 1930.

Lempicki, Sigmund von. *Geschichte der deutschen Literaturwissenschaft.* Göttingen, 1920.

Leslie, Shane. "The Percy Library," *Book Collectors' Quarterly,* XIV (1934), 11.

Lewis, Saunders. *A School of Welsh Antiquarians.* 1924.

Longaker, Mark. *English Biography in the Eighteenth Century.* Philadelphia, 1931.

Lounsbury, Thomas R. *Studies in Chaucer.* 3 vols. New York, 1892.

Lounsbury, Thomas R. *The Text of Shakespeare.* New York, 1906.

Lovejoy, A. O. *The Great Chain of Being: A Study of the History of an Idea.* Cambridge, Mass., 1936.

Lovejoy, A. O. "Monboddo and Rousseau," *MP,* XXX (1933), 275.

Lovett, David. *Shakespeare's Characters in Eighteenth Century Criticism.* Baltimore, 1935.

MacClintock, W. D. *Joseph Warton's Essay on Pope: A History of the Five Editions.* Chapel Hill, N. C., 1936.

McCutcheon, R. P. "Addison and the *Muses' Mercury*," *SP*, XX (1923), 17.

McKerrow, Ronald B. *The Treatment of Shakespeare's Text by his Earlier Editors*. Oxford, 1933.

McKillop, Alan Duglas. "A Critic of 1741 on Early Poetry," *SP*, XXX (1933), 504.

Mann, Elizabeth L. "The Problem of Originality in English Literary Criticism, 1650–1800," *PQ*, XVIII (1939), 97.

Marburg, Clara. *Sir William Temple: A Seventeenth Century Libertine*. New Haven, 1922.

Marshall, Roderick. *Italy in English Literature, 1755–1815*. New York, 1934.

Martin, L. C. *Thomas Warton and the Early Poems of Milton*. Oxford, 1934.

Martin, Roger. *Essai sur Thomas Gray*. Paris, 1934.

Marwell, Heinz. "Percy und die Ossian-Kontroverse," *Anglia*, LVIII (1934), 392.

Marwell, Heinz. *Thomas Percy: Studien zur Entstehungsgeschichte seiner Werke*. Göttingen, 1934.

Meinecke, Friedrich, "Die englische Präromantik des 18. Jahrhunderts als Vorstufe des Historismus," *Historische Zeitschrift*, CLII (1935), 256.

Meinecke, Friedrich. *Die Enstehung des Historismus*. 2 vols. München, 1936.

Miller, Frances S. "The Historic Sense of Thomas Warton, Jr." *ELH*, V (1938), 71.

Miller, G. M. *The Historical Point of View in English Literary Criticism, 1570–1770*. Heidelberg, 1913.

Milner-Barry, Ada. "A Note on the Early Literary Relations between Oliver Goldsmith and Thomas Percy," *RES*, II (1926), 51.

Milner-Barry, A., and Powell, L. F. "A further Note on Hau Kiou Choaan," *RES*, III (1927), 218.

Monk, Samuel S. *The Sublime: A Study of Critical Theories in Eighteenth Century England*. New York, 1935.

Murray, R. H. *Erasmus and Luther*. 1920.

Nethercot, A. H. "The Reputation of Donne as Metrist," *Sewanee Review*, XXX (1922), 463.

Nethercot, A. H. "The Reputation of the Metaphysical Poets During the Age of Johnson and the Romantic Revival," *SP*, XXII (1925), 81.

Nethercot, A. H. "The Reputation of the Metaphysical Poets During the Age of Pope," *PQ*, IV (1925), 163.

Nichols, John. *Illustrations of the Literary History of the Eighteenth Century.* 8 vols. 1817–1858.

Nichols, John. *Literary Anecdotes of the Eighteenth Century.* 9 vols. 1812–1816.

Noyes, Robert Gales. "Ben Jonson Masques in the Eighteenth Century," *SP*, XXXIII (1936), 427.

Noyes, Robert Gales. *Ben Jonson on the English Stage, 1660–1776.* Cambridge, Mass., 1935.

Ogburn, Vincent H. "The Wilkinson Manuscripts and Percy's Chinese Books," *RES*, IX (1933), 30.

O'Leary, Gerard. *English Literary History and Bibliography.* 1928.

Oras, Ants. *Milton's Editors and Commentators from Patrick Hume to Henry John Todd, 1695–1801.* Tartu, 1931.

Osborn, James M. *John Dryden: Some Biographical Facts and Problems.* New York, 1940.

Osborn, James M. "Thomas Birch and the *General Dictionary* (1734–41)," *MP*, XXXVI (1938), 25.

Parry, J. J. "Dr. Johnson's Interest in Welsh," *MLN*, XXXVI (1921), 374.

Paul, H. G. *John Dennis.* New York, 1911.

Peardon, Thomas P. *The Transition in English Historical Writing, 1760–1830.* New York, 1933.

Perkinson, Richard H. "The Polemical Use of Davies' *Nosce Teipsum,*" *SP*, XXXVI (1939), 597.

Powell, L. F. "Hau Kiou Choaan," *RES*, II (1926), 446.

Powell, L. F. "William Huggins and Tobias Smollett," *MP*, XXXIV (1936–1937), 179.

Rae, John. *The Life of Adam Smith.* 1895.

Raleigh, Sir Walter. *Six Essays on Johnson.* Oxford, 1910.

Ralli, Augustus. *A History of Shakespearean Criticism.* 2 vols. Oxford, 1932.

Raysor, Thomas M. "The Downfall of the Three Unities," *MLN*, XLII (1927), 1.

Raysor, Thomas M. "The Study of Shakespeare's Characters in the Eighteenth Century," *MLN*, XLII (1927), 495.

Reichwein, Adolf. *China and Europe: Intellectual and Artistic Contacts in the Eighteenth Century.* 1925.

Reynolds, Myra. *The Learned Lady in England, 1650–1760.* Boston, 1920.

Rinaker, Clarissa. *Thomas Warton: A Biographical and Critical Study.* Urbana, Ill., 1916.

Rinaker, Clarissa. "Thomas Warton and the Historical Method in Literary Criticism," *PMLA*, XXX (1915), 79.

Robertson, J. G. *Studies in the Genesis of Romantic Theory in the Eighteenth Century*. Cambridge, 1923.

Roekerath, Netty. *Der Nachruhm Herricks und Wallers*. Leipzig, 1931.

Saintsbury, George. *A History of Criticism and Literary Taste in Europe*. 3 vols. Edinburgh, 1900–1903.

Scheffer, John D. "The Idea of Decline in Literature and the Arts in Eighteenth Century England," *MP*, XXXIV (1936), 155.

Schütt, Marie. *Die englische Biographik der Tudorzeit*. Hamburg, 1930.

Scott, W. R. *Adam Smith as Student and Professor*. Glasgow, 1937.

Seaton, Ethel. *Literary Relations of England and Scandinavia in the Seventeenth Century*. Oxford, 1935.

Seitz, R. W. "Goldsmith and the *Literary Magazine*," *RES*, V (1929), 410.

Shepard, Odell. "Clarissa Rinaker: Thomas Warton," (review), *JEGP*, XVI (1917), 153.

Sisam, Kenneth. "The Authenticity of Certain Texts in Lombard's *Archaionomia*," *MLR*, XX (1925), 253.

Smith, Audley L. "Richard Hurd's *Letters on Chivalry and Romance*," *ELH*, VI (1939), 58.

Smith, David Nichol. *Shakespeare in the Eighteenth Century*. Oxford, 1928.

Smith, David Nichol. *Warton's History of English Poetry*. Oxford, 1929.

Smith, Logan Persall. *Four Words: Romantic, Originality, Creative, Genius*. Society for Pure English Tract, No. 17. Oxford, 1924.

Snyder, E. D. *The Celtic Revival in English Literature, 1760–1800*. Cambridge, Mass., 1923.

Spranger, Eduard. "Die Kulturzyklentheorie und das Problem des Kulturverfalls," *Sitzungsberichte der preussischen Akademie der Wissenschaften*. Berlin, 1926.

Spingarn, J. E. *A History of Literary Criticism in the Renaissance*. New York, 1899.

Spurgeon, Caroline S. *Chaucer devant la critique*. Paris, 1911.

Spurgeon, Caroline S. *Five Hundred Years of Chaucer Criticism*. 3 vols. Cambridge, 1925.

Stauffer, Donald A. *English Biography before 1700*. Cambridge, Mass., 1930.

Stephen, Sir Leslie. *A History of English Thought in the Eighteenth Century*. 2 vols. Third ed. 1902.

Stern, L. C. "Die ossianischen Heldenlieder," *Zeitschrift für vergleichende Literaturgeschichte*. Neue Folge, VIII (1895), 82.

Straus, Ralph. *Robert Dodsley*. 1910.

Teggart, F. J. "A Problem in the History of Ideas," *Journal of the History of Ideas*, I (1940), 494.

Tennery, Grace R. "Ballad Collections of the Eighteenth Century," in *MLR*, V (1915), 283.

Thompson, E. N. S. "Milton's Part in *Theatrum Poetarum*," *MLN*, XXXVI (1921), 18.

Thüme, Heinrich. *Beiträge zur Geschichte des Geniebegriffes in England*. Halle, 1927.

Tinker, Chauncey Brewster. *Nature's Simple Plan*. Princeton, 1922.

Tobin, James E. *Eighteenth Century English Literature and its Cultural Background: A Bibliography*. New York, 1939.

Toynbee, Paget. *Dante in English Literature from Chaucer to Cary*. 2 vols. 1909.

Toynbee, Paget. "Gray on the Origin and Date of *Amadis de Gaul*," *MLR*, XXVII (1932), 60.

Traube, Ludwig. "Einleitung in die lateinische Philologie des Mittelalters," *Vorlesungen und Abhandlungen*. Vol. II. München, 1911.

Troeltsch, Ernst. *Der Historismus und seine Probleme*. Tübingen, 1922.

Tupper, Caroline F. "Essays erroneously attributed to Goldsmith," *PMLA*, XXXIX (1924), 325.

Tuve, Rosamund. "Ancients, Moderns and Saxons," *ELH*, VI (1939), 165.

Van Tieghem, Paul. *Le Préromantisme*. 2 vols. Paris, 1924.

Vincent, Howard P. "Warton's Last Words on the Rowley Papers," *MLR*, XXXIV (1939), 572.

Walcott, F. G. "Dryden's Answer to Thomas Rymer's *Tragedies of the Last Age*," PQ, XV (1936), 194.

Warren, Austin. *Alexander Pope as Critic and Humanist*. Princeton, 1929.

Warren, Austin. "Pope's Index to Beaumont and Fletcher," *MLN*, XLVI (1931), 515.

Wasserman, Earl Reeves. "Elizabethan Poetry 'Improved,'" *MP*, XXXVIII (1940), 370.

Wasserman, Earl Reeves. "Henry Headley and the Elizabethan Revival," *SP*, XXXVI (1939), 491.

Wasserman, Earl Reeves. "The Scholarly Origin of the Elizabethan Revival," *ELH*, IV (1937), 213.

Watkin-Jones, A. "Bishop Percy and the Scottish Ballads," *Essays and Studies* (English Association), XVIII (1933), 110.

Watkin-Jones, A. "Langbaine's *Account of the English Dramatick Poets* (1691)," *Essays and Studies* (English Association), XXI (1935), 75.

Watkin-Jones, A. "A Pioneer Hispanist: Thomas Percy," *Bulletin of Spanish Studies*, XIV (1937), 3.

Watkins, W. B. C. *Johnson and English Poetry before 1660.* Princeton, 1936.

Watson, John Selby. *A Life of William Warburton.* 1863.

Wellek, René. "The Theory of Literary History," *Travaux du Cercle Linguistique de Prague*, VI (1936), 173.

Wellek, René. "Vývoj anglické literární historie (The Development of English Literary History)," *Slovo a Slovesnost*, (Prague), IV (1938), 96.

Whitney, Lois. "English Primitivistic Theories of Epic Origins," *MP*, XXI (1924), 337.

Whitney, Lois. *Primitivism and the Idea of Progress in English Popular Literature of the Eighteenth Century.* Baltimore, 1934.

Whitney, Lois. "Thomas Blackwell, a Disciple of Shaftesbury," *PQ*, V (1926), 193.

Williams, Robert D. "Antiquarian Interest in Elizabethan Drama before Lamb," *PMLA*, LIII (1938), 434.

Wollstein, Rose Haylbut. *English Opinions of French Poetry (1660–1750).* New York, 1923.

Wood, Paul Spencer. "The Opposition to Neo-Classicism in England between 1660 and 1700," *PMLA*, XLIII (1928), 182.

Wright, H. "Lapp Songs in English Literature," *MLR*, XIII (1918), 412.

Wright, Herbert H. *Studies in Anglo-Scandinavian Literary Relations.* Bangor, 1919.

Wülker, Richard. *Grundriss zur Geschichte der angelsächsischen Literatur.* Leipzig, 1885.

Wurtsbaugh, Jewel. "Digby's Criticism of Spenser," *RES*, XI (1935), 192.

Wurtsbaugh, Jewel. *Two Centuries of Spenserian Scholarship (1609–1805).* Baltimore, 1936.

Yeowell, James. *A Literary Antiquary: Memoir of William Oldys, Esq.* 1862.

Young, Karl. "Samuel Johnson on Shakespeare: One Aspect," *University of Wisconsin Studies in Language and Literature.* No. 18. Madison, Wis., 1923, p. 146.

Zilsel, Edgar. *Die Enstehung des Geniebegriffes.* Tübingen. 1926.

Zimansky, Curt Arno. Introduction and Notes to an Edition of Thomas Rymer's *Critical Works.* MS, Princeton Doctoral Dissertation. 1937.

Zobel, A. "Darstellung und Würdigung der Sprachphilosophie John Lockes," *Anglia,* LII (1928), 289.